Blue Jays 1, Expos 0

Blue Jays 1, Expos 0

*The Urban Rivalry That Killed
Major League Baseball in Montreal*

DAVID LUCHUK

McFarland & Company, Inc., Publishers
Jefferson, North Carolina, and London

LIBRARY OF CONGRESS CATALOGUING-IN-PUBLICATION DATA

Luchuk, David.
    Blue Jays 1, Expos 0 : the urban rivalry that killed Major League baseball in Montreal / David Luchuk.
    p.   cm.
    Includes bibliographical references and index.

    ISBN-13: 978-0-7864-2812-0
    (softcover : 50# alkaline paper) ∞

    1. Toronto Blue Jays (Baseball team)   2. Montreal Expos (Baseball team)   3. Sports rivalries—Canada.   I. Title.
II. Title: Blue Jays one, Expos zero.
GV875.T67L83   2007
796.3570971—dc22   2006039758

British Library cataloguing data are available

©2007 David Luchuk. All rights reserved

No part of this book may be reproduced or transmitted in any form or by any means, electronic or mechanical, including photocopying or recording, or by any information storage and retrieval system, without permission in writing from the publisher.

On the cover: Jarry Park, first home of the Montreal Expos
(Canadian Baseball Hall of Fame and Museum)

Manufactured in the United States of America

McFarland & Company, Inc., Publishers
  Box 611, Jefferson, North Carolina 28640
    www.mcfarlandpub.com

Acknowledgments

In the years since I first launched this project, I have received many kinds of support from many different people. Looking back on the whole process, from inception to publication, it is humbling to consider how much I have leaned on others and how little chance there was of this book becoming a reality without their help. I am truly grateful.

Thanks to my mom and dad in particular, and my whole family in general, for their confidence in the value of spending so much time and energy on what was, for many months, a labor of love with little prospect of finding an audience. Thanks to my lovely wife for showing me the merit of making this effort, regardless of its outcome, and for being the first to celebrate the discovery of a publisher willing to take a chance on the book. To my dear friends, who never tired of indulging me by enduring countless digressions into the minutia of Canadian history and baseball lore (or, at least, my versions of both), I owe you many, many hours of undivided attention. To Osgoode, my confidante through countless mini-crises, a particular note of gratitude.

The list of people who kindly offered their encouragement and shared their ideas on topics related to this book is especially meaningful to me. I am very proud, and tremendously lucky, to have counted you all as supporters in this endeavor: Jonah Keri at *Baseball Prospectus*, Alan Schwarz at *ESPN*, Jim Callis at *Baseball America*, Doug Pappas (RIP), Neil de Mause at *Field of Schemes*, Dewey Knudson and Bill King at *Sports Business Journal*, Seth Livingstone and Paul White at *USA Today*, Dr. Jeanne Wolfe at McGill University, Dr. Andrew Zimbalist at Smith College, Stephanie Myles, Jack Todd, and Bill Brownstein at the *Montreal Gazette*, Roy MacGregor at the *Globe and Mail*, Dr. Gordon McOuat at King's College, Dr. Hok-Lin Leung and Dr. David Gordon at Queen's University, Dr. Mark Seasons at University of Waterloo, and Craig Burley at *Hardball Times*. A hundred times, thank you.

Illustrations for this book were drawn from Library and Archives Canada and the Canadian Baseball Hall of Fame. Thanks to Debbie Brentnell and Daniel Potvin at the Archives and thanks to Scott Crawford at the Hall of Fame.

Contents

Acknowledgments v
Preface 1

April 3
May 30
June 54
July 77
August 103
September 128
October 158

Bibliography 185
Index 191

Preface

This book is about the respective fates of the Toronto Blue Jays and Montreal Expos, which veered onto permanently divergent paths during the summer of 2002. It is also about the historic rivalry between the cities of Toronto and Montreal, which stretches back at least as far as rebellions in the 1800s and the creation of Canada itself. What does one have to do with the other? That is the central question.

In answering that question, the book asks readers to consider conditions for success, and even survival, in Major League Baseball as it existed in 2002. At that time, a wave of public financing for new stadiums was in full swing. So much so that a team's ability to squeeze stadium subsidies out of increasingly skeptical governments was an important factor in determining how the league perceived its stability. Those with little hope of receiving this financial support were vulnerable to the threat of contraction and relocation.

The moribund Expos faced stadium problems that, in their severity and persistence, dwarfed those of other teams. These problems contributed to a sentiment of perpetual crisis surrounding the franchise. As was revealed in 2005, they were also coming to a head at a time when public money was being spent more recklessly than ever in Montreal.

Between 1994 and 2003, as the Montreal Expos spiraled into disarray, Canada's government reportedly paid around $150 million to supporters of the prime minister's Liberal Party under the pretense of combating separatism in Quebec. These supposed service contracts were channeled through a complex web of kickbacks under the influence of the prime minister's office, and exploded into a national scandal exposing political officials, senior bureaucrats and party supporters to censure and even criminal conviction. Canadians were shocked by these revelations, all compiled in a public report issued by a Commission of Inquiry in 2005.

The scandal broke after research for this book was completed but, nonetheless, it offers a useful frame of reference for readers launching into the story. What if the kind of patronage described by the commission actually reflects practices established as far back as the very first Canadian government? What if those practices were responsible for launching and maintaining a rivalry that has lasted over a hundred years? Finally, what if this illegitimate yet enduring dynamic is relevant to the viability of large-scale projects like baseball stadiums?

The Blue Jays and Expos played in separate leagues. There has never been a baseball rivalry between the cities. However, as soon as public stadium financing shifted the conditions for major league success into the politial sphere, the historic rivalry between the cities became a factor in baseball.

This book tells the story of how that factor was revealed in 2002. It is not intended as a lament for the Montreal Expos. Rather, through a mixed present and past tense narrative, it seeks to revisit the turmoil of an unforgettable season and frame a larger story about the rise of two cities and the people who set them against each other.

April

> "I [have] pledged to concentrate on two areas ... competitive balance on the field and the economic stability of the clubs and baseball as a whole."
> —*Commissioner Bud Selig to the U.S. House of Representatives, Dec. 6, 2001*

The 2002 season opens on April Fool's Day in Boston with the Toronto Blue Jays facing the hometown Red Sox. During pre-game ceremonies, new Red Sox owner John Henry raises an outfield banner celebrating 90 years of baseball at Fenway Park, which he has proposed to renovate using his own money rather than replace using public funds. Both the banner and the planned upgrades are fitting gestures. Fenway Park is a true monument that recalls an era when privately financed baseball stadiums contributed to the health of American cities.

In the mid–19th century, Boston was basically an island jutting into Massachusetts Bay at the end of a narrow strip of land. Disconnected and overcrowded, the city had become uninhabitable to the poor and inhospitable to the rich.

In response, local officials took radical action, allowing countless trainloads of debris to be dumped into the marshy swamp that separated the city from shore. This enormous infill not only connected Boston to the mainland, it paved the way for residential and commercial development in what was called the Back Bay.

Though the daring infill was a success, it was a messy success. Small, primarily immigrant communities sprouted to life but the Back Bay was prone to noxious flooding when heavy rains backed up the sewer system. Something had to be done to keep Boston's newest neighborhood from drowning in sewage.

The solution came from a man named Frederick Law Olmsted who devised a network of interconnected paths and carriageways around a large flood basin that locals named the Back Bay Fens. His design saved homes from being submerged in wastewater and established a winding park that benefited the entire city. This section of Boston came to be known as Fenway.

By 1910, Fenway had evolved into a dynamic enclave. Bounded by rail yards and warehouses, it featured a hodge-podge of schools, businesses, hospitals and even the local symphony. Given its location, near the old city core, it was judged by local financier Charles Taylor as the perfect location for a new baseball stadium.

Taylor, a newspaper magnate and owner of the Red Sox, was tired of renting space at nearby Huntington Grounds where outfield spectators stood behind a rope that marked the end of the playing surface. He decided to build a new facility in the Fenway district instead. This decision was motivated primarily by financial gain.

Taylor was sick of baseball. The Red Sox had been abysmal since repeating as champions in 1904-05 and he had purchased the team only as a plaything for his son. Plans were in place for him to sell the franchise but he'd paid enough rent at Huntington to know there was still money to be made in baseball. He built a new stadium, sold the Red Sox and rented his new park to his former team.

Fenway Park fit right into its host neighborhood. Residents accepted it as a grand structure in a mixed community that had a little of everything. In fact, improved transit service between downtown and Fenway was an asset to the whole district and, necessitated by the popularity of the ballpark itself, helped establish a long-standing affection between local residents and the home of the Red Sox.

Fenway Park is a tribute to baseball at its best. Sure, Taylor was a cutthroat but he took his chances like everyone else and made a positive contribution to one of Boston's most vibrant districts. It is a shining star in baseball's increasingly checkered legacy.

Plans to replace Fenway Park with a new, publicly financed stadium have sparked outrage. John Henry, in his first season as owner, has tried to ease these tensions by endorsing a proposal to renovate rather than replace the crumbling facility. This is an awkward tactic.

The team's previous owners explored the same option and determined that it wasn't worth the trouble. Furthermore, Henry is the same man who once spooked fans in Florida into thinking their team was on the verge of collapse so he could force a stadium-financing bill onto the state. All evidence suggests that Henry has backed off plans to replace Fenway Park because government officials have buckled under grassroots opposition. He is biding his time.

Fenway's murky future offers a fitting introduction to both the John Henry era in Boston and the current state of baseball. Henry is a wildly successful stock trader who acquired the Red Sox in a deal that the Massachusetts attorney general described as a crooked swindle. In this, he courted the assistance of Major League Baseball every step of the way.

April

This past winter, the Red Sox were available to be purchased and Henry wanted in on the bidding. He had committed most of his free money to the ugly-duckling Florida Marlins so, before making a move in Boston, he had to unload the Marlins on somebody else. Searching for a solution, Henry found an ally in Commissioner Bud Selig.

Selig is the car salesman and condo renter whose capacity to absorb the fury of fans and media has made him popular among major league owners. His integrity in light of a secret loan he received from Twins owner Carl Pohland has been questioned by the United States Congress. He's also been accused of providing blatantly false financial information to the United States House of Representatives and was asked to resign from his post by one of those same elected officials. But he's the commissioner. Certain indiscretions, it seems, come with the job.

Selig intervened to help John Henry. The commissioner had recently been convinced that Major League Baseball should contract two franchises: the Montreal Expos and Minnesota Twins. This strategy was temporarily knocked off course by a lawsuit filed by the Minnesota athletics commission that prevented him from axing the Twins. Nonetheless, the Expos were dead in the water and this fact could be levered in Henry's favor.

Two years prior, Selig had supported a man named Jeffrey Loria in wrestling control of the Montreal Expos away from penny-pinching local owners. Frustrated and disillusioned after a pair of awful seasons with the Expos, Loria was open to the idea of getting out.

Selig, Henry and Loria agreed on a swap that saw Major League Baseball buy the Montreal Expos for $120 million, Loria buy the Florida Marlins for $158 million and Henry buy the Boston Red Sox and Fenway Park for $700 million. This involved the radical depreciation of Marlins assets to create tax savings for Henry along with the reinvestment of millions by Red Sox investors who had supposedly been bought out.

In the end, Major League Baseball took control of the Expos, Loria turned his meager investment in Montreal into $120 million while Henry snapped his fingers and found himself in control of a $700 million investment of other people's money in the Boston Red Sox. This is baseball in 2002. It is a dodgy business in which governments are squeezed for money, fans are threatened with contraction and the commissioner helps make it all happen. Mercifully, the first day of the season offers a welcome distraction in the form of the game itself.

On opening day against the Blue Jays, former Expo ace Pedro Martinez takes the mound for Boston. Martinez looks a fair bit chunkier than he ever did while dominating the National League with Montreal. He's always been a physical aberration, a beanpole with an overpowering fastball, so it's not a bad thing that he's put on weight. The extra pounds add character.

To the dismay of Red Sox fans, Pedro seems unbalanced by all his new character. He is not himself against Toronto, giving up 8 runs before being pulled in the 4th inning.

Normally, Pedro Martinez doesn't leave a game before thoroughly demoralizing his opponents. On opening day, the only demoralizing thing that happens with Martinez on the mound is a bonehead fan racing onto the field to have his picture taken next to Nomar Garciaparra. The game turns into a circus.

Blue Jay first baseman Carlos Delgado is hit twice in the back. A Toronto bench coach named Cookie gets tossed, which the Canadian announcers think is hilarious. The Blue Jays manage not to record any outs with an infielder standing on second base, holding the ball, next to two disoriented Red Sox runners. Twenty-two runs later, the whole thing seems vaudevillian.

With the game tied at 11, the Red Sox bring another former Expo into the game. Ugueth Urbina used to be Montreal's closer, wildly pumping his fist every time he finished a game with a strikeout. Now playing the same role in Boston, Urbina doesn't pump any fists against Toronto. The Blue Jays force one last run across the plate and win 12–11.

It's a peculiar way for Toronto to start the season. The Jays stick it to two former Expos.

A day later, the current Montreal Expos open their season at home in front of a respectable if not capacity crowd at Olympic Stadium. Roberto Clemente, who once played for the minor league Montreal Royals just like Jackie Robinson, is honored in a brief ceremony that adds a sense of history to the occasion. With much emphasis on the threat of contraction, fans and media alike are happy to focus on the past.

Representing the Florida Marlins for the first time this summer, for example, Tim Raines stretches his legs along the third base line and waves to Montreal fans who still adore him. And why not?

At last year's home opener, while pinch-hitting for the Expos during a crucial late-inning rally, Raines thrilled the crowd with his mere presence at the plate. He later admitted to taking extra time between pitches because he didn't want the electric ovation to come to an end. The mood is more somber today, and fans dislike seeing him in a Florida uniform, but he seems at home just the same.

In a season described humorlessly by Expos officials as a celebration, fans are eager to cheer the dearly departed. If former manager Felipe Alou were in attendance, current manager Frank Robinson would be a forgotten man. Despite Robinson's impeccable major league credentials, the Expos' faithful would happily toss him on his ear in exchange for Alou.

There have been plenty of low points for the Expos. The strike in 1994 robbed them of a chance at postseason glory. Their ambitious downtown stadium plan was hung out to dry by an owner who abandoned the franchise.

The prime, skyline-view property on which the stadium was to be built fell into the hands of a condominium developer. These stand as minor insults compared to the day Jeffrey Loria fired Felipe Alou.

Felipe had a reputation for drawing blood from stones. In 1994, he led the young Expos to the best record in baseball and won Manager of the Year. In 1996, he outdid himself by leading a less talented squad to a second place finish, narrowly missing both the playoffs and another Manager of the Year award. He had not been able to pull such tricks in 1999, 2000 or 2001.

But fire Felipe? Above all else, this is why fans in Montreal despise Jeffrey Loria.

At the 2002 home opener, Loria is the only former Expo who doesn't receive any face-time on camera. He once suggested, in response to questions about the plan to build an outdoor stadium in chilly downtown Montreal, that fans in New York didn't mind sitting outside in October. Thrilling stuff, World Series talk in Montreal. The thrill didn't last. Today he sits in the background watching his new team play against the one he pledged to save.

None of this lamenting makes a lick of difference once the first pitch is thrown, of course. It's up to the young stable of current Expos to tell the tale. They fall behind Loria's Marlins 6–1 before rallying in sporadic bursts to pull within striking distance in the bottom of the 9th inning.

With runners at second and third, Andres Galarraga is lifted so Henry Rodriguez can bat in his place. As he is apt to do, Rodriguez fouls off ball four then promptly strikes out.

One strikeout later, Jose Vidro represents the Expos' last chance. Vidro delivers a single up the middle that he stretches into a double when an errant throw home fails to keep the Expos from tying the game.

With the crowd still cheering, All-Universe outfielder Vladimir Guerrero is walked intentionally, giving Orlando Cabrera the chance to slash a double that rolls to the wall and ends the game. The Expos win 7–6.

Fans go crazy. French announcers scream in joyous incoherence. Frank Robinson dances around the field. Valder-y, Valder-a.

While the Expos scramble for a tight win under the patchwork roof of Olympic Stadium, rain pours down in Boston canceling the final game of Toronto's opening mini-series. This sends the Blue Jays home to SkyDome where 40,000 fans turn out for an afternoon game against the Minnesota Twins, a team that probably wouldn't exist if not for a legal injunction that quashed Bud Selig's contraction scheme before it could rack up any victims.

The Twins have their heads in a noose. Supposedly, the Twins are no longer viable in Minneapolis, just like the Expos in Montreal. However, in the case of Montreal, two factors stand out as justifications for dissolving the team: awful attendance and uncompetitive play. In Minnesota, these don't apply.

For one thing, while the Expos were last in home attendance in 2001, the Twins were 25th out of 30. Florida, Tampa Bay, Kansas City and Chicago

(White Sox) all posted worse attendance figures without being targeted for contraction. As for competitiveness, the Twins were in the hunt for a division title deep into last season's second half. What gives?

It's a stadium thing. There's little support in Minneapolis for financing a new baseball stadium out of the public coffers and the only solution the state has proposed is to cover the interest on a loan that would allow the team to build its own facility. That's the same formula the Quebec government proposed for Montreal two years ago. It didn't fly then and it doesn't fly now so the Twins find themselves in Selig's crosshairs.

They also find themselves in Toronto where the Blue Jays have almost no hope of making the postseason, play in a concrete mausoleum on artificial turf and placed 23rd out of 30 in attendance last year. It's strange to think that the Blue Jays voted in favor of contraction since they look as much like a target as the Twins.

The Jays haven't done a lot to counter this perception, recently behaving like a franchise no longer capable of competing with the big boys. They have installed a new general manager this summer. J.P. Ricciardi leveraged his association with the frugal Oakland Athletics organization into his big chance in Toronto. Ricciardi has wasted no time charting a cost-cutting course.

He traded the Blue Jays' closer to Oakland in exchange for a little known prospect named Eric Hinske, regarded as one of the least talented infielders entering the league. He also traded Toronto's shortstop, designated hitter and sole Canadian player in exchange for prospects. He is crafting a lineup consisting primarily of raw talent.

Some say the Blue Jays could have the league's worst defense. Others are critical of the pitching rotation, which rests on the shoulders of players like Roy Halladay who was in A-ball last season. Many point to the outfield and say the trouble is just beginning.

Raul Mondesi is a former All-Star. Jose Cruz Jr. and Shannon Stewart both posted good offensive stats last summer. Vernon Wells brings defense and speed to his first full season in the league. These players constitute a very promising outfield but there's room for only three of them.

To deal with this problem, Ricciardi has asked Shannon Stewart to be the designated hitter. Stewart is sulking. Ricciardi handles questions about possible trades involving the young outfielder on a daily basis. His dilemma is that Stewart is a quality offensive talent on a team that eventually needs to replace Mondesi in right. He's got to keep Stewart but doesn't have anywhere to put him.

These are the types of questions facing Ricciardi in his first season at the helm. The success of the Blue Jays will depend on his answers.

In the Jays' home opener, pitcher Roy Halladay gives the new general manager something to smile about by looking nothing like a kid who just came up from the minors. He works deep into the late innings against Minnesota and gives up just a single run. In his support, Blue Jays hitters serve up a rousing comeback victory worthy of thousands of skipped classes and corporate hours lost to the city.

Carlos Delgado, one of the most reliable offensive terrors in the game, extends an unlikely streak by reaching base for the tenth consecutive time. Eric Hinske impresses skeptical observers by racking up three doubles. Finally, Raul Mondesi cashes Hinske in with a home run that puts the game on ice. The Blue Jays win 7–2.

It's enough to make people forget that the doomed Twins are in town and that the Blue Jays, a less competitive franchise that draws as poorly at home, voted in favor of contraction to help seal their fate. A win is a win and Toronto will take it.

Like the Blue Jays, the Expos also have a new general manager. Omar Minaya was appointed shortly after Jeffrey Loria took Montreal's entire front office with him to Florida.

Minaya has a thankless job, charged with caretaking the league's cynical investment in a franchise that it openly plans to dismantle. He is in a world all his own, divorced from the long-term success on which other general managers focus.

How can he safeguard the best interests of his club when it is owned by a consortium of individuals who benefit directly from its failure? What would stop other teams from picking the Expos to pieces in a series of lopsided trades prior to dissolving the team? These questions hang over Minaya's head and color the rotten filter through which all his decisions are perceived. Omar Minaya not only has to deal with this absurd relationship between himself and the league, he also faces the same daunting challenge that has dogged general managers in Montreal for a decade: getting fans behind his team.

There is a lot to like about the 2002 Expos. Vladimir Guerrero patrols right field, menacing base runners with powerful throws overshadowed only by his unstoppable presence at the plate. Jose Vidro plays good defense at second base while hitting over .300. Shortstop Orlando Cabrera bats bigger than he looks, filling in as clean-up hitter from time to time. Javier Vazquez is again the centrepiece of the Expos' rotation after being one of the National League's most dominant pitchers in the second half of 2001. This is the nucleus of what could be a good ball club.

Still, to no one's surprise, the carnival atmosphere of the Expos' home opener is replaced, the very next day, by the echo of plastic horns in the bleachers. These are lonely sounds floating around a near empty stadium like whale music. Around 35,000 fans come out to watch the first game of 2002. Only 3,500 turn up for the second.

"How many hot dogs do they cook here? I mean, precook before a game? Five?"
—*Bill Cosby, on baseball in Montreal, 2002*

Across North America, images of empty seats flicker momentarily on television screens before a thousand sportscasters sitting at a thousand teleprompters get their digs in at the Expos. At the opener, at least it was comedy legend Bill Cosby taking shots. On the second day of the season, every nameless sports journalist from Coquitlam to Kalamazoo gets a turn to make a crack.

It's fitting. Star talent never turns out for a crowd so small.

The Expos will not be the only team in Canada facing attendance problems this season. The Blue Jays have a long way to go before recapturing the fan support they enjoyed during the early 1990s. That said, the Expos attract so few fans that the team is capable of drawing hundreds, not thousands.

All signs point to imminent failure. It's a good thing that Montreal fans have thick hides. They have seen their team reach the end of the proverbial road several times. Plus, that road has been pretty rocky right from the start.

Many more fans cheerily crowded into Jarry Park thirty years ago than currently make the trek out to Olympic Stadium. Those first Expos fans welcomed baseball to Montreal in the midst of a looming emergency poised to explode into outright revolution.

Looking back on where the Expos franchise came from offers a view of where it's going. These glances into the past also point to trouble bearing down on Toronto where crises facing the Expos are just a few years away from descending on the Blue Jays.

The 1960s are a good place to start because the Expos were born during that volatile period. The chaos of those years, however, pushes the story back much further. The future of baseball in Canada is tangled in two centuries of corruption and bloodshed through which Toronto and Montreal have come to know one another as rivals.

"Canadians do not need to be liberated."
— *Prime Minister Lester Pearson, 1967*

In the spring of 1969, Canada was still basking in the afterglow of its 100th birthday and the glamorous international spotlight of Expo '67 in Montreal. To some, Canada was justly being recognized among the world's elite. To others, Canada was embarking on the early days of a life and death struggle over the presumed rights of an oppressed people.

Some waved and others burned Canada's new maple leaf flag as the Montreal Expos joined Major League Baseball. Adding unwelcome drama to this hopeful expansion, Montrealers cheered their new team in the exploded debris of political violence.

In February 1969, a single bomb was detonated at the Montreal Stock Exchange. In March, several went off at public places and private businesses alike. In Montreal's commercial shipping port, hub of an international distribution network at the heart of the city's economy, 30 people were injured in another blast. It hardly seemed a welcoming home for baseball.

In truth, Montreal was never regarded as an ideal choice. It had been home to the minor league affiliate of the Los Angeles Dodgers for 40 years, which worked in its favor. The Dodgers' president was head of the expansion committee in 1968. Local fans had shown real commitment and the government of the day seemed determined to make the experiment work so Montreal became big league baseball's first nervous venture outside the United States. No one was prepared to believe that the political climate could turn sour so quickly. What most failed to recognize was that it had been turning sour for over a hundred years.

Prior to the inaugural 1969 season, Montreal appointed former prime minister Lester Pearson as the team's honorary president. This gesture acknowledged Pearson's consistent support for efforts that eventually brought the expansion team to Montreal in spite of shaky finances and the ire of the United States Congress.

Pearson was a known baseball fanatic. He played semi-pro ball in Toronto prior to serving in World War I, brokering a peace deal in the Arab-Israeli war, winning the Nobel Prize, rising to prime minister and taking over as president of the United Nations. Baseball fan, peacemaker, prime minister: Lester Pearson.

During his time in office, Pearson became acutely aware of growing political unrest in Quebec. In a speech before members of the exclusive Empire Club in Toronto, Pearson outlined his vision for Canada's future, explicitly acknowledging that within Canada there was "a French-speaking sector which ... has the nature of a national community with the Province of Quebec as its heart and center."

"This fact," he said, "must be recognized."

Three years after his speech, dozens of foreign dignitaries descended on Montreal for Expo '67. The world's fair drew an estimated 50 million visitors and went down as one of the most financially successful ventures of its kind.

For Pearson, who had worried the event would be an utter disaster due to construction delays, Expo was at the heart of Canada's centennial celebration. For that national community Pearson was so eager to recognize, Expo offered an ideal backdrop against which their most desperate hopes were given a voice by a visiting war hero who unsettled all of Canada by encouraging the revolutionary sentiment he sensed in Montreal.

In the aftermath of Charles de Gaulle's now infamous "Vive le Québec libre!" rally at City Hall, Prime Minister Pearson did his best to assure Canadians that the country would resist any effort to tear it apart from within. Sadly for Pearson, this line of reasoning didn't ring true with voters and his perceived tolerance for nationalism in Quebec cost him his power the very next year.

By the time Pearson left office in 1968, the groundwork had been laid for major league expansion into Montreal. The bid was submitted just months before Pearson was replaced by Pierre Trudeau as prime minister. The following year, he watched from his idle post as honorary team president as two phenomena sprung to life: Expos baseball and the modern separatist movement in Quebec.

> "Make your revolution yourselves.... You alone can build a free society."
> —*Manifesto of the Front de Libération du Québec, 1970*

The Montreal Expos did some remarkable things during the summer of '69. Less than two weeks after the team played its first game, future pitching ace Bill Stoneman threw a no-hitter against the Philadelphia Phillies. At rickety Jarry Park, with the smallest seating capacity of any stadium in the league, the team hosted over a million fans. Baseball was all the rage.

Still, the Expos were a lowly expansion team and cobbled together only 52 wins. They tied a record by losing 20 straight games, failing to win during the entire month of May.

As a result, from the beginning of the 1970 season, the Expos focused on improvement. The slogan "70 in 70" became a rallying cry.

Behind a converted outfielder named Carl Morton, the second most popular redhead on the team after "Le Grand Orange" Rusty Staub, the Expos surpassed that goal in their sophomore year. Montreal won 73 games in 1970 and Morton was voted National League Rookie of the Year.

That summer, the baseball season ended just in time for political tensions to boil over into a national emergency. The days of conciliation for Quebec nationalists under Lester Pearson were over.

Flamboyant new prime minister Pierre Trudeau didn't bother hiding his dismissive attitude about separatism. He turned Canada into an officially bilingual country and emphasized the importance of its cultural diversity. If Trudeau hoped such measures would reassure radicals in Quebec that his Canada could be theirs as well, he was sorely disappointed.

Throughout the summer of 1970, violence rocked the streets of Montreal. English boroughs near the downtown core became frequent targets for bombings. In the fall, British trade delegate James Cross and Quebec politician Pierre Laporte were kidnapped.

While the Mets and Orioles battled for the World Series, Trudeau invoked the obscure War Measures Act granting his government sweeping powers to impose martial law over Montreal. Laporte was soon discovered, murdered in the trunk of a car. In the weeks that followed, over 400 people were detained as political radicals. Less than 20 would ever be convicted of a crime.

A wave of paranoia swept across the nation. One politician was quoted as saying that separatists had "infiltrated every strategic place in the province." Buoyed by this mania, most Canadians supported the repression of political activism in Quebec.

Canadians would always remember those days as the FLQ Crisis, named after the group responsible for Laporte's murder. Quebecers would always remember that the rest of the country stood glibly by while the army marched on Montreal.

None of this had anything to do with baseball. The fact that Expos owner Charles Bronfman was cited as an enemy of Quebec by the FLQ (Front de Libération du Québec) was little more than an accidental overlap.

The uprising was not related to baseball and had no impact on the perceived stability of the Expos franchise. Relocation was never seriously discussed. The league was committed to seeing the young team through these ugly events.

On the other hand, what the league couldn't bear was Jarry Park. While a revolution ran amok in the streets, the Expos' biggest worry was its stadium. This would haunt the franchise for years.

In 2002, little has changed. Baseball still finds a home for itself in such awful turmoil and is now more obsessively preoccupied with stadiums than ever before.

"I'm very confident in all of our security measures."
—*Commissioner Bud Selig on the safety of baseball facilities, 2001*

Two days before Selig's announcement, in autumn 2001, New York and Washington suffered a calamity broadcast live around the world. People struggled to make sense out of that dark September morning and baseball was there to offer a familiar distraction.

Security at baseball stadiums, like all sports venues, has been dramatically increased since the terrorist attacks. At times, these places have seemed like giant bull's-eyes on an American landscape filled with possible targets. They are certainly treated as such by military and law enforcement officials.

It would be a blow to more than just the infrastructure of America for one of its many sports cathedrals to come under attack. The mythology of the American people is rooted in professional sports. Americans tell sports stories with the same reverence as biblical tales. Sports figures are always cast in the light of heroes.

In this context, a bomb blast at Fenway Park or Yankee Stadium would have a greater symbolic impact than an attack at a nuclear station or hydroelectric dam. To a lesser extent, the same would be true of a gunshot from the stands or an assault on the field. Americans would feel it in their bones.

Responding to this reality, America has bolstered security at most professional sports venues. Whenever spectators and athletes come together, police and military personnel will not be far behind.

One has to wonder how safe Nomar Garciaparra felt on opening day when a man ran out from the stands and stood beside him to have his picture taken. One has to wonder how safe Derek Jeter felt a week later when a woman raced out to his position, forced a piece of paper into his hand and escaped back into the anonymity of the stands.

Nomar Garciaparra and Derek Jeter are more than just two of the best young players in a sport desperate to attract new fans. They are among the biggest stars on baseball's most legendary clubs. If Nomar had blown into a million pieces or Jeter had dropped to his knees with a switchblade in his gut, the country would have gone into shock.

Stadium security has come a long way since September 11, 2001. It's clearly got a long way to go if officials are serious about preventing something outrageous from happening. This challenge is magnified when teams like the Yankees travel to Canada.

After hosting the Minnesota Twins, Toronto welcomes the Yankees to SkyDome. Former Blue Jay David Wells pitches for New York in front of a paltry crowd. On television, broadcasters show only those camera angles in which the smattering of fans fills the screen.

As this season wears on, tiny crowds in Toronto will almost certainly generate comparisons to embarrassing totals in Montreal. In both cities, the league may soon start asking serious questions about steps being taken to ensure that those crowds are secure.

Canada is not a military nation. It does not spend much money on soldiers. Ethnic profiling is a taboo. Under these conditions, a clever malcontent could concoct a fairly reliable plan for sneaking dangerous materials into Olympic Stadium or SkyDome and find enough privacy to use them. As teams like the Yankees criss-cross America they are moving targets. When they come to Canada, they are worryingly exposed.

In the second week of April, the Yankees blow out the Blue Jays. All the while, deep recesses of SkyDome abound with empty corridors largely unpatrolled by fans or stadium staff.

There's something unnatural about discussing these scenarios in the context of a Canadian crowd. Canadians are supposed to be docile, friendly people. And they are. Within the cultural mosaic, however, there are as many loony-bin types as anywhere and the country's short history is spattered with its share of blood, particularly where Toronto and Montreal come into play.

The year 1970 wasn't the first time Canada's army descended on Montreal to quell a political uprising. Rather, contrary to how many Canadians regard their history, it was the first time such an action was taken in Montreal alone, and helped engender the now popular myth that separatism has always had something to do with French Quebec.

Before Canada came into existence, Toronto and Montreal were both focal points for separatist violence. Conventional wisdom has it that the two cities have been at loggerheads since the army of England pushed the army of France out of the new world but, prior to the idea of Canadian nationhood, Toronto and Montreal weren't rivals at all. It was only when their revolutions failed, and power was centralized in a new political reality that Canada's most familiar collision course took shape.

"Up then, brave Canadians! Get your rifles and make short work of it."
—*William Lyon Mackenzie, separatist agitator in Toronto, 1837*

The English-French thing was not central to rebellions that flared in Toronto and Montreal as Canada crept closer to nationhood. Radicals in Upper (Ontario) and Lower (Quebec) Canada were simply desperate for greater accountability and independence.

In 1841, the British Parliament formally united Upper and Lower Canada. The new province of Canada, still under the authority of a parent government in England, was created through the forced merger of what had once been the warring settlements of Britain and France.

During this era, economic crises sent farmers and laborers to the poor house, gross political patronage was the order of the day and liberal-democratic thought was taking shape among the growing middle class. Unrest was inevitable.

In some quarters, there was a call for more responsible government. In others, there was a call for an American-style republic. In Toronto and Montreal, the idea of sweeping reform was gathering strength.

Toronto was the colloquial name used by British officers negotiating with First Nations chiefs over the purchase of a quarter-million acres of land abutting a huge waterway that extended as far as the city of Kingston to the east. By the early 1830s, the town that was constructed on this site had grown into a self-sufficient shipping and merchant community.

It had also been granted official city status thereby allowing for a kind of representative government. This paved the way for regulations aimed at fixing broken streets and cleaning up deplorable sanitary conditions generating deadly outbreaks of cholera.

Toronto's strategic location on the shore of Lake Ontario encouraged property development in close proximity to the harbor. Inland development was driven by property subdivision up Yonge Street, near the center of town, while the waterfront continued to be the primary focus of construction activity. Government buildings, boarding houses, jails, hotels and shops of all kinds

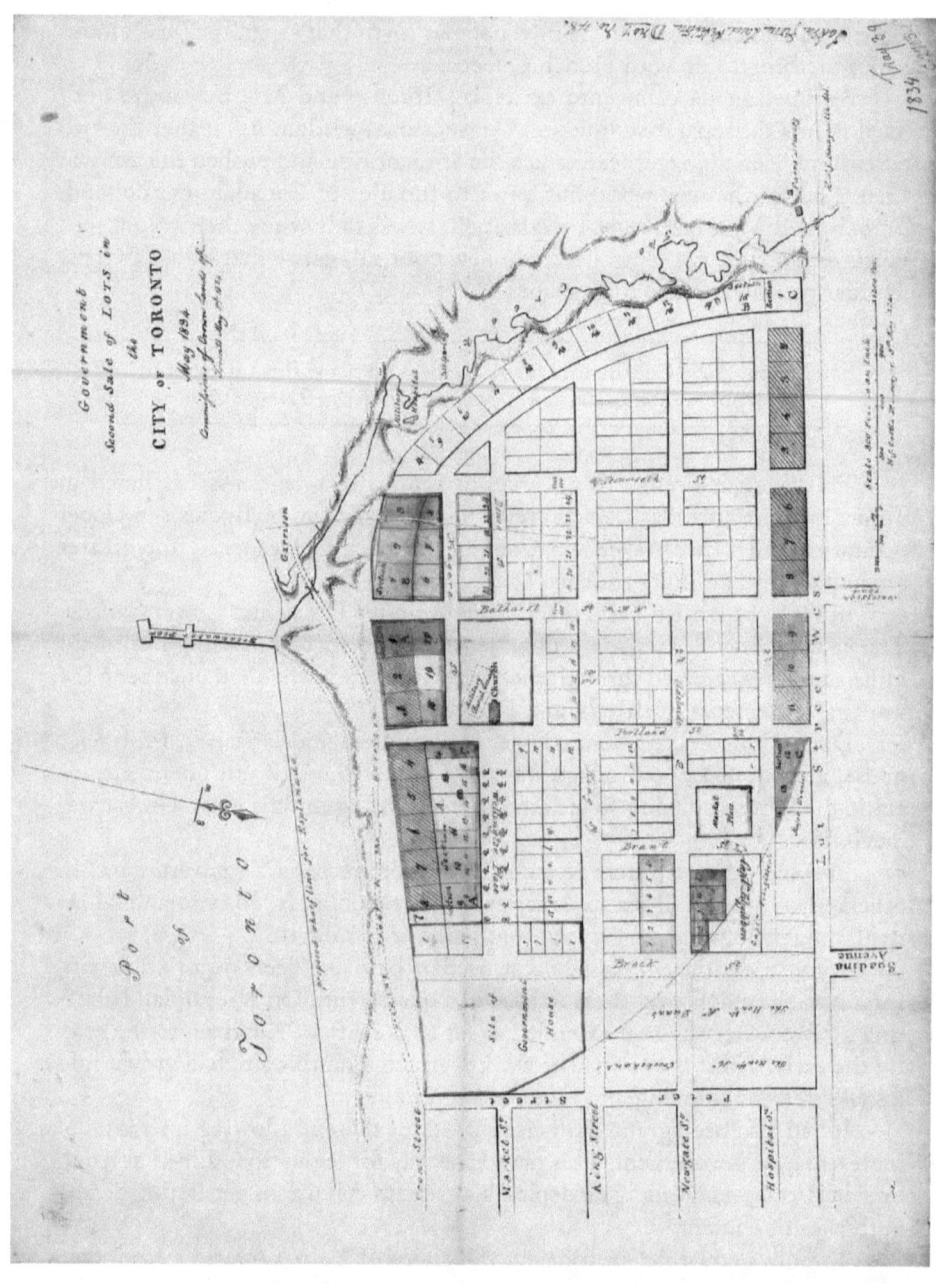

Modest beginnings for the city of Toronto (1834), which gradually expanded into more than a shipping and commercial outpost dependent for its existence on other cities across Lake Ontario, like the capital in Kingston (Henry James Bonnycastle / Library and Archives Canada / NMC-5038).

crammed together close to the harbor's many wharves. By 1837, Toronto had grown to almost 12,000 inhabitants.

Official city status was awarded and the new government took steps to modernize essential public works. These measures did little to satisfy local activists who felt that truly responsible government had not been established.

With people and money pouring into town, those merchants who were not making fortunes riding the coattails of public officials were calling for reform. There were enough idealists around to manufacture angry mobs in the streets.

In 1837, William Lyon Mackenzie proclaimed that, since no revolutionary movement had ever failed in the Americas, it was time for Upper Canada to break away. Mackenzie organized a military uprising that swelled to include a revolutionary army of between 600–800 volunteers.

Their plan was to coordinate attacks throughout Toronto and, thus, capture both the city and region. Instead, they discovered that a volunteer army is not always strong on coordination. The rebels split, some fragments attacking prematurely and allowing the British army to defeat individual pieces one at a time. The result was utter chaos.

Mackenzie fled to the United States where he failed to relaunch his attack. In the end, those of his revolutionary allies who were not able to escape to America were hanged in Toronto. The rebellion was put down.

The issue at the heart of this turmoil, for which some were willing to fight and die, was economic stability and the principle of responsible government. Linguistic and cultural differences among the many groups living in the city weren't primary motivators. Not even in Montreal.

When Toronto came into its own during the 1830s, Montreal was already almost 200 years old. A century prior to the purchase of the land that eventually became Toronto, the walled city of Montreal was at the heart of the international fur trade by virtue of its location on the primary waterway connecting Europe to the colonies.

By the 1820s, that business had fallen apart and officials in Montreal were scrambling to save the local economy by focusing on the exploitation of natural resources and the expansion of existing shipping connections. The strength of the Bank of Montreal ensured that the capital necessary to make this transition happen was accessible. Backed by this financial giant, the city reinvented itself.

After the fortifying wall was finally torn down, Montreal expanded in all directions between the hill that locals deemed a mountain and the rough waters of the St. Lawrence River. The city grew many times larger and several suburbs developed both east and west along the town's main arteries as well as up towards the mountain looming behind the harbor.

Like in Toronto, the early 1830s featured a significant change in the governance of Montreal, which was incorporated under its own city charter for

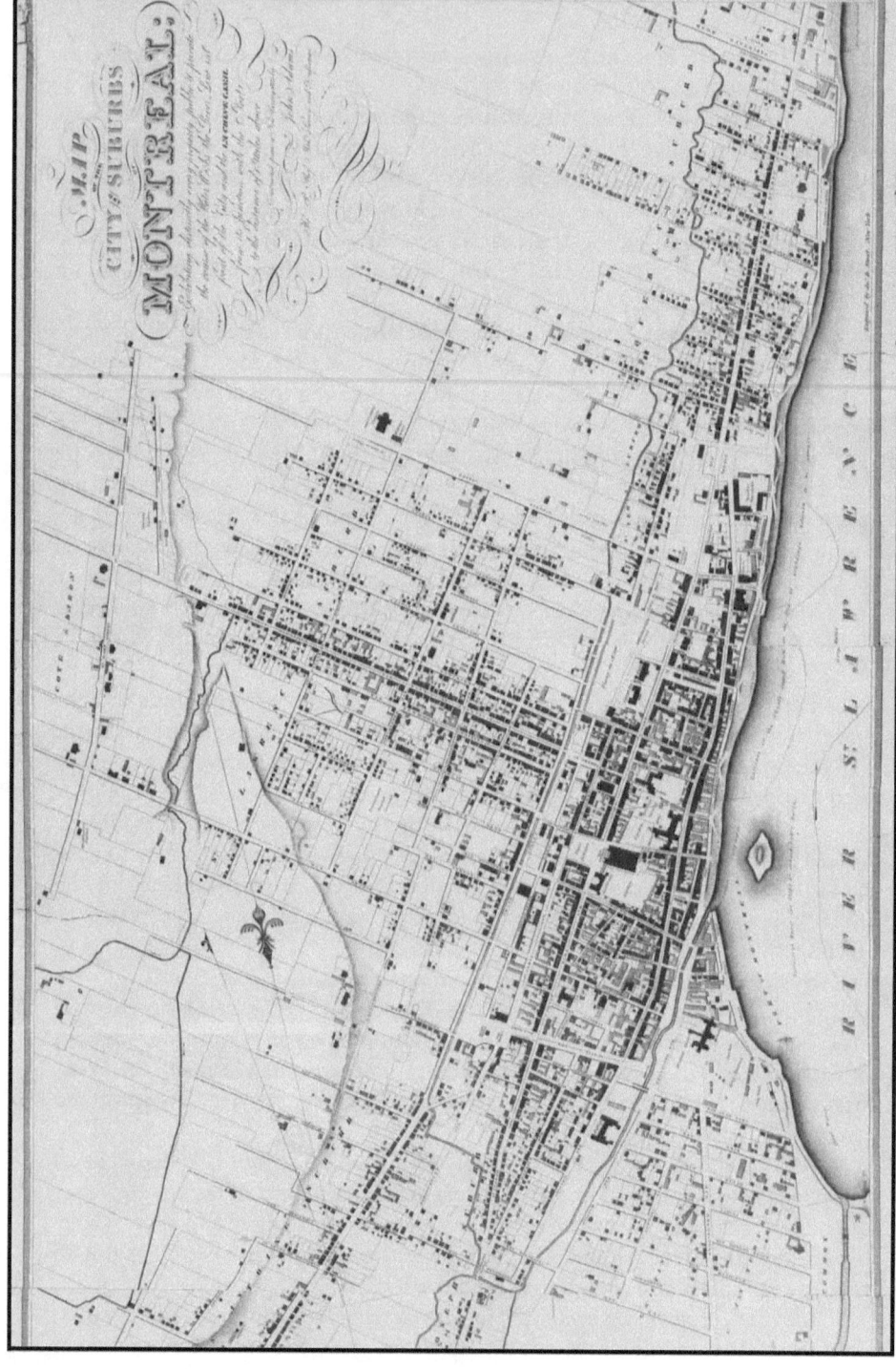

the first time. This allowed for the establishment of an elected council and regulations that, in part, were intended to address Montreal's own cholera epidemics. It was an important step forward as it established the first quasi-independent government in the city.

The charter didn't last. It was repealed in 1836 and the sudden return of the old guard, totally unaccountable to the city's nearly 20,000 inhabitants, was received with scorn from reformers of all stripes. Local elections became occasions for violent confrontations in the streets, including blind assaults by army regiments desperate to regain order.

Politicians in Quebec City ineffectually bickered over their own proposals for legislative reform, rendering themselves irrelevant to people in Montreal. Clashes between rival factions were commonplace. Innocent bystanders were shot dead. The Bank of Montreal was threatened with imminent attack. In the absence of true government, anarchy often carried the day.

In this raucous and adversarial climate, at roughly the same time that Mackenzie's rebellion was being put down in Toronto, a variety of different communities threw support behind a political group led by both English and French idealists in Montreal, known as the Patriotes. Inspired by revolutionary events in Europe and America, the Patriotes movement was a reaction to economic failure along the St. Lawrence River, mass emigration to the United States and the sentiment of assimilation perceived to be emanating from Upper Canada.

The Patriotes took to the streets of Montreal in a show of open disdain for British authority. They rebelled violently and hopelessly. The rabble-rousers were assembled and, just like in Toronto, hanged by the neck for all to see.

The rebellion wasn't about English-French. It was a patchwork, enjoying support in Montreal's Irish community among others. People wanted out of what they saw as a bad deal.

This same idea was at the heart of a declaration of independence that was written the following year and helped spark a second rebellion in Montreal. That, too, was put down and had as much to do with economic failure as with language and culture.

A decade later, English and French businessmen issued the Montreal Merchants Manifesto, endorsing complete annexation to the United States. To some, just about anything seemed preferable to the chaos of local government and the cross-section of power offered inside the British province of Canada.

In both Toronto and Montreal, the very idea of Canadian union was a cause for alarm. For these people, the trouble was only beginning.

Opposite: Sprawling city of Montreal (1825), well established as a critical shipping throughway for international goods destined for markets across North America (John Stout Adams / Library and Archives Canada / NMC-12938).

By the late 1850s, the concept of confederation was gaining popularity. Plans for a cross-country railway establishing Toronto as a gateway to the breadbasket of the west were developing. Canada would extend itself to the seas and become a nation under its own constitution.

This was the new vision and it suited the surviving political leadership in Toronto nicely. The queen had assented. Confederation was coming. The queen had also settled the question of where the new country's capital would be located, a matter of much interest in Toronto and Montreal.

Competition among candidate cities was believed by the queen to be so fierce that if the capital were established in Toronto, Kingston, Montreal or Quebec City the remaining three would harbor lasting, damaging resentments. As capital of the former province of Canada, Montreal had already paid its dues to the union. Those dues had been harsh.

Following the rebellions and the Montreal Merchants Manifesto, the Canadian government based in Montreal introduced the Rebellion Losses Bill, compensating those who'd incurred financial damages during the uprising. Incensed by this action, a mob descended on the capitol buildings.

The legislature was ransacked and the assembly set on fire. With fire-fighters blocked from the scene by rioters, little could be salvaged. The capital was subsequently moved out of Montreal, exchanged between Toronto, Kingston and Quebec City.

The fiasco devastated Montreal's chances of being selected as Canada's permanent capital. Toronto and Kingston, in turn, were judged as being too close to the United States, a former enemy whose forces had once come close to capturing Quebec City as well. So the queen selected Ottawa, a cut-rate city on the skids with a picturesque site for Parliament buildings along its river.

Toronto and Montreal, united in mutual disdain for Ottawa and their stifled ambition to pull out of the Canadian experiment altogether, moved forward from that point in history along divergent paths. Canada's classic rivalry came to life along the way.

They were never rivals before. Toronto had more of a rivalry with Kingston just as Montreal was more frequently at odds with Quebec City. It was Canada that turned the two onto each other.

Western expansion would eventually solidify Toronto's position as a center of growing economic and political influence. Revolutionary voices were drowned.

In Montreal, Canadian union would bring riches to some but would also become a vehicle for political careerists who saw the city as a pawn to be played. Revolutionary voices, rather than being drowned, changed their tune.

Both cities had to be dragged into Canada. People today have a hard time understanding this, partly because it's not a popular aspect of the country's history and partly because they think the two cities have maintained a cute rivalry that has something to do with hockey. Like it or not, activists in both Toronto and Montreal risked the gallows to keep Canada from happening.

No one gets hanged in Canada anymore. What a mess.

Instead, Canadians ignore political activism and, from time to time, make fun of it on public television. Because the country thinks of politics as little more than a source of satire, it's also become easy to think of the rivalry between Toronto and Montreal as being about something as simple as language or as banal as sports.

The 2002 baseball season is doing what it can to support this silly idea, kicking off with the Blue Jays and Expos registering identical 5–5 records. There's little to choose between the two clubs, running neck and neck albeit in different leagues.

More important than any tenuous links to the underlying rivalry, these records reflect the fact that both teams still have their heads above water. Compared to teams like the Detroit Tigers, still yet to win a single game, this modest success speaks to an important truism in baseball: you can't win anything in the first month of the season but you can lose everything. The Blue Jays and Expos still have respectability in their sights.

Montreal carries its record into New York to face the Mets, a team built around expensive free agent sluggers Jeromy Burnitz and Mo Vaughn. New York's offense will surely be better as a result of these signings. They'll still need pitching and defense if they want to contend.

Early on, those prospects seem remote. A pile of errors help the Expos build a commanding 7–0 lead before New York storms back into the game. Burnitz earns some of his enormous paycheck by chasing Expos starter Javier Vazquez from the mound with a 7th inning hit that extends a key rally.

After that, more bad signs for New York. Scott Strickland, freshly acquired from these same Expos just a week ago, comes into the game.

Expos general manager Omar Minaya didn't waste any time answering the question of how he was going to improve his marked team. He dealt from the Expos' strong suit, its bullpen, in order to shore up the starting rotation.

Minaya traded reliever Scott Strickland and a couple of prospects to the Mets in exchange for young starter Bruce Chen. The theory is that the Expos can afford to trim their stable of competent relievers in order to protect against the possibility of injuries to their starters.

Minaya jumped at the opportunity. Nagging questions about how to balance future prospects against existing talent on a team that is perceived as having neither a future nor a present are answered. The move is widely expected to have a modest, positive impact. Everyone breathes a little easier, except perhaps the Mets.

In the 11th inning, Strickland gives up a home run to Vladimir Guerrero, sinking New York. On this day, poor pitching and awful defense hand the Expos another win.

Despite the dramatic victory, Montreal has reason to worry. The team loses two players to injury. Catcher Michael Barrett, who has been a hitting machine over the first two weeks, is forced out of the game with a strained hip. Second baseman Jose Vidro leaves the game as well with an injured groin. Vidro is essential to the Expos' offense. These injuries threaten all of Montreal's limited success.

By contrast, the injury story in Toronto is just the opposite. For a team whose biggest question mark is its young pitching staff, the news that two comparatively experienced starters, Esteban Loaiza and Steve Parris, are expected to return by early May couldn't come at a better time.

These two pitchers will immediately improve Toronto's rotation and, by allowing manager Buck Martinez to move some of his current starters into the bullpen, will also create an improved corps of relief pitchers. It's good news for the Blue Jays. Almost as good is the fact that they're in Tampa Bay facing the Devil Rays, one of the most awful franchises in professional sports.

Against the D-Rays, Carlos Delgado goes off. He hits a home run and a double, draws a pair of walks and scores twice, raising his batting average to a team-leading .432. When Delgado is at his best, it's hard for Toronto to lose.

Both the Blue Jays and Expos push their records over .500 with wins. True, 6–5 is nothing special but, this early in the year, the only thing teams really need to guard against is the type of start the Tigers are having. A record of 0–11 is devastating. So devastating that Detroit has coaxed former Expos manager Felipe Alou out of retirement to help turn the team around.

Felipe's got his work cut out because the Tigers need an emergency overhaul. It's tempting to think of Alou as the sort of manager to deliver. His mysterious Midas touch and grizzled charm used to attract at least as many fans to Olympic Stadium as any of his players. Drawing fans to the stadium during his tenure in Montreal was no small feat.

Not that Olympic Stadium always had a reputation as a tough building to fill. When it first opened its doors to baseball, 58,000 people were in the stands.

Back then, Olympic Stadium was a good sight to see. There was no silly roof and the arching tower leaned over crowds from high above. Montrealers didn't feel burdened by its location. The stadium reminded them of a great moment on the international stage and held the promise of more good times in the major leagues.

In mid–April, the building celebrates 25 years of baseball but only 4,700 people turn out to see the Expos play the Cubs. These days, most Montrealers regard Olympic Stadium as an eyesore and a financial sinkhole. Residents continue to pay for the facility, sometimes referred to as the Big Owe, through property taxes. People perceive it as being in the middle of nowhere.

Against the Cubs, on baseball's 25th anniversary at the Big O, the Expos surrender a massive home run to slugger Sammy Sosa. His towering blast clears the oval security ring below the Kevlar roof before ricocheting off a speaker over the outfield fence. It is a staggering shot, brought down to earth by the constraints of the stadium. Some will say that this is fitting; baseball limited by the Big O itself. They won't say that too loudly.

After losing to Chicago, the Expos get back on track and pull into first place in the National League East. In front of 11,000 fans, the biggest crowd in Montreal since the home opener, the Expos exploit the sloppiest defense in baseball and beat the New York Mets again to move into a tie for the division lead.

The Expos have their star hitters to thank for being at the top of the table. Vladimir Guerrero and Jose Vidro are the gears that make Montreal's engine turn and, though players like Michael Barrett were hot early on, the team is not in first place because of its plucky catcher. The core of the Expos' offense is explosive. People will eventually turn up to see a show like that even if it means traveling out to the Big O.

The inadequacy of Olympic Stadium continues to be the biggest obstacle standing between the Expos and permanence in Montreal. This is somewhat ironic since this is the same facility that was supposed to get the league off Montreal's back and ensure that the Expos stayed in town forever.

"Most people who frequented Jarry Park still love the 'Spos but never warmed up to the concrete toilet bowl."
—*Jonah Keri, senior writer,* Baseball Prospectus, *2002*

Prior to joining the league, backers of Montreal's expansion franchise promised baseball's front office that the city would build a permanent domed stadium for the team. This was perceived as being absolutely necessary given the chilly weather in Montreal and was a key condition upon which the franchise was awarded.

After the city turned down a proposal through which seven million dollars in public money would have been set aside to finance such a stadium, the Expos were forced to consider alternatives. As a temporary measure, Jarry Park was hastily retrofitted.

By 1972, when the team originally expected to move into a permanent domed facility, no such project was even looming on the horizon. Improvements and adjustments continued to be made at Jarry Park but it was clearly not a suitable long-term site for baseball. The relationship between the team and the league strained over the issue. Where was the new stadium?

At the time, there was no appetite in Ottawa for talk of federal intervention to help Montreal and the Expos. Prime Minister Trudeau was embroiled in plans to transform the aging Toronto waterfront into a vibrant mixed-use district including a massive downtown park for all to enjoy. For decades, this

Jarry Park was poorly suited as a host for Major League Baseball but, by necessity, it was put to use and, to the surprise of many, was embraced by local fans (Canadian Baseball Hall of Fame and Museum).

would turn federal attention to the renewal of Toronto's waterfront. Baseball in Montreal was not on the agenda.

With tensions over this issue rising, fans watched Bill Stoneman pitch his second no-hitter at Jarry Park in 1972. Carl Morton had already begun his slide into obscurity but young Mike Torrez picked up the slack by winning 16 games. The team struggled with only 70 wins but the pitching staff showed promise.

In 1973, that staff fell to pieces. Only the phenomenal stats of 23-year-old Steve Rogers stood out among Expos pitchers. Luckily, the batters finally hit their stride.

Third baseman Bob Bailey and outfielder Ken Singleton both had breakthrough seasons, hitting 26 and 23 home runs respectively. Along with consistent hitting from both Ron Hunt and Ron Fairly, this offensive coming of age kept the Expos in the chase for a division title right to the end of the season. They recorded 79 wins, the team's best showing ever.

In 1974, while Steve Rogers emerged as a workhorse on the mound, Singleton and Bailey had disappointing summers. The offense slumped, hampering the Expos' overall progress. Montreal matched its previous year's total of 79 wins, which was a disappointment of sorts.

The organization looked to young players such as Gary Carter, Larry Parrish and Warren Cromartie for hope moving forward. The team's future, however, was a topic of much debate.

There continued to be no new stadium in Montreal. Major League officials had seen enough baseball at Jarry Park. The pressure was on and serious discussions took place about whether or not to revoke Montreal's expansion franchise in response to the stadium debacle.

In this adversarial climate, the words of International Olympic Committee (IOC) president Lord Killanin offered a ray of hope. Speaking in 1974, Killanin emphasized the importance of designing Olympic facilities to accommodate post–Olympic uses and prevent cities from being saddled with "stadia in which the seats ... remain empty forever."

The IOC had awarded Montreal the 1976 Olympic Games. Facing the wrath of a league that had run out of patience, he also awarded Montreal a way of keeping its baseball team.

This hope and relief will be familiar to those in Toronto who reacted similarly to the development of SkyDome 15 years after Montreal started planning Olympic Stadium. These days, Montrealers shake their heads at the sight of their decaying public liability. Torontonians are not far from having to confront this same reality. In 2002, fans in Toronto rock themselves to sleep thinking that SkyDome and the Big O are in different classes altogether, telling themselves that the only thing the buildings share is a home team with pitching problems.

The Blue Jays have surrendered more runs than any other team in baseball. The inexperienced starting rotation has been kicked around so badly that, according to manager Buck Martinez, it is starting to have an adverse impact on the team's hitting.

Martinez claims that, constantly having to come back from significant early deficits, his hitters have been thrown out of synch and are trying to do too much at the plate. It's the sort of comment one expects from a former television commentator with no managerial experience at any level. He is adept at recognizing patterns, less so at specifics.

Only Roy Halladay stands out as a reliable arm in Toronto's rotation. Halladay has struck out twenty batters while giving up three walks in 22 innings. That's first rate. As good as he's been, the Blue Jays will need more than just Roy Halladay as they embark on another series against the Yankees.

Blue Jays-Yankees games are interesting for more than just the obvious reasons. Yes, these are divisional rivals and, since the Yankees payroll is more than double that of the Blue Jays, it is a kind of big market-small market showdown. Beyond that, the Jays and Yankees also share some of the same baseball history.

At different times, both teams have been almost universally despised among American fans for the success they've enjoyed. In fact, one could say that Toronto didn't really "arrive" in the league until the popular magazine *Baseball Weekly* featured a cover story on the team entitled "Damned Blue Jays" during their World Series runs in 1992 and 1993.

America was rooting for any team but the Blue Jays because Toronto had dramatically exported the World Series north of the border. Though it would be impossible to accurately measure such a thing, it could not be far from the truth to say that the Blue Jays of the early 1990s were one of the most disliked teams in modern major league history.

For the New York Yankees, the two measly years of scorn directed at the Blue Jays are mere drops in the bucket of comparative exasperation that has been directed at the Bronx Bombers for decades. The Yankees are the most popular and most reviled baseball club in America. It's been that way forever.

The Yankees are one of those rare franchises whose success and excess have reached such extreme levels that it is sometimes unclear whether the team exists as part of its league or the league exists as an extension of the team. It is an oft-quoted cliché that no individual or team is bigger than the game. In New York, they seriously doubt whether this could be the case.

In Toronto, fans do not share the luxury of such willful self-delusion. Blue Jays fans, like all sports fans in Canada, are a jittery lot starving for recognition. It is a disproportionate blow when a free agent leaves town and a lopsided rush when a free agent signs on. Toronto is characterized by this perpetual little-big-man image crisis.

On a Saturday afternoon in the Bronx, the little big men meet the real big men. The Jays count on Roy Halladay to be at his best.

Early on, things look bad. Bernie Williams takes the young Blue Jays starter out of Yankee Stadium with a home run in the 1st inning. Staking the Yankees to a lead at home is never a good idea. For a struggling team like the Blue Jays, it's suggestive of total disaster.

Halladay shrugs it off and gets back to work. From that point forward, he gives up only two more hits and eventually leaves with the game tied 1–1. Following his exit, Blue Jays hitters put up three runs and surge comfortably ahead. Cue the rest of the Blue Jays pitching staff.

The Yankees are down to their last strike with the bases empty in the bottom of the 9th inning when closer Kelvim Escobar does what Blue Jays pitchers seem to do best. He blows it. Two walks and three hits later the Yankees tie the game. Watching from the bench, Roy Halladay must feel like a tired old man.

Mercifully, the self-destructive Toronto pitching staff doesn't cost them this game. Instead, rookie third baseman Eric Hinske picks an opportune moment to hit his first career home run, winning the game. Nonetheless, Toronto is playing like a team waiting to implode.

In Montreal, the Expos face similar challenges. Pitching has not been the team's strong suit but Expos hitters have been outstanding and it's made up for some of these woes.

General Manager Omar Minaya holds his breath as recently acquired Bruce Chen takes the mound against New York with the Mets pressing in the midst of a 4th inning rally. Chen was the key player in a deal that sent reliever Scott Strickland to New York and has since led to some rather brash speculation about the integrity of Minaya's office.

As expected, he not only has to deal with the pressure of finding solutions to his team's problems but also has to deal with the stigma of being the general manager of a team owned by its competitors. Unnamed sources have come forward to criticize Minaya's deal for Chen.

Claiming to be National League general managers who would have given Montreal much more for Strickland than he received from the Mets, these mysterious whistleblowers have asked what alliances might still remain between Minaya and his former employers in New York. The implication is that Minaya gave the Mets a better deal than necessary.

Set aside the fact that Minaya is operating on less than a shoestring budget and probably could never have afforded the overpaid pseudo-talent that other teams would have tried to dump on Montreal. Forget that young starting pitchers like Chen are a commodity that every team wants. Aside from all that, it's just bizarre to hear major league executives lecture about integrity.

With two outs in the 4th inning, Montreal holds a slim lead. It'll make for bitter headlines if Chen falls apart and costs Montreal both the game and its place atop the division. Instead, Chen sparkles.

Not only does he smother the Mets' rally, he shuts them out and helps himself by hitting a single and scoring behind Jose Vidro's RBI double. Chen's performance propels Montreal into sole possession of first place in the National League East.

"I think this team is one year away from being the '94 Expos."
— *Omar Minaya, 2002*

The Blue Jays don't have to deal with the same bitter scrutiny that follows the Expos. They aren't enjoying the same success either.

Toronto stumbles through a 14-game road trip as the month of April grinds to a close. They face the Texas Rangers at The Ballpark in Arlington, a facility constructed with public money that also inadvertently financed the political campaign of President George W. Bush.

Coming in, the Jays have lost seven out of their last ten games. Carlos Delgado's average has dropped below .300 while Raul Mondesi's has plummeted to the mythic Mendoza line. Only Shannon Stewart, demoted to designated hitter, is putting up consistent numbers. These are tough times.

In Texas, things don't get any easier. Fans in Arlington seem to follow opposition stats pretty closely. Persistent hecklers, taking a certain glee in Delgado and Mondesi's respective struggles, are audible all day long. The Jays respond with a strong early showing. They jump out to a quick lead and carry a 4–3 advantage into the bottom of the 9th inning, sending closer Kelvim Escobar out to finish things off.

The first hitter Escobar faces nails the second pitch he throws. The solo home run forces extra innings and the frustrated Jays trudge back out for another hour of baseball.

They take a lead again in the 15th inning, thinking they've outlasted the Rangers' heroics. That is, until little known David Eckstein delivers his first hit of the day in the form of a grand slam home run in the bottom of the inning. The Rangers win 8–5. The Blue Jays drop to 8–15 on the season.

The Expos are holding together by doing the very thing that the Jays still fail to accomplish. When their pitching falters, their hitting takes over.

Montreal leads the National League in batting average, hits, runs and RBIs. Jose Vidro and Vladimir Guerrero are killing and the team continues to receive contributions from a variety of sources.

Most recently, first baseman Lee Stevens stepped into the spotlight by hitting homers in consecutive games. If nothing else, this suggests that the offense is healthy. They're spreading it around.

The Expos' team ERA is also top 10 in the National League so the pitchers are beginning to get their act together. If Javier Vazquez returns to form, the Expos won't need to lead the league in offense all season long. That'd be good. They're not likely to lead the league in offense all season long.

As it stands, their success has people asking whether contraction is really such a good idea. Even Bud Selig is slightly moved, acknowledging that he would not be inclined to contract a division winning team at the end of the year. Six wins in a row sure do a lot for a team.

On the last weekend of April, the Expos beat the St. Louis Cardinals 5–2. Vladimir Guerrero hits two homers, which is the fifteenth time in his young career that he's hit more than one dinger in a game. The feat also gives him 28 RBIs, pushing him into the National League lead and surpassing the previous Expos record for RBIs in April, originally set by teammate Henry Rodriguez.

Rodriguez is back with the Montreal Expos in 2002, five years after he was last at home in Olympic Stadium where he enjoyed his greatest success. Rodriguez started the 1996 season on an offensive tear that would become legendary among Expos fans.

For a brief period, it literally seemed like Henry Rodriguez hit a home run every day. He obviously didn't, finishing that first month with 10 blasts and 27 RBIs. Still, it ranks among the most impressive temporary assaults ever put together by an Expo. Furthermore, Henry delivered his performance with such panache that it was thrilling and controversial.

During that improbable run, Henry once took a step out of the batter's box and raised one hand off his bat to call for a time-out in the midst of the opposing pitcher's windup. The umpire refused to grant his request so Henry stepped back into the box and cranked the ensuing pitch over the fence. On another occasion, he was justly accused of sneaking a peek back at the catcher's position or sign prior to drilling a home run.

At Olympic Stadium, Rodriguez's position was, and often is, littered with Oh Henry! chocolate bars. Fans still have a soft spot for the memory of that remarkable spring.

"I love playing for the Expos. Montreal fans treated me better than any others."
—*Henry Rodriguez, on his decision to return to Montreal, 2002*

May

> "The result [of not using any public money] is that we won't have any pro sports."
> —*Houston mayor Bob Lanier, 1996*

Compared to the threat of relocation, the threat of contraction is new. Until this summer, contraction was dismissed as a misguided and ineffective response to problems shared by many teams. The league preferred to support individual owners threatening host cities with franchise relocation instead.

They are distinct strategies in the coercion of local officials but the threats of relocation and contraction share at least one thing in common. Both turn on public stadium financing.

The threat of relocation is usually empty. There simply aren't that many viable and available markets for professional sports in North America. Nonetheless, in 1996, Houston discovered just how serious those threats can sometimes be when the local football team moved away, in part, over the government's unwillingness to cough up money for a new stadium.

Prior to this move, politicians in Houston opposed the crowded bandwagon of American cities committing taxpayer money to new sports facilities. Following the football team's relocation, these same people began laying the groundwork for tax deferral schemes and vague referendums, clearing the way for a new baseball stadium to be built.

As a result, in 2000, the Astros received a new facility that represented the failure of Houston's attempt to stem the tide of public subsidization for professional sports. The stadium also reflected close ties between the city and Enron Corporation, an energy sector giant poised to dissolve in international scandal.

At the time, Enron's sponsorship of the new stadium put a welcome private sector face on what was otherwise an enormous public sector payoff. It offered the franchise a figurehead partner with which most Houston residents could identify.

Enron was a major employer in a city where half the population worked in the oil and gas industries. Energy has always been a huge part of Houston's history.

At the turn of the 20th century, Houston's economy was driven by the distribution of agricultural goods and the exploitation of natural resources such as lumber and cotton. As these industries withered, the city's long-term prospects looked bleak. Luckily, Houston got a shot in the arm from two unexpected sources.

First, in 1900, a vicious hurricane tore through Texas and all but destroyed the city of Galveston. Prior to this catastrophe, Galveston drew most of the nearby Gulf Coast's lucrative shipping activity away from Houston, situated further inland. With the annihilation of Galveston, Houston was back in the shipping business.

Second, in 1904, prospectors discovered oil north of Houston. Serious oil exploration had been underway in Texas for almost a decade prior to this discovery but, with it, Houston underwent a dramatic transformation.

Oil wells were hastily erected. Machine shops and factories were opened. The revived shipping business spurred the construction of several refineries. Financiers from all around Texas moved their businesses to Houston. This sudden agglomeration led to a wave of takeovers and mergers. Houston became the home of big money energy in America.

A hundred years later, Houston's fortunes still extended from these same unpredictable factors, albeit not necessarily in its favor. In 2001, $6 billion in damage was done to the city core by a tropical storm that caused mass flooding. Making matters worse, as energy prices plummeted, Enron went bankrupt amidst the biggest corporate scandal in American history. Houston was hit hard.

Enron Field quickly became more than just the flagship of Houston's unwilling venture into stadium financing. Two years after the facility opened, as it became clear that Enron executives had artificially inflated the value of the company's stocks by hiding losses as capital expenditures in make-believe subsidiaries, Enron Field stood as a public monument to the country's biggest con artists.

Houston has yet to replace Enron as naming sponsor for the stadium. The Astros were forced to pay $2 million just to get the company name off their building. For all the money residents forked over to get the thing built, they now have a nameless, infamous stadium in which to welcome Montreal.

The Expos ride into Texas on the coattails of National League Player of the Month Vladimir Guerrero, and the team seems to be picking up a fresh head of steam. Their best pitcher has yet to come around, their slugging third baseman has just recovered from his most recent injury but the offense keeps rolling so, with these pieces falling into place, everything is coming up Expos.

Javier Vazquez has not played up to his obvious potential this summer.

Facing Houston, the future-star version of Montreal's young ace makes a welcome appearance.

Staked to an early 4–0 lead, he pitches a complete game and gives up just a single run. The encouraging performance suggests that he may be reaching his stride.

A day later, Guerrero leads the charge. With the Expos trailing 3–1 in the 7th, he nails his second home run of the game and sparks a torrid comeback. Afterwards, Houston pitchers admit they weren't even trying to throw him strikes. It's an approach that many have tried. The tactic fails because Guerrero swings at everything. He is an equal opportunity slugger.

Adding fuel to this fire, Montreal adds another potentially dangerous weapon in the form of third baseman Fernando Tatis. Tatis has spent the better part of a year rehabbing from injuries. Now back in the lineup, he could turn the league's most potent offense into an irresistible force.

This is exactly what the Expos need. A winning formula is coming together while the current lineup remains hot enough to carry them when all else fails. They jumped out of the gate quickly this summer. The grueling marathon ahead will challenge them to keep it up.

Just like the Expos, the Blue Jays kick off the month of May against a Lone Star opponent. Unlike the overachieving Expos, the Jays are scrambling to get themselves under control. After a listless road trip, they return home to face the Texas Rangers and hopefully turn their season around.

They'd better not look to their fans for a lift in this direction. So few people turn up at SkyDome upon the team's return that, when Eric Hinske drills a home run in the early innings, the cheers aren't loud enough to drown out the sound of the ball bouncing off the bleachers.

The Jays are not enjoying much in the way of home field advantage. They are also not asserting themselves, even against the most questionable talent in baseball.

For many teams, the sight of Hideki Irabu wobbling in from the bullpen is like the sight of steaks grilling on the bar-b. After being chased out of New York and shipped to the Expos in a bamboozling deal that saw two blue-chip prospects go to the Yankees, Irabu spent almost three years being hurt or downright awful in Montreal. Some pitchers stop losing streaks. Irabu is a losing streak unto himself.

The Texas Rangers, unable to afford a pitching staff after paying their shortstop a quarter of a billion dollars, figured they might put him to good use as a closer. If the Blue Jays are any indication, the experiment is paying off.

Losing 5–3 and facing Irabu, the Blue Jays fail to make anything happen. They don't even put a runner on base. Though Irabu usually looks dazed, like he just finished an enormous meal, he is unfazed by the Jays.

It's another demoralizing loss for Toronto, indicative of just how differently 2002 has been coming together for Canada's teams. While the Blue

Jays fold in front of the league's most debatable talent, the Expos prepare for a showdown against the best team in the world.

A quick trip to Arizona gives Expos hitters an opportunity to establish some credibility against Curt Schilling, one of the league's most overpowering pitchers. Along with former Expo Randy Johnson, Schilling makes up half of baseball's most feared pitching duo.

Faced with this daunting offensive challenge, Expo pitchers forget that they have work to do as well. The Diamondbacks rip three consecutive home runs off starter Bruce Chen, surging into an early 4–0 lead and reminding everyone that it wasn't just clutch pitching that won them a World Series.

After that, Schilling goes through the motions of striking out 14 batters. Vladimir Guerrero and Michael Barrett both homer but the beauty of a pitcher like Schilling is that so few batters reach base against him that his mistakes are never very costly. Guerrero and Barrett both hit their home runs with no one on base.

The Expos eventually lose 6–3 and the team's offense has its shine scuffed away in the process. If they arrived in Arizona hoping to cement themselves as a top team in the National League, they leave wondering how to respond to a harsh wake-up call. Swept out of Arizona by the champs, the Expos bubble looks like it may just have burst.

Under manager Frank Robinson, the Expos have exceeded all expectations. They have turned the depressing buildup to possibly their final year in Montreal into calls for a revision of the contraction strategy. Still, they haven't shaken their status as a doomed team. Most agree that it is only a matter of time before the long grind of the season takes its toll.

The Expos have succeeded so far because the monster at the core of their lineup is delivering. Take Vladimir Guerrero away and the wheels fall off. This is a tenuous position for a baseball team, and is a topic on which the Toronto Blue Jays could lecture at length since one of the biggest factors in their continued slide is the disappearance of Carlos Delgado.

At his best, Delgado is the sort of hitter that can turn a good team into a great one. He is also the sort of hitter who, when he stumbles, can turn a mediocre team into an awful one just as quickly.

Delgado started the season on a tear, showing both patience and power over the first couple of weeks. Since then, he has become a major contributor to Toronto's spiritless downward spiral. His batting average has fallen to .255. Along with power outages from Raul Mondesi and Jose Cruz, this has grounded the Blue Jays' offense.

Such is the relentless pressure of a full major league season. If a team's offense turns on the contribution of one superstar, that player had better perform. If not, the constant weight of scrambling to manufacture wins will wear a team down. The Blue Jays are living in this environment and the Expos are one injury or slump away from joining them.

A lot has to go right for Montreal to follow through on the limited success they've enjoyed so far. Only one or two things have to go wrong for it all to turn into a fiasco. This is the sort of story that sports fans in Montreal know all too well. Montreal is the city that transformed the world's biggest sports spectacle into the country's most notorious sports debacle.

"The Olympics can no more have a deficit than a man can have a baby."
—*Montreal mayor Jean Drapeau, 1973*

The 1976 Olympics were such a disaster that, in their aftermath, Los Angeles ran uncontested in its bid to host the event eight years later. Every other potential host was scared away.

The legacy of the 1976 Olympics is one of missed deadlines, exploding budgets and allusions of corruption. Many facilities, including Olympic Stadium, were still under construction during the opening ceremonies. Montreal's Olympics were a grand idea, buoyed by the optimism of the late '60s, scuttled by shortsightedness and ego.

In the years leading up to the event, construction on all Olympic facilities proceeded as planned. Projects were underway as early as 1973 and within two years the support structure had been removed from Olympic Stadium, signaling its near readiness.

The Olympics were in good shape until the kingpins of Montreal labor decided to hold the event for ransom in May 1975. Construction workers went on strike, derailing the entire project. They didn't return to work until late October. By that time, the Olympics were in a state of crisis, hopelessly off schedule and over budget.

Olympic Stadium architect Roger Taillibert watched his bold vision stutter, unfinished towards each deadline. Though many locals characterized his retractable-roof concept as too flimsy to handle Montreal's blustery winter, Taillibert's design was never truly realized. Unfinished venues were hastily thrown together as the Olympics began, and the massive tower from which his roof was to extend would not be completed for almost a decade.

It is unclear whether Olympic Stadium would have turned into the financial sinkhole it eventually became if Taillibert's concept had been delivered. What is clear is that his design was never meant to accommodate the Montreal Expos.

"You built a stadium that looks like a giant bidet."
—*Former Expos pitcher Bill "Spaceman" Lee, 1998*

In the summer of 1976, as Montrealers watched their Olympic dream stagger forward in disarray, the people of Toronto turned their own Olympic

Olympic Stadium, spectacularly over-budget and converted for baseball with only limited success, earned its reputation as Canada's most notorious sporting investment (Canadian Baseball Hall of Fame and Museum).

experience into a modest success. The Paralympic Games were held in Toronto and featured more athletes, events and media coverage than ever before. It was an important step forward for the Paralympics. For Toronto, it was a small accomplishment in a year filled with talk of good things to come.

In March, Major League Baseball selected Toronto as a site for further expansion into Canada, redressing the last-minute injunction that had prevented local businessman Paul Beeston from purchasing the San Francisco Giants. Heading a group of investors, Beeston put the new franchise in position to start playing the very next summer. Though the speedy turnaround seemed rushed to some, the idea of bringing big league baseball to Toronto had been percolating for almost 20 years.

Back in 1959, at an aging fairground near the waterfront, a football stadium had been constructed for the Toronto Argonauts. This facility, designed in a manner that was totally incompatible with baseball, stimulated dogged enthusiasm for the idea of attracting a major league team. Exhibition Stadium's inadequacy would cause Toronto to be overlooked as a potential expansion site for a full decade.

In 1974, politicians decided to bite the bullet and borrow $18 million to renovate Exhibition Stadium. After incorporating the original grandstand into outfield bleachers, situating home plate in the corner of a football end zone and laying down the largest artificial field in North America, Toronto completed its makeshift baseball stadium in 1976. The city would be awarded its expansion franchise later that year.

When play began in 1977, some of the drawbacks of Exhibition Stadium came to light. The best seats were in left field while the most expensive seats were totally exposed to the elements. There were no seats at all down the third base line and home runs to right bounced into an empty field beyond. It was a strange place for just under 2 million fans to watch baseball that first season.

For all the problems, the fact that Toronto succeeded in bringing a second major league team to Canada was a source of pride for fans who'd supported baseball in the city for decades. What few fully appreciate is that the establishment of major league teams in Montreal and Toronto ought to have been regarded as perfectly natural and was probably long overdue, given the role that both cities played in the creation of the game itself.

> "The chief event ... was a baseball match." —*Letter to* Sporting Life *magazine, recounting 1838 holiday festivities in Canada*

Exhibition Stadium lacked the creature comforts of other major league facilities but stalwart fans in Toronto were undeterred (Canadian Baseball Hall of Fame and Museum).

In the years leading up to the forced union of Upper (Ontario) and Lower (Quebec) Canada, and in the aftermath of separatist rebellions in Toronto and Montreal, the game of baseball was invented. By all accounts, the basic rules of baseball were cobbled together based on the rudiments of two British games: cricket and rounders. The story of its evolution from a mere variation on these themes into the unique game that is played today is fraught with conflicting accounts. Canada has as strong a claim to its invention as the United States.

In the late 1700s, impromptu games similar to early forms of baseball were not uncommon in the streets of Montreal. The burgeoning middle class strove to improve its social standing through participation in organized sports like lacrosse, ice hockey and football. Baseball was perceived as a low pursuit and was reluctantly introduced into the structure of organized sport. Nevertheless, if one traces the rudiments of the game back to its earliest days, some of that history unfolded in the alleys of Montreal.

Some suggest that formal, organized baseball was born in New York during the summer of 1839. Most historians dismiss this account as a popular convention rather than a true record. However, the date is interesting in that it falls a year after the first reported baseball game played in Canada.

In a letter to the editor of *Sporting Life* magazine, a Colorado resident reports being in Upper Canada during holiday celebrations in 1838. His detailed account of the game, its players and outcome leaves no doubt as to the fact that baseball was coming together in Canada at the time.

From that point forward, organized baseball is known to have spread throughout eastern Canada. By the 1870s, baseball had become a regular feature of Dominion Day, Canada's most patriotic annual event. Over time, it would come to be recognized as an integral aspect of American culture exclusively but even after America laid its final claim to the game itself, the history of baseball would continue to cross the northern border.

At Hanlan's Point in Toronto, for example, the baseball world caught a glimpse of its future when then-pitcher Babe Ruth showcased improbable power, hitting his first professional home run into the harbor. Ruth openly acknowledged that the man who originally pointed him towards the game was his grade-school mentor, a Canadian with a homegrown love for the sport. Finally, when Ruth's legend was spent in New York, he was replaced by a Canadian named "Twinkletoes" who filled Babe's outfield position for nearly a decade. Regardless of how deeply entrenched baseball would eventually become in the lore of Americana, the roots of its greatness will always stretch back to Canada.

The fact that Canada's role in the history of baseball has been reduced to less than a side note illustrates that there's nothing about the game that prescribes fairness. It was never supposed to be fair. It was always just a game with winners, losers and more than a few dramatic injustices along the way.

Blue Jays 1, Expos 0

Fans in Montreal may be tempted to believe that 2002 represents the end of all fairness in baseball. In truth, there's nothing special about their hardship this summer. Fans have eaten dirt before. Teams have come and gone.

The Expos have no special claim to martyrdom in baseball; 2002 is still treating the Toronto Blue Jays a lot more harshly so far as day-to-day injustices go.

The Blue Jays leave SkyDome and travel to Seattle where they face a Mariners team that won 110 games last season. The good news for Toronto is that Roy Halladay is in top form against this menacing Seattle offense.

Halladay consistently throws strikes early in the count and keeps leadoff hitters from reaching base almost every inning. This holds the Seattle offense incheck. With Toronto's big bats still missing in action, the team leans on rookie Eric Hinske whose three hits pace the Jays to a 4–0 lead.

In the 8th inning, the Mariners finally get to Halladay as Ichiro Suzuki and Mike Cameron string hits together, chasing him from the game. For a welcome change, Blue Jays relievers do not unravel under the sudden pressure and the Jays hold on for a win. Just in case they have ideas about using this as a stepping-stone with greater things in mind, enter a minor injustice for good measure.

The following night, Hinske is at it again. In the 2nd inning, he ties the game by hitting his fourth home run of the season. In the 5th inning, he ties the game again with an RBI double. In the 7th inning, he singles to start a rally and eventually scores the go-ahead run that puts Toronto on top 3–2.

Snakebitten, this team finds ways to turn outstanding performances into futile gestures. Against Seattle, it's the umpires who intervene to scuttle Toronto's hopes.

In the 10th inning, Ichiro Suzuki charges home from third base after a weak groundball is tapped up the middle of the infield. Suzuki is extremely quick but Toronto infielder Joe Lawrence, playing in the place of underachieving Homer Bush, is even quicker with his throw home.

Catcher Tom Wilson, playing in the place of injured Darrin Fletcher, blocks the plate and applies a clean tag. Ichiro, with a reputation as one of the fastest runners in the league, is called safe. The Mariners win 5–4. It's a slap in the face, as if Toronto needed one.

By stark contrast, the Montreal Expos have been the recipients of occasional good luck this summer and, along with strong hitting, it's kept them over .500. No one really thinks the Expos are much better than Toronto. In a game that often turns on the half-inch between a ball landing fair or foul, good luck makes a big difference.

Critics of the Expos openly question how long this can last. Good teams may look lucky but woe is the team that counts on being lucky. The Expos look like the former but most expect them to morph into the latter. It is already happening.

Montreal's bats go silent. Since being swept by the Diamondbacks, Vladimir Guerrero has only two hits, Henry Rodriguez has been released and hotheaded Troy O'Leary has been nervously added to the lineup. This is not the same team that had Bud Selig reconsidering contraction less than a month ago.

With the Colorado Rockies in town, the Expos cross their fingers and send Carl Pavano to the hill. Montreal has been waiting for Pavano to make good since acquiring him in exchange for Pedro Martinez. Pavano has been hurt numerous times and looks to be in a perpetual state of rehabilitation even when healthy.

Against Colorado, he pitches respectably well until the 7th when he fails to record any outs as Colorado adds four runs to a slender lead. With no support coming from the Expos' offense, Pavano is tagged with a 5–0 loss.

This extends the Expos' sudden losing streak to six games. Adding insult to injury, the team is passed in the standings by Jeffrey Loria's Florida Marlins. Seemingly out of nowhere, it's crisis management time.

The baseball season is so long that tracking any one team is an exercise in looking for long-term trends as they reveal themselves on a day-to-day basis. This is much easier when it comes to really good and really bad teams because they tend to be predictable.

Teams like the Blue Jays and Expos, on the other hand, are amalgams of occasional heroism and minor disasters. Daily swings in performance could point to trends that extend over the whole summer or be forgotten as blips on what will eventually be the real story.

Take the Expos. Six wins in a row and league officials were talking about scrapping contraction. Six losses later and there is no more talk of the team's long-term survival in Montreal.

Take the Blue Jays. They give up more runs than any other team but there's still hope for a winning season. Their tendencies have been towards self-destruction and failure. Yet, it's still only May.

Watching these teams through an entire schedule begs the question, when do these tendencies become trends that really expose the quality of a major league team? This is a rhetorical question for fans and observers. It's a bread-and-butter issue for people like Omar Minaya and J.P. Ricciardi.

Minaya stills lives in the absurd bubble of Montreal's baseball limbo. Any move he makes is guaranteed to generate a media frenzy because the only story journalists want to write about the Expos is the apocalyptic contraction story. All of Minaya's trades immediately become the source of conspiracy theories and wild speculation. For him, spotting trends is only the beginning.

Life is no easier for J.P. Ricciardi. He is trying to turn the disinterested Toronto public back onto baseball while meeting the demands of owners who understandably balk at losing millions of dollars every year. He has the benefit of knowing that his club will be around for at least the next few summers. That's cold comfort when faced with the expectations of owners who want him to succeed with a wink and a few handshakes.

The Blue Jays badly need pitchers. Will their rookie general manager cripple an already struggling offense to get them? The Expos are in danger of turning contraction into a self-fulfilling prophecy. Will their rookie general manager turn to risky pick-ups like Troy O'Leary to keep it from happening? For both, these questions are overshadowed by more worrying developments consuming the entire league.

In mid-May, the players' union gets serious with the owners. The collective bargaining agreement between these two adversaries expires at season's end. Rather than sitting at a bargaining table to hammer out a new deal, the union is kicking around tentative dates for a strike that many feel is inevitable in 2002.

The reason that so many feel the players will strike this summer is that the owners will run out of revenue sources after the season ends, and might therefore impose a lockout after the World Series. The players aren't stupid. They know that the season itself is their biggest leveraging tool. Strike during the season and they hit the owners where it hurts. Most expect this to happen in mid-August because that's late enough to threaten the remainder of the season but early enough for a settlement to be negotiated. Baseball is about to be gripped by yet another labor war.

This power struggle between players and owners won't break any hearts in Montreal because contraction looms large over it all. In Toronto, there are no such distractions. If there's a strike this year, the Blue Jays and their fans will be hit just as hard as the rest of the league.

The Expos face imminent dissolution. The Blue Jays face potential disaster. Though their situations differ, both are being twisted into knots by powers beyond their control.

For Toronto and Montreal, this story is so old that it stretches back to the earliest days of the Canadian experiment. Major League Baseball can do its worst in 2002. So long as there has been a Canada, there have been powers pulling these cities in different directions.

"Truly the public men of Canada are ambitious. Bismarck and Louis Napoleon are pigmies in comparison."
—*Joseph Howe, premier of Nova Scotia, 1866*

After Canada came into existence on July 1, 1867, the hangover of confederation set in almost immediately. A separatist movement in Nova Scotia challenged the Canadian government right from the start. Rebellions in Toronto and Montreal had failed and, once the reality of nationhood took hold, those left behind shifted their focus to manipulating Ottawa. Influence and control became focal points. In Nova Scotia, people had few illusions about being able to dictate decisions in the capital so, while the issue of separation moved to the background in Ontario and Quebec, the maritime independence movement was born.

In the first provincial election following confederation, a separatist leader named Joseph Howe was voted in as premier of Nova Scotia and traveled all the way to Britain to plead for the independence of his province. He openly predicted the ruin of the Atlantic region within a state whose policies served only the interests of central provinces and cities.

Howe was opposed by politicos like Charles Tupper who, with the support of lobbyists in Ottawa, forced him to either accept a seat in cabinet or accept being ignored by the new government. Howe consented and, as a result, Nova Scotia was bamboozled into Canada by the empty promise of a more positive influence within confederation than without.

With Nova Scotia in tow, the Canadian government quickly withdrew from the long-standing Reciprocity Treaty that guaranteed the free trade of goods between Canada and the United States. This was the first step in the realization of Howe's dark prediction.

Maritime trade dropped 40 percent while trade in Ontario and Quebec jumped 100 percent. Canada had been a gamble and Nova Scotia had been wise in its reluctance to anteup.

Illusions that greater autonomy might be promoted in the new country were also vividly dispelled in Ontario and Quebec. Expansion was the order of the day. Federal leaders in Ottawa drooled over the great, untapped frontier to the west while pitting financiers struggling through international depression against one another in Toronto and Montreal.

By the 1870s, both cities were changing and expanding. Protective tariffs imposed on the United States worked in their mutual favor by limiting American access to Canadian markets linked by rail networks that started in Montreal and ran through Toronto. Montreal had surpassed Quebec City, and Toronto was outpacing Hamilton, in the race to become the dominant metropolitan power center of the new country.

"All aboard for the west."—*George Etienne Cartier, celebrating Canadian Pacific Railway expansion, 1872*

Business leaders in Toronto and Montreal lobbied aggressively for the favor of the new federal government. In 1871, the controversial Bank Act granted broad new lending powers to financial institutions in Toronto, a direct challenge to the financial dominance of the Bank of Montreal. The battle lines over this legislation reflected a new adversarial reality. Toronto and Montreal had only each other with which to compete.

In this combative environment, massive foreign and local investments were pumped into a plan to open the western prairies to rail service in the hopes that wheat exports would stabilize the national economy. Industrialists in both cities knew that this would mean riches for some and ruin for others. As it played out, only one man truly understood how to turn the opportunity to his advantage.

In the same year that the Bank Act controversy was unfolding, Prime Minister John Macdonald negotiated a daring pact with the territory of British Columbia. In exchange for the agreement of Pacific leaders that they would submit to the rule of Ottawa, Macdonald swore that within a decade he would connect British Columbia to the rest of the country by rail.

He made this deal without knowing how he was going to follow through on the promise. His solution not only shocked Canadians and exacerbated the growing rivalry between Toronto and Montreal, it also challenged the legitimacy of Canada's infant government.

In 1872, Montreal financier Hugh Allan made significant campaign contributions to John Macdonald. Allan was a member of Montreal's business elite, among whom influential positions in the Bank of Montreal, the Board of Trade and the Hudson's Bay Company were routinely exchanged. Other members of this cabal included George Stephen, a merchant who elevated himself to bank president, along with the McGill and Molson families. These individuals captured permanent control over Montreal's most powerful institutions, giving them a huge stake in commercial activity across Canada.

From inside this privileged community, Hugh Allan made his offering to the prime minister. In exchange, Allan received lucrative contracts to turn the Canadian Pacific Railway into a reality. He gambled that the prime minister would value cash in hand over fairness in the awarding of massive public contracts. He was right.

The shady deal promised to turn Allan into a veritable tycoon at a time when an international depression was just beginning to take hold. Manufacturing activity was tailing off and anyone with the connections to make a move into rail development funded by the federal government was keen on doing so. Hugh Allan not only made himself the big winner in this sweepstakes, he also ensured that the gigantic project created complementary spin-offs for his compatriots in Montreal.

Not everyone necessarily stood to benefit from Allan's success. The city was divided along clear cultural and geographic boundaries that came into sharp relief during the 1870s.

The fault line splitting Canada's traditional linguistic communities stretched up from the old waterfront, running the length of St. Laurent Boulevard. The city's south side, abutting the bustling harbor, was home to a mixed bag of immigrant households amidst the belching factories and tangled rail lines. Radiating out in all directions were new residential neighborhoods, such as Hochelaga in the east, necessitated by the doubling of Montreal's population.

Tucked into the heart of these boundaries, the central west end was home to the prosperous and the focus of much development.

Montreal was Canada's most important city. Its control of international shipping and continued dominance in the banking sector proffered wealth and fame to the influential men who controlled these industries, and marquee status on the west end district where they lived.

In the 1870s, after years of difficult property negotiations, Montreal made a public park out of Mount Royal. During this same period, majestic City Hall was constructed within a stone's throw of the commercial port and the bustling business district. Though pigs and other livestock roamed the streets of other neighborhoods, the west end that people such as Hugh Allan called home featured the young country's most exclusive addresses.

As such, when it became known that the prime minister had awarded the Canadian Pacific Railway contract to Allan and had leveraged his own gamble in British Columbia to make the rich men who funded his political career even richer, people were not amused. In particular, Allan's railway competitors in Toronto, accustomed to struggling against the power brokers in Montreal but

Montreal Harbor (1874) was a source of considerable wealth and political influence for the insider society that controlled the local economy (Alexander Henderson / Library and Archives Canada / PA-149728).

outraged by the prime minister's audacity in the face of a deepening economic depression, turned the issue into a national scandal that disgraced Macdonald and forced his withdrawal from politics in 1873. The growing rivalry between Toronto and Montreal, launched by Canadian nationhood itself, brought down the federal government.

The outrage of Toronto's business leaders should not be mistaken for helplessness. Toronto had its share of rich industrialists. The only real difference between powerful financiers directing the national economy in Montreal and powerful financiers trying to draw favor towards Toronto was the stability of banks and shipping in the former and a ravenous, combative entrepreneurial spirit in the latter.

> "[a] lively dashing place."—*Walt Whitman on Toronto, 1880*

By the time John Macdonald's government collapsed in 1873, the volume of rail traffic regularly passing through Toronto had become so hard to manage that Union Station was completely renovated. Canada's westward push was passing through Toronto.

The Bank Act affair and railway scandal signaled the willingness of local businessmen to fight for the favor of the pliable government in Ottawa. The expansion of Union Station signaled their readiness for the windfall that was coming.

As it had in Montreal, the physical expansion of Toronto radiated out from the waterfront where industrial and manufacturing activity was centralized. Unlike in Montreal, Toronto's expansion was not driven by the dominance of local banks but, instead, by fierce competition among local shopkeepers and tradespeople who gave birth to Canada's most vibrant commercial district.

Yonge Street stretched up from the harbor and was serviced by the city's only horse-drawn streetcar as far north as Bloor at the city limits. This was Toronto's backbone. Frequently the site of bloody rampages between Catholics and protestants, assigned the infamous title of Rebel's Corner at its intersection with Queen Street, and having spawned a working class aristocracy of ruthless shopkeepers living hand to mouth in the tough neighborhood abutting the waterfront, Yonge was the platform from which Toronto's commercial success leapt forward.

It was a proving ground for businesses. Timothy Eaton opened his first shop on Yonge in 1869. Robert Simpson opened a rival store on this same throughway in 1872. Following local convention, both moved away from Yonge as soon as their fortunes allowed but not before they made their bones in the heart of the action.

This spirit of aggressive competition also characterized dealings on the

Yonge Street (1890), where only the strong survived during Toronto's rise as a commercial and industrial player on the national scene (Merrilees Collection / Library and Archives Canada / PA-166917).

waterfront. Following the construction of a new wharf serving rail traffic, and fueled by the expansion of train services connecting Toronto to the rest of Canada, conflict among rival companies routinely created and destroyed the fortunes of tycoon hopefuls. Like all Toronto industries, transportation was a sink-or-swim proposition. There were always plenty of vultures ready to pick a fresh corpse clean.

The waterfront was the site of much risky business among shippers feeding goods into the local marketplace. Storms continually battered the breakwaters that shaped the harbor, creating new channels and hazardous bars in the notoriously shallow water. These were assets to the lucky and the downfall of the reckless.

Shipping conditions became so hazardous that in 1879 a government report recommended closing several sections of the harbor. In the midst of a continental depression, this recommendation stood little chance of being implemented. Given that every other merchant in Toronto lived under the constant threat of imminent disaster, there was little sympathy for shippers who had to do the same.

Bankruptcy and failure were common occurrences. Few who survived in this environment had a stomach for protecting anything other than their own access to local markets against the perceived challenge of American distributors. Though there was strong support in Toronto for stiff tariffs against goods produced in the United States, there was no support for recommendations that would close part of the harbor to protect shippers. Such was the schizophrenic nature of the budding commercial power center during those difficult years.

The lobbying efforts of these pitiless new capitalists were not limited to stifling the perceived threat of competition from America. There was also little patience in Toronto for the ambitions of powerless dissidents in other parts of Canada. When westward expansion created unrest in the farthest reaches of the new country, merchants in Toronto provided special discounts on fuel so that local gangs could stomp it down.

As Canada extended to the west, it inflamed tensions still bubbling under the surface. Unwilling to accept domination by Ottawa, for example, the French–Aboriginal Métis community in northern Manitoba rebelled and appointed its own leader, Louis Riel.

Riel enraged English Canadians by executing an Ontario settler who supported confederation. When the Métis uprising again captured national attention in 1885, French Canadians were outraged by the presence of Toronto ruffians and the federal government's decision to execute Riel himself.

Canada left a trail of bloodshed in its wake as the government relentlessly pushed westward. By 1887, the provinces had seen enough.

The premier of Quebec called a conference to re-write the legislation that created Canada and curtail the powers of the federal government. Nova Scotia sought to redress the inequities created by their mistaken entry into the confederation. Ontario and Quebec had their eyes set on capturing a greater portion of manufacturing work necessitated by the continued development of the west. The provinces all agreed on a resolution calling for the resumption of free trade with the United States.

The federal government brazenly ignored them. Ottawa had tasted the power of nationhood and would continue to dictate the shape of national development.

Canada might have been a grand success. With one city providing an open door to the boundless potential of the west, and another maintaining a thriving shipping link to the Old World, there ought to have been nothing to stand in Canada's way.

Unfortunately, the insiders who concocted the idea of Canadian union did not recognize, in these two places, a dual foundation for national greatness. They saw competing power centers that could be played to their advantage. In this way, Canada's success was hindered by individuals whose ego and ambition got mixed up in the destinies of two great cities.

Major League Baseball would be a richer league, by far, if the respective problems of the Blue Jays and Expos could be resolved. The individuals who view the league as a vehicle for their own aggrandizement will happily break the Expos into digestible pieces and hide the swallowed assets as a capital expenditure. They will humor the Blue Jays in their financial misery without shedding any tears. The free market sometimes has casualties, they will say.

The only factor that really distinguishes the powers at play in the survival of the Blue Jays and Expos from those that have been shaping the destinies of Toronto and Montreal since confederation is the context of baseball itself. Outside the boundaries of this silly, charming game, corruption and petty intrigue still carry the day. Inside the chalk lines, it's still just baseball.

Things may finally be going right for the Blue Jays. After a month and a half of bad breaks, they look like a team that might actually start stringing wins together. Best of all, they're playing their best baseball of 2002 at home.

With the Oakland Athletics in town, the Blue Jays face an opponent that has been awful away from the sandy beaches of southern California. After being small-market poster boys for the last three years, the A's have been severely hampered by the off-season loss of free agent MVP candidate Jason Giambi. They are not playing like a team that has driven the New York Yankees to the brink of elimination the past two postseasons.

The A's face pitcher Roy Halladay who stays true to form by giving up a lone run over 8 innings. At present, he is pitching as well as anyone in the American League.

The A's breathe a sigh of relief knowing they'll only have to face him once. What they fail to realize is that losing to Halladay stings a lot less than losing to players they shipped to Toronto themselves.

Eric Hinske, the rookie third baseman, and Justin Miller, one of Toronto's young starters, both came from Oakland in trades that many observers criticized as salary dumps on Toronto's part. Against the A's at SkyDome, these youngsters make the moves look like pure shrewdness.

Hinske tags a three-run home run that puts Toronto ahead 6–0 while Miller cruises to an easy victory that guarantees the Blue Jays their first series win at home this summer. Pretty sweet.

Sweeter still, the Blue Jays welcome back one of their injured pitchers. Esteban Loaiza is among Toronto's best but has spent the first month of the year in rehab.

Loaiza makes a strong statement in his first start of the season. He pitches a complete-game shutout. It is an overwhelming performance that he later describes as the best of his career. With Carlos Delgado showing signs of life by hitting his 12th home run, the Blue Jays give Loaiza more than enough support. Toronto wins 11–0, sweeps Oakland and improves to 16–25 on the season.

If the rest of the batting order can follow Delgado's resurgence and generate consistent run support for pitchers like Loaiza and Halladay, watch out. The season is still young and the Blue Jays are getting hot. Heading to the

Bronx for a series against the Yankees, the Blue Jays will need to get hotter still.

On the flip side, facing the Dodgers in balmy Los Angeles, the Montreal Expos are ice cold. The Dodgers pound Montreal pitchers relentlessly and build a 10–1 lead. L.A. hitters run so wild that even Dodgers pitcher Andy Ashby gets into the act, hitting a solo home run. The laugher is Montreal's sixth loss on an awful California road trip.

This extermination at the hands of the Dodgers is disheartening. The fact that Montreal has lost most of its recent games by just one or two runs is much more troubling. Every team gets blown out now and again. Good teams win close games more often than not.

The Expos have been close in almost every game on this trip and have come up empty almost every time. This is the infamous death of a thousand cuts that many teams suffer. If Montreal doesn't find a way to start winning again soon, they may end up being one of them. Heading home to face the Atlanta Braves, things aren't going to get any easier.

Both the Blue Jays and Expos prepare to compete against the best talent in their respective divisions. The Yankees and Braves are the cream of the crop.

Over the past decade, no team has made more World Series appearances than the Yankees or won more consecutive division championships than the Braves. These are elite teams, difficult tests for the inconsistent and unpredictable Canadian clubs.

Playing the best makes for good points of comparison but will neither make nor break the Jays and Expos. Montreal was stunned by their sweep at the hands of the Diamondbacks but it's been the subsequent losses against mid-level opponents that have dropped them below .500.

This is the perpetual challenge: to prey on mediocre clubs. This will be true even if the Blue Jays whip New York or the Expos humble Atlanta. It's one thing to challenge the best over a short series. It's another to victimize the rest over six long months.

Watching young teams like the Expos and Blue Jays ride this learning curve is frustrating. Watching expansion teams do it can be downright painful. The only nice thing about being an expansion team in this situation is that fans usually cut a new franchise plenty of slack. In many cases, this forgiveness is the only reason a team survives its first years in the league. Such was certainly the case in Toronto.

> "We were a team with a lot of heart, little talent and mediocre results ... in Exhibition Stadium, perhaps the worst facility in baseball."
> —*Paul Beeston, on the Blue Jays' early years, 1990*

The Toronto Blue Jays spent the latter part of the 1970s trying to slide under the dubious 100-loss plateau. During their first three seasons, they were the archetype of a struggling expansion team. However, through these lean years, the Jays cultivated at least one legitimate slugger and witnessed the emergence of many young players who would become the building blocks of their success.

In 1977, the troubles of the Toronto Blue Jays started on the mound. No pitcher in the Jays' rotation recorded an ERA below 4.00, racking up more losses than any other squad. Combined with the fact that the team generated the second fewest runs and hits in the league, these stats accounted for Toronto's 107 losses. None of this could dampen the enthusiasm of local spectators who still broke the attendance record for an expansion club after just 50 home games.

In its second year, the team didn't fare much better even though first baseman John Mayberry emerged as a legitimate offensive threat by leading the team with 22 home runs. Despite another 100-loss season, 1978 was a building-block year. Lloyd Moseby was drafted and Ernie Whitt played on the club along with Willie Upshaw. The team had started to stockpile talent.

In 1979, the Jays suffered a setback of sorts. Few, other than Mayberry, stood out for the club. The pitching was hopeless and the team lost more games than ever before.

While enduring 109 losses, the Blue Jays' talent pool nonetheless deepened. Jesse Barfield emerged as a blue-chip prospect and shortstop Alfredo Griffin won Rookie of the Year. It seemed just a matter of time before the club turned around.

That turnaround began in earnest the very next season. Twenty-two-year-old Dave Stieb joined 24-year-old Jim Clancy in the starting rotation, combining for 25 wins. Mayberry enjoyed his best season as a Blue Jay, cranking 30 home runs. Ernie Whitt and Lloyd Moseby were inserted into the everyday lineup, and Willie Upshaw joined the club from the minor leagues. After drawing a record 6 million fans to Exhibition Stadium over the first four seasons, the Jays finally looked like they were heading in the right direction.

In the early 1980s, the Blue Jays were deep in young talent, showing plenty of promise and drawing tons of fans. None of that could insulate them against the labor problems that loomed on the horizon and would come to stigmatize baseball for the next 20 years.

No sport has suffered so much, and gained so little, from the bad faith between its players and owners than baseball. This self-destructive dynamic exploded like a powder keg in the 1980s. Since then, the issues driving labor conflict have changed substantially but baseball continues to be a breeding ground for distrust and insincerity that is killing it from within.

"The credibility of [players'] performances ... is at stake here."
—*U.S. Senator John McCain, on steroid use in baseball, 2002*

Dramas at play in major league labor negotiations have changed over the past twenty years. Case in point: Jose Canseco is poised to release a tell-all book about the ugly side of baseball and claims that 85 percent of Major League Baseball players use steroids. Ken Caminiti, who recently admitted to using steroids during his MVP season in 1996, figures it's closer to 50 percent. Buck Martinez, manager of the Toronto Blue Jays, says it's an internal issue that ought not to be discussed in public.

Major League Baseball does not test its players for steroids. The players' union won't allow it. This effectively legitimizes steroid use, which has surely been a factor in the offensive explosion that has seen almost every significant record in baseball history fall, then fall again, then get demolished altogether.

Despite the fact that steroids are dangerous, the players' union has chosen to see this issue as a question of power. Union leaders perceive mandatory testing as an infringement of players' privacy rather than a necessary safeguard. A player will presently be fined or suspended if he's caught smoking a reefer but it's not even possible to catch a player using steroids.

Just as callous as the players' union, Bud Selig and the rest of baseball's owners don't seem to care if Ken Caminiti's testicles shrivel up either. No one has benefited more from the recent heroics in baseball than the owners. They have little to gain from a drug-free game.

One of two things is going to happen now that the question of steroid use has gained prominence on the eve of labor talks. Either the players' union is going to agree to mandatory testing, claim they've made a major concession then dig their collective heels in on economic issues, or the owners are going to drop the issue altogether, claim they've made a major concession and insist that they have no choice but to hold firm on economic issues. This is about to become a bit-piece in the grand charade that is leading baseball headlong into another labor disaster.

These are distractions that the Blue Jays don't need as they travel to New York. A few days in the Bronx cannot erase all the damage this team has done to itself so far in 2002. After sweeping the A's, it could be a confidence builder.

Things don't turn out that way. The Yankees don't even put their best on the field. Relief pitcher Sterling Hitchcock makes a rare start in the first game and Mike Mussina pitches on unusually short rest in the second. It's a bad sign for the Jays, that New York treats the series as an opportunity to conduct experiments. This is a chance to gain some respect by punishing the Yanks.

Instead, the Blue Jays crumble, failing to score beyond the 3rd inning of either game. New York gives its elite pitchers a rest and it doesn't hurt them a bit. Key home runs by Yankee third baseman Robin Ventura and former Expo Rondell White break both games open. While Yankees experiments pay off in spades, Blue Jays pitchers cannot hold New York's hitters at bay.

Despite these failings at unforgiving Yankee Stadium, the third game of the series belongs to Roy Halladay. This story is becoming familiar. When the Jays need someone to stop the bleeding, Halladay is there.

In the 1st inning, he gives up hits to the Yankees' first four batters before settling down and retiring the side. He escapes having given up only a single run. From that point forward, he sprinkles a handful of hits over the next five innings. The Blue Jays win 8–3.

Toronto heads home to host the Cleveland Indians and get back to the business of trying to straighten out their record. A series against the Yankees makes good headlines but isn't as crucial as taking advantage of teams like the Indians, which have been struggling all season long.

Cleveland is a total mess coming into SkyDome. The Indians still burn a half dozen Blue Jays pitchers in the course of a 5–2 win. The next night, things get even worse.

The Jays' offense is shut down completely, ruining a fine pitching performance from rehabbed Esteban Loaiza who pitches into the 8th inning but receives no support. It's characteristic of bad baseball. One night the pitching stinks. Another night, the bats go missing.

Closing out the series against Cleveland, the Jays face pitcher Bartolo Colon. Colon is the ace of the Indians' staff. He pitches a complete game, giving up one run on four hits. Raul Mondesi sees his batting average drop close to .200 again and Carlos Delgado is held hitless for the fourth time in the last six games. Cleveland sweeps the series at SkyDome.

This drops the Blue Jays to 17–30 on the season. What a difference one week can make.

In Montreal, the Expos face a tough test as well. Atlanta and Philadelphia, which both finished ahead of Montreal last season, each visit the Big O. Luckily, some of the Expos' bats have been getting hot again.

The Braves are sure to be in the thick of things when this season closes. With pitchers like Maddux and Glavine still throwing very effectively, and hitters like Chipper and Andruw Jones still at the heart of the batting order, it is only a matter of time before Atlanta surges into championship form.

In the first game, the Expos kick a very bad habit they'd recently picked up: losing one-run games. The tenacity of hitters like Guerrero and Vidro pulls them out of this funk.

People around the league are taking notice of the streak that Vidro has put together. He has hit safely in 15 consecutive games. Though much of this streak stretched over a disastrous West Coast road trip, Vidro has raised his batting average from .292 to .324. He's on fire.

Against the Braves, he shows no signs of slowing down. With Javier Vazquez having another difficult outing, the Expos lean on Vidro. He comes through with three hits, including an RBI single in the 9th inning that ties the game against former Cy Young winner John Smoltz. Vidro extends his hitting streak to 16 and the Expos are rewarded with extra innings, a rare second chance against the Braves. Montreal makes it count.

In the 10th, the Expos get lucky. With the bases loaded, young outfielder Brad Wilkerson taps a weak ground ball to the infield. He hits it so weakly, in fact, that no Braves are able to get to it before Wilkerson reaches base and the winning run crosses home plate. Montreal wins 5–4.

The following night, the Expos are victimized by a top pitcher in top form. Tom Glavine is totally overpowering. He pitches a complete game shutout that drops his ERA down to an incredible 1.67. Of the few hits given up by Glavine, one is tallied by Jose Vidro who keeps his personal streak going despite the 2–0 loss. Atlanta leaves town after a brief series, split one game apiece.

Just like Toronto, the Expos shift from playing against a marquee team to playing a middle-of-the-road opponent that will have a much greater impact on its final place in the standings. Unlike Toronto, the Expos can once again count on their big bats to carry them.

Against the Phillies, Montreal goes on an offensive binge in an old-fashioned slugfest. The Expos and Phillies combine for 22 runs on 24 hits. The most effective batter in the midst of this explosion is Jose Vidro who tags a dramatic 10th inning, game-winning grand slam home run.

Also making a solid contribution, Troy O'Leary, recently called up from AAA, has his best game. O'Leary is a wild card in the Expos' lineup. He is reputed to be extremely self-centered but also has the talent to help Montreal win.

He impresses with two more hits and RBIs the following night but it is Jose Vidro's turn to steal the show once again. Vidro hits safely four times, raising his batting average to an eye-opening .348 and extending his hitting streak to 20 games, the best in the Major Leagues this season.

Nineteen thousand fans at Olympic Stadium cheer the Expos' sweep of Philadelphia. Things are headed in the right direction again for Montreal. What a difference one week can make.

These are the ebbs and flows that the Blue Jays and Expos must endure. Few in Toronto want to hear any talk about the good habits that the Jays could pick up from the Expos even though they could clearly use some pointers from their doomed cousins down the road. Better that than continue to co-opt only the worst parts of the Expos' legacy, which is exactly what Toronto does at the end of May by becoming another Canadian ward of the league's commissioner.

When Toronto set a record in 2001 by losing $53 million dollars in one season, fans comforted themselves by saying that at least Toronto's owners were willing to spend money, which was better than in Montreal where the Expos could only get by on hand-outs.

Blue Jays supporters have stridently maintained that this is why baseball works in Toronto but not Montreal. No longer.

The Toronto Blue Jays have formally joined the Expos among the ranks of baseball's have-not franchises. The ownership group running the Toronto

Blue Jays on a $15 million quarterly deficit announced that it would partially defray those losses by accepting a $5 million handout from Bud Selig's office.

Referring to Canadian currency as the peso, Blue Jays owner Ted Rogers put a light spin on the announcement and backpedaled from recent statements about looking for alternatives to remaining in Toronto. This sudden subsidization of Blue Jays operations could not feel more ominous, especially in light of developments in Minnesota.

Attendance at SkyDome continues to plummet as the team slides out of contention with the season less than two months old. Those quarterly losses are not a one-time problem. They are ongoing.

Now the league has decided to give the Jays $5 million, which will not even begin to address the team's financial shortfall but will be counted among the clearest signs that this team is not surviving in its current market. Meanwhile, the State of Minnesota is poised to save the Twins by ponyingup a $330 million stadium.

Minnesota governor Jesse Ventura has agreed to pay for a new stadium. If Twins owner Carl Pohland succeeds in making this deal work, Commissioner Bud Selig will have to look elsewhere for an American League contraction candidate. That search could begin in Toronto.

Late inning meltdowns and financial handouts are not the sorts of things Blue Jays fans want to hear about. The season is supposed to be about building for a bright future, not sliding back to the woeful status of the Montreal Expos. Of course, being the Expos isn't such a bad thing at the moment.

The Expos are a streaky team. This makes fans nervous because they never know what to expect. It also makes opponents nervous because just when Montreal seems down and out, one streak invariably ends and another begins.

So it is in Atlanta. After beating up on the Phillies at home, the Expos are in tough against the Braves. They lose the series' first two games. Jose Vidro's hitting streak is snapped in the process.

In the 9th inning of the final game, the Expos are losing again. With the bases loaded and two outs, they face John Smoltz on the mound. Smoltz jumps ahead of Jose Vidro with a pair of quick strikes. Down to their last pitch, the Expos are party to the collision of yet another set of streaks changing direction.

Vidro is hitless since his streak ended. The Braves have not lost a game in the 9th inning since the first weeks of the season.

With these factors as a backdrop, Smoltz delivers an 0–2 pitch out of the strike zone, trying to induce Vidro to swing. Vidro lunges forward, lifting a double into the outfield and driving three runners home. The Expos win 4–3. Going into the last day of May, they even their record at 26–26.

"That's a tough one because I never felt at all I was going to give up another hit."—*John Smoltz, post-game interview, 2002*

June

"I don't know that you can link too much economic activity to what we've done."

—*Tigers CEO John McHale,
on downtown renewal in Detroit, 2001*

Arguments in favor of public stadium financing lean heavily on the idea that new ballparks pay for themselves in positive spin-offs for host cities. The fact, therefore, that officials in Detroit had visions of waterfront revitalization in mind when they gave the Tigers land and money is not especially remarkable. That they hoped this contribution would undo decades of downtown abandonment, stimulated by realities that extend far beyond the playing field, makes this a telling case.

Detroit has been trapped in a cycle of perpetual decline since the 1970s when it earned the nickname Murder City and entered such deep distress that its population dipped to turn-of-the-century levels. By the 1990s, as a sign of just how tough times had gotten, the city annually issued 100 times as many permits for demolition as for construction because property owners were desperate to keep derelict structures from being torched on Devil's Night. Formerly the flagship of the automotive revolution, Detroit has become the model of urban decay in America.

As this spiral stretched into the new millennium, an ambitious pizza vendor convinced local officials that a new entertainment district would lead to widespread redevelopment along the waterfront where, all the while, this same man was strategically acquiring properties. The hub of his proposed renewal scheme was a sparkling new home for the Detroit Tigers, which he also happened to own. What neither he nor the city seemed interested in acknowledging was that this hopeful plan hinged on factors stretching back to the very roots of the city.

Detroit came into its own during the 1920s when consolidation among auto manufacturers stabilized the industry and turned Detroit into a destination of choice for immigrants and working families. This fueled rapid expansion not just within Detroit proper but also in outlying areas.

City planners scrambled to fill empty gaps between Detroit's traditional boundaries and the booming towns on its outskirts. Struggling to keep up, they radically altered their strategy in the '20s by opting to simply absorb the satellite towns instead. Annexation became the primary tool for reeling in Detroit's new suburbs.

It was impossible to know just how far the suburbs would extend in future years so, when the annexation of towns beyond the infamous 8-Mile boundary failed, planners gambled that they'd already amalgamated enough to sustain Detroit proper. That gamble was a complete disaster.

In the 1950s, the population of Detroit peaked at 2 million but outlying towns also continued to swell. A precarious balance was established between demand for roads, pipes and services in the city core and the continued exodus of tax revenue to towns that Detroit had failed to annex. When the auto industry was turned on its head by the arrival of Japanese imports in the '70s, and hundreds of thousands of jobs were lost, this balance tipped.

Buildings in the city were abandoned as businesses opted for lower taxes in the suburbs. The population of Detroit tumbled while the surrounding areas exploded. People couldn't get out of Detroit fast enough.

A decade later, this is the desperate environment in which Mike Ilitch emerged as a savior. Owner of the Detroit Tigers as well as a national chain of pizza joints, Ilitch renovated a decrepit old theater and moved his corporate headquarters back to the city. Local officials celebrated him, along with a handful of other financiers gobbling up downtown properties, as a hero.

Bolstered by the enthusiasm of a city in crisis, Ilitch proposed to build Comerica Park as part of his plan to resuscitate Detroit. All the city had to do was put up $115 million for the acquisition of waterfront land, expropriate property from those who wouldn't sell and grant Ilitch generous commercial licenses to cover his part of the deal. The city bought in and, in 2000, Detroit received its new stadium.

What all have since discovered is that it doesn't matter how many baseball fields, snooty theaters and gaudy casinos are crowded into an entertainment district when taxes are six times higher in the city compared to the suburbs. Detroit's fortunes have receded since Ilitch's deal was cobbled together. Its troubles are numerous.

The few remaining developable parcels of land near the core are contaminated. Most new jobs and homes continue to be created in the suburbs. The population continues to fall.

Even at Comerica Park, the glitter has faded. Attendance is near the bottom of the American League because fans pay far too much to watch a terrible team play. The very presence of the stadium is driving rent up in surrounding buildings and preventing new businesses from moving in.

The stadium has not been the engine of a downtown revival. It has been the petri dish in which the theory of renewal through stadium development has come crashing back to reality.

In the first days of June, the Toronto Blue Jays visit the empty splendor of Comerica Park and the lonely streets of downtown Detroit. These are welcome changes. The stadium and city may be depressing to locals but they are comforting reminders that things can always get worse for a visiting team in dire straits.

Blue Jays players have all but given up on manager Buck Martinez. The team's poor play, combined with outlandish contracts tied to underachieving players, has aggravated this situation by making it difficult for General Manager J.P. Ricciardi to purge the malcontents.

Outfielder Raul Mondesi ought to attract offers from other teams but his pitiful batting average and $11 million salary make him virtually impossible to trade. The Jays are stuck. Change is clearly in the cards and manager Buck Martinez stands out as the only viable target.

Against the Tigers, Toronto enjoys rare success on the road. Comerica Park is a mirage in this way. Even teams falling to pieces win when they visit the Tigers. Detroit is a temporary reprieve.

While the Blue Jays try to forget their many troubles in Detroit, the Expos travel to Philadelphia where June kicks off with a blast. Several blasts, actually.

Since sweeping Philadelphia at home last month, the Expos have dropped five of seven games, including one in which Jose Vidro was intentionally walked to load the bases for Vladimir Guerrero. When opposing teams seek out Guerrero in the batting order, something is wrong. Against Philadelphia, the Expos continue to slide.

The Phillies not only score 10 runs in the 1st inning but pitcher Robert Person twists the dagger by hitting a grand slam. On this day, that's just the beginning. Before being lifted in the 5th, Person drills another home run. The Phillies eventually win 18–3.

Following Montreal's farcical loss, the axe falls in Toronto. The Jays return home after sweeping Detroit only to announce that manager Buck Martinez has been fired.

Martinez will be remembered as resilient but out of his depth. The determination that allowed him to turn mediocre power and sore knees into a 17-year playing career did not allow him to succeed as a manager. Martinez is gone and his former base coach, Carlos Tosca, is in. Tosca has 1700 minor league games under his belt as a manager.

Unsettled by managerial upheaval in Toronto and a crisis of uncompetitive play in Montreal, Canada's teams prepare to face one another at Olympic Stadium in the first of two interleague series this summer. This offers perhaps the final opportunity, beyond the outside chance that they meet in the World Series, for the Jays and Expos to play head-to-head.

Five years after its introduction, interleague play is still controversial for a variety of reasons. The most ridiculous is that it offends the purity of the game. The most pragmatic is that it unbalances the schedule and provides advantages to teams that play easier opponents compared to divisional rivals.

Prior to hosting Toronto, for example, the Expos face the Chicago White Sox who play them very tough. This is what makes interleague play awkward. While the resurgent Braves are in Texas facing the deadbeat Rangers, the Expos are duking out nail-biters against the White Sox.

These discrepancies are supposed to even out because every team theoretically plays an equal number of strong and weak opponents. As baseball mixes and matches series to retain certain rivalries and initiate others, however, the schedule becomes increasingly unbalanced.

Some fans still get a kick out of seeing new rivalries develop. Others still bitterly stew over any change to the traditions of the game. The debate lingers on in 2002, an aftershock from a time when interleague play was the most controversial issue facing Major League Baseball.

That time has passed. There are now much larger dramas unfolding.

Baseball is a numbers game. Its fans tend to be stat-junkies and masters of the obscure. Of late, the numbers that have captured the most attention focus on disparities between financial statements offered by Bud Selig and analyses offered by *Forbes* magazine with respect to how much profit baseball owners actually generate.

Three hundred nine million dollars. That's the difference between the total net loss that major league owners claim they suffered last season and the total net profit that *Forbes* estimates those owners enjoyed during the same period. These numbers paint two very different pictures of profitability in baseball.

Bud Selig suggests that existing financial woes could lead to the outright collapse of up to eight major league franchises. This is universally accepted as posturing in advance of labor negotiations. The legitimacy of his claims is challenged by the *Forbes* study which suggests that, outside of Montreal, the only two franchises in any real danger seem to be the Devil Rays and Blue Jays.

Selig is on a quest to re-capitalize baseball using government money. In this, he is supported by developments such as Jesse Ventura committing $330 million for a facility that will raise the Twins' head off the contraction chopping block. Selig's focus will soon shift to other cities where taxpayers have yet to cough up. If that happens, the numbers will point in one of two directions: Tampa or Toronto.

In 2002, the Expos are being ground to dust and the Blue Jays are holding their breath hoping not to be next. This has been the status quo for 25 years. From the very beginning, the Expos have been more directly impacted by the league's off-field drama than the Jays.

> "I think the bankruptcies will start in two or three years."
> —*Whitey Herzog, 1981*

In 1981, names that would eventually become synonymous with the Blue Jays' coming of age penetrated the everyday lineup. Lloyd Moseby led the team in hits and RBIs. Alfredo Griffin led the team in extra-base hits. George Bell, Jessey Barfield and Willie Upshaw all played support roles. Dave Stieb established himself as the pitching staff's premier starter.

The foundation of much future success was laid. Glimmers of that potential were overshadowed, just the same, by a miserable record and the most destructive labor dispute baseball had seen to that point.

The summer of '81 began with a dismal stretch of awful play in Toronto. Attendance at Exhibition Stadium was near the bottom of the American League as the Blue Jays posted a 16–42 record. All this on-field trouble came to an abrupt end on June 12th.

On that day, for the first time in the history of Major League Baseball, the players went on strike. It came as no surprise to owners who had collectively taken out a $50 million insurance policy but fans were stunned. Over the next seven weeks, those same fans watched as the adversarial dynamic between owners and players created the infamous split-season schedule.

At issue between the rival camps was free agency. The owners had proposed a controversial new system for providing compensation to any team that lost a player through free agency. Their system allowed the team losing a free agent to select any player from the other team's roster other than the top 15. It became known as the "16th Man" proposal and was totally unacceptable to the players' union, which regarded it as a crippling disincentive.

In truth, the whole proposal was a non-starter because the "16th Man" model would only have limited the mobility of middle-of-the-road players. For two full months, baseball was stalled over the movement of mediocre talent.

Near the end of July, the owners' insurance ran out and a mediated compromise was reached. It was decided that teams signing sign free agents would be allowed to protect 24–26 players on their respective rosters and all remaining players would be included in a draft pool from which teams losing free agents would be allowed to select. This system was soon abandoned.

When baseball finally resumed, there was no way to make up all the lost games so the split-season was concocted. Under this scheme, records from the first half of the season were treated as final and the top teams guaranteed a playoff against those that finished the second half atop the standings.

This created certain injustices. The Cincinnati Reds and St. Louis Cardinals finished the season with the best overall records in their respective divisions. Neither would compete in the playoffs because they failed to finish first in either of the season's two halves.

The split season had no impact on the Toronto Blue Jays. Though the second half was considerably more positive for Toronto, and the Jays managed a respectable 21–27 record after the strike, they were never really in the playoff picture. The same could not be said of the Montreal Expos.

Nineteen eighty-one fell in the middle of five consecutive winning seasons in Montreal. At the time, many predicted they would rise to championship form as the "Team of the '80s."

Gary Carter, Andre Dawson, Tim Raines, Larry Parrish and Tim Wallach were all regulars in the lineup, which would come to be regarded as among the best to ever play for the Expos. Steve Rogers and Bill Gullickson were at the heart of Montreal's pitching rotation. Legendary closer Jeff Reardon joined Woodie Fryman and Bill Lee in the bullpen. The Expos were peaking and their second half record of 30–23 was enough to put them in the playoffs.

The Expos' postseason began with a series against the defending World Series champions, the Philadelphia Phillies. It was the most promising debut fans could possibly have expected, eventually decided in Philadelphia where Steve Rogers pitched a complete game shutout. Gary Carter led Montreal with eight hits and two home runs. Closer Jeff Reardon recorded saves in the series' first two games but lost Game 4 in extra innings.

This forced the deciding game at Veterans' Stadium, in which Rogers carried the team to victory, and may have contributed to a pitching decision that would become the most lamented mistake in team history. Montreal advanced to the League Championship series against Los Angeles.

On offense, the Dodgers featured Dusty Baker, Steve Garvey and Pedro Guerrero along with a frequently injured outfielder named Rick Monday who'd once gained national attention by pulling an American flag away from a fan he thought was going to burn it. Monday had come to Los Angeles in 1977 and was a regular run producer for two seasons before being hobbled by injury.

Despite these quality hitters, the Dodgers were led by two pitchers: Burt Hooton and rookie sensation Fernando Valenzuela. Hooton was a pitching menace, shutting the Expos out over 14+ innings, keeping L.A alive up to the deciding game at Olympic Stadium. With a trip to the World Series on the line, the Dodgers sent Valenzuela to the mound. After giving up a run in the 1st inning, he held the Expos in check. The game was tied going into the 9th.

Expos manager Jim Fanning had Jeff Reardon in the bullpen. Reardon was well rested, having not pitched since the series' first game. One of the reasons he hadn't pitched since then was that he'd given up three runs in that appearance and, together with his loss against the Phillies in the previous series, looked shaky.

Fryman and Lee had both pitched in the previous game so Fanning faced a difficult decision. Who to bring in to pitch the 9th? What he decided to do was bring in Steve Rogers, a starting pitcher who had not made a relief appearance all season.

Baseball is funny in this way. Managers are often tempted to make decisions in the playoffs that they would never seriously consider during the regular season. A sport that is so often characterized by sticking to a system for 162 games induces managers to become risk-takers when the most is at stake. Rogers was an excellent pitcher but he was not a closer. The Expos' three closers sat on the bench as Rogers took the mound.

The rest is Expos history. Rick Monday hit a two-out solo home run to the deepest part of Olympic Stadium sending the Los Angeles Dodgers to the World Series. It would be the closest Montreal would ever come to reaching the Fall Classic, and the first of many times that the awkward logic of Major League Baseball shaped the fate of the franchise.

The split-season model benefited Montreal by putting the Expos in the playoffs where they fell to the devastating disappointment of what came to be known as Blue Monday. Surely, none of the Expos complained when the strange split season gave them an opportunity to compete for a championship. They simply fell one dubious pitching decision short.

Montreal has not always been on the losing end of controversial decisions generated by the war between players and owners. Only recently has Montreal become a place where the whims of the commissioner never work in its favor.

In this way, Major League Baseball mirrors the history of Toronto and Montreal. Though the tables have turned in the century since, the 1880s were a period in which both cities struggled to manage unprecedented growth but Montreal continued to benefit from the intervention of central authority more directly than its newfound rival.

"Get their money ... before they have time to invest it somewhere else."—*George Stephen, advising Prime Minister Macdonald, 1880*

Politicos in Canada learned very quickly that no matter how flagrantly they abused the public trust, if they greased the right wheels things would work out to their advantage. Canada's first generation of leaders established a culture of patronage so widespread that the disbursement of government revenues became the key tool for wresting and retaining power in the capital.

Forced to resign in disgrace in 1873, John Macdonald turned an astonishing trick by regaining the position of prime minister in the election of 1878. This dramatic about-face, surely one of the most baffling moments in Canadian democracy, sent a clear signal to the country's political elite: patronage was the name of the game. This directly impacted the development of Toronto and Montreal.

A crippling depression came to its end in the early 1880s. With the essential character of both cities remaining largely unchanged, the welcome turnaround further entrenched their rivalry.

It shouldn't have. Toronto and Montreal were hit hard by the depression but the resilience of local industries, underscoring how needless their rivalry had always been, got them through. Only when the depression came to an end, and Ottawa resumed its practice of playing the two against each another, did the rivalry pick up again.

In Toronto, bank failures during the depression made it difficult for manufacturers to raise capital, and the fall of iron prices brought down huge companies. For all this strife and failure, aggressive merchants seized certain opportunities.

Local markets opened to wheat from the western prairies, introducing a new product to the bustling commercial corridor running along Yonge Street. Some entrepreneurs took advantage of the depreciated value of iron to manufacture new products. The cheap price of labor allowed the physical development of the city itself to continue.

The depression showed that Toronto was capable of surviving global economic catastrophe because its industries were diverse enough to adapt to changing conditions. The commercial port was, as always, also a focal point.

The harbor was expanded and upgraded in 1882. Risky throughways, created by storms and erosion, were widened to encourage shipping and a new dike was constructed to repel the forces of nature; 40 new wharves were added.

These were direct investments by the city and private financiers. For the most part, the federal government did not participate. The absence of federal support for these upgrades was reflected in other areas as well.

A health crisis still plagued Toronto's central neighborhoods, which were becoming dangerously overcrowded. The city's water and sewer systems were not suitable for the masses of new people flooding to the city. Local government struggled to keep Toronto from becoming a breeding ground of disease. Affluent residents fled the congested city core, giving rise to Toronto's first suburb in the form of Yorkville, an independent town just beyond the Bloor Street city limit.

Yorkville was a pleasant alternative to the city. Residents valued its rural appeal. To live in Yorkville was a sign of having freed one's self of Toronto. City officials viewed this luxury as a real problem.

With little help coming from higher levels of government and urgent demand for sewer and water upgrades, it didn't suit Toronto to have its richest residents move beyond the limit of its tax authority. In 1883, due in part to critical infrastructure demands, and in response to an exodus of affluent taxpayers, Toronto annexed Yorkville outright.

Similar factors were also at play in Montreal. The local economy relied heavily on a busy commercial port but the depression brought shipping to a near standstill. The chairman of the harbor commission publicly bemoaned a lack of federal investment in upgrades to the port, which was expanded and became the only one of its kind in North America to be lit by electricity in 1882. All without Ottawa's help.

Like Toronto, Montreal was consumed by business failure. The lumber industry collapsed. Railway construction slowed. The banks in Montreal were generally older and controlled much more capital than their counterparts in Toronto, though, so it was easier to keep the city's most important industries afloat.

The strength of Montreal's financial institutions allowed local industrialists to survive. Montreal shared Toronto's disdain for Ottawa's lack of support in areas such as port modernization but the federal government's relentless push to expand westward ensured that the prospects of Montreal's well-connected elite were still quite rosy.

The collapse of John Macdonald's government after the Canadian Pacific Railway scandal led to a commitment that Ottawa would build the railway itself. By 1880, efforts to manage the massive undertaking through the public works department were in shambles. Ottawa was still committed to connecting the Pacific region to the rest of the country but was incapable of making this happen on its own.

When Macdonald returned to power, he immediately revived the railway scheme under the exact same model that had previously cost him his position as prime minister. In an act of pure audacity, no sooner had Macdonald recaptured his post at the head of federal politics than he, once again, awarded the railway contract to a member of Montreal's prosperous inner circle.

George Stephen was a successful investor who founded a major insurance company and rose to the position of president of the Bank of Montreal. His partners in the revamped railway endeavor included the general manager of the Bank of Montreal and the principal shareholder at the Hudson's Bay Company.

In effect, the same cast of characters that had been so controversial when the first contract was issued remained for this second go-around. The only difference was that, this time, the public swallowed the deal without complaint.

The contract was awarded in 1881 and the headquarters of the Canadian Pacific Railway was established in Montreal. The rail line was completed by 1885 and Macdonald met his commitment to British Columbia as planned.

George Stephen replaced Hugh Allan but, despite this cosmetic change, the project benefited the same privileged community with which the prime minister had dealt all along. Business as usual officially resumed in Canada.

Ottawa was just as reluctant to get involved in port modernization in Montreal as it had been in Toronto. George Stephen's successful bid to recapture railway contracts from the federal government helped soften this blow by ensuring that the commercial port boomed through the next two decades.

The port of Montreal underwent unprecedented expansion. Wharves were extended, occupying twice as much space as before the depression. The number of ships using these facilities remained largely unchanged but the amount

The continued expansion of Montreal's commercial port (1890) was critical to the city's fortunes, particularly in times of econmic uncertainty (W. Notman / Library and Archives Canada / PA-149196).

of goods being processed and distributed more than tripled. With this increased activity also came an expansion in the manufacturing industry in districts abutting the city core.

Hochelaga, for example, was an eastern neighborhood just beyond the boundaries of Montreal proper. With the boom that followed the end of the depression, residences and factories spilled into this area creating new pressure on the tiny municipality's infrastructure as well as a significant drain on tax revenues for Montreal.

The lingering threat of smallpox encouraged affluent residents to seek housing as far from the core as possible. This combination of factors, as it had in the case of Yorkville, created the conditions in which annexing Hochelaga made sense for Montreal.

Hochelaga could not afford to pay for the infrastructure necessitated by its sudden growth. Montreal needed to extend its tax base in order to pay for its own expansion. The concept of amalgamation was born out of pure necessity. In 1883, the City of Montreal officially expanded to absorb Hochelaga.

In both Toronto and Montreal, the 1880s ushered in an era of rapid expansion. With the return of John Macdonald, financiers in Montreal were guaranteed to succeed through the final development of the Canadian Pacific Railway but the federal government continued to shy away from directly funding ports or infrastructure in either city.

The port of Montreal boomed partly as a result of railway construction while both Toronto and Montreal gobbled up surrounding districts to address critical shortfalls in tax revenues necessary for infrastructure upgrades. The federal government's inconsistent intervention and relentless bias in favor of Montreal permanently changed the shape of both cities.

John Macdonald's grip on power was nearly absolute. His whim was law. Once again sitting at the head of the federal government, he discovered that the practice of Canadian politics had not changed in the few years since his temporary downfall. It had just taken a quick depression to scare his constituency into thinking it was good government.

It remains unknown whether Macdonald's grip on Canadian politics would have survived a subsequent economic downturn that again hit in the early 1890s. He died in office in 1891. His legacy, however, was secure. For the entire century that followed, politicians in Ottawa would fall over themselves trying to recreate the dominance that Macdonald enjoyed.

He was succeeded by a string of prime ministerial pretenders that became known as the Futile Four. Even Charles Tupper, the man who duped Nova Scotia into the country, was incapable of hanging onto the power that Macdonald wielded so effortlessly.

In the election of 1896, Tupper and his party were put to the test. The outcome would be decided by two Quebecers who learned more from Macdonald than any of his failed successors.

"Leave Quebec to Laurier and me."
—*Joseph Tarte, strategizing for Wilfred Laurier, 1896*

Wilfrid Laurier was a Montreal lawyer who understood the power of patronage in federal politics. Laurier campaigned for the prime minister's job in partnership with a close political ally, a Quebec newspaper editor named Joseph Tarte.

Tarte's influence on the federal election of 1896 began years earlier when, as editor of *Le Canadien*, he turned John Macdonald's renewed railway project into a front-page story that brought down the incumbent minister of public works. Tarte gambled that Macdonald's party would not be as resilient in the face of public scandal as the powerful prime minister had been prior to his death, and the payoff went straight to Laurier waiting in the wings.

Tarte's newspaper ran stories harshly critical of then public works minister

Hector Langevin. Specifically, he cited evidence that seemed to prove Langevin had been paid to award construction contracts to a pre-selected firm. The accusation led to a public court hearing in which Langevin was found guilty of negligence and was forced to resign.

In 1896, leaning on these allegations of widespread corruption, Wilfred Laurier was elected as prime minister. He immediately appointed Joseph Tarte as, of course, minister of public works.

In the years that followed, Tarte would show that his campaign against patronage in the public works department had been the work of a clever opportunist, not the act of a principled man who opposed government kickbacks. In fact, the port of Montreal finally received federal funding towards important upgrades as a result of Tarte's willingness to send business in the direction of his supporters back home.

Together, Tarte and Laurier had manufactured a scandal that allowed them to snatch power from John Macdonald's former party then turn the benefits of government patronage over to their own supporters instead. The face of Canadian politics had taken shape. As always, whether they liked it or not, Toronto and Montreal were along for the ride.

During this era, the rivalry between Toronto and Montreal officially extended beyond politics and commerce into the field of sports. At the time, baseball was still in its infancy. Though growing in popularity, it lagged behind sports such as curling, rowing and snowshoeing. Insofar as heated, elite-level competition was concerned, baseball could not hold a candle to the undisputed national game of choice: lacrosse.

Lacrosse ushered in the tradition of Toronto-Montreal sports confrontations. It featured the most clubs, tournaments and players of any organized sport and also offered the requisite level of controlled violence necessary for stirring the emotions of participants and spectators. It was perfect. Canadians felt that it was their game.

When Canada held the lacrosse "championship of the world" in the 1870s it was serious business. When one such final pitted the Dominion Club of Montreal against the Tecumseh Club of Toronto, the stage was set for the 130 years that would follow. That championship game ended in a 2–2 draw. Ever since, the two cities have knocked themselves out trying to break the tie.

> "It's pretty sad because I'm sure a lot of fans look forward to this series"—*Carlos Delgado, on the possible end of Jays-Expos interleague play, 2002*

Few players on either the Toronto Blue Jays or Montreal Expos can place the upcoming interleague series at Olympic Stadium within the context of a sporting rivalry that stretches back over a century. The only player that even comes close is Blue Jays catcher Darrin Fletcher.

Fletcher is an oft-injured Blue Jay who spent the better part of six seasons playing for the Expos. Fletcher has seen enough ups and downs on both sides of the classic Canadian rivalry to look forward to these upcoming interleague games as a confrontation between two proud cities that get very uptight when their teams meet. He will be among the few players for whom this could be the case. For the most part, the only ones who really care are the fans.

Fans of the Toronto Blue Jays justly point to back-to-back World Series championships in the early '90s and crow with self-assurance. Fans of the Montreal Expos point to numerous occasions in which labor strife, a lack of money or bad luck relegated their best teams to the ranks of perennial also-rans.

These people will be a focal point of the Canadian interleague series partly because so few are likely to turn up at the Big O. If the whole series draws 30,000 fans it will be a success.

The first game features young pitchers on the mound. Tohmo Ohka is trying to keep a hot streak going which has seen him emerge as the Expos' second best starter. For Toronto, Justin Miller is trying to find the consistency necessary to turn occasionally brilliant performances into a regular place in the Blue Jays rotation.

From the outset, Miller is not in control and Montreal takes advantage. In the 1st inning, he is unable to find the strike zone and weak-hitting Lee Stevens draws a bases-loaded walk to open the scoring. In the 3rd inning, Miller is victimized by Stevens again as the infielder tags a two-run home run. In the 5th inning, Miller's nightmare continues as Stevens rips an RBI triple into the right field corner. It is the best night Lee Stevens has seen in a long while, and one that Miller may take just as long to forget.

By contrast, Tohmo Ohka is having a near ideal night. His few mistakes have only a marginal impact on the score as the innings roll along.

It's not entirely smooth sailing but Ohka manages to hold things together. In the 2nd inning, he allows Toronto to cut the Expos' lead in half by giving up a solo home run. In the 6th inning, he makes a similar mistake against young outfielder Vernon Wells who tags a solo blast. Ohka leaves the game after 7 innings, having given up just those two runs. The Expos win 8–2. All but two of the players in Montreal's lineup record hits, exactly the type of balanced attack that they need on a night when Vladimir Guerrero is less than his dominant self.

Saturday night at Olympic Stadium sees the pitching tables turn. Toronto sends Esteban Loaiza to the hill while Montreal counters with Carl Pavano. Loaiza has been a standout since his return from a shoulder injury and, other than Roy Halladay, whom the Expos will not face this weekend, has been Toronto's most reliable starter. Pavano, on the other hand, is described by his own manager as having great pitches but as being unable to pitch. In fact, Pavano has been one of the main reasons that Expos general manager Omar

Minaya has been so desperate to add depth to the team's pitching rotation. Everything would be easier if Pavano would come around.

Against Toronto, this fails to occur. Pavano barely lasts 3 innings, giving up six walks and two home runs. Luckily for the Expos, he hits the showers before too much damage is done. Blue Jays hitters lick their collective chops seeing Pavano's replacement, rookie Zach Day, wander in to make his major league debut. With a 3–0 lead, it looks like blast-off time.

A pitcher making his major league debut is an unknown commodity. Day is likely to be unsure how to pitch to celebrity batters such as Carlos Delgado but, at the same time, these hitters don't have any idea what to expect from him either. A pitcher like Day, in a scenario like this, is a real wild card. He escapes the 4th inning, pitching around a pair of base runners with nobody out, and his teammates then come to life at the plate.

The Expos chase Loaiza in the 6th inning when Fernando Tatis launches a 400-foot blast into the bleachers, turning the game into a contest between bullpens. As it has been all season long, this scenario is unfriendly to the Blue Jays. While Day goes about the business of throwing near perfect innings, Toronto's relievers get ripped.

The Expos eventually win 9–3, setting up a possible series sweep on Sunday afternoon. The Blue Jays have a date with Javier Vazquez.

Staring out at a top pitcher on the mound and brooms waving in the stands, the Blue Jays respond. Outfielder Shannon Stewart, among the only Blue Jay hitters this season to play up to his potential, starts the game with a very loud bang. He takes Vazquez out of the Big O with a solo home run that sets the stage for a three-run 1st inning. It's exactly what Toronto needs.

Unfortunately for Blue Jays fans, the Expos show that they know a thing or two about starting games off with a bang. Center fielder Brad Wilkerson follows Shannon Stewart by hitting a leadoff home run of his own. The Expos proceed to one-up the Jays as Jose Vidro delivers another shot over the wall. With back-to-back blasts, the Expos cut the Blue Jays' lead to 3–2.

The hit parade peters out for a while as both pitchers settle down. Then, in the 6th inning, things get ugly as Blue Jays manager Carlos Tosca dips into his bullpen.

Lee Stevens singles. Orlando Cabrera doubles. Brian Schneider doubles. Javier Vazquez singles and, finally, Brad Wilkerson hits a sacrifice fly. Three runs later, the Expos jump into the lead.

Under Carlos Tosca, it has not been so easy to put these Blue Jays away. Facing a 5–3 deficit, the Jays get to work. Their first order of business is Vazquez.

After Tom Wilson beats out an infield single and Shannon Stewart doubles, the Jays manufacture a run. Vazquez is lifted. The second order of business is tying the game. They accomplish this the very next inning with a single, double and RBI ground out. The Blue Jays are right back in it.

Another battle of the bullpens carries forward into the 9th inning with the game tied 5–5. Toronto leads off in style, receiving a double from Shannon Stewart, who collects his third extra-base hit of the afternoon. Tosca then employs some classic National League little-ball, bunting Stewart over to third base. The Blue Jays need just a fly ball or grounder to take the lead.

Raul Mondesi steps to the plate ahead of Carlos Delgado. This is Toronto's most menacing duo. Mondesi's hard grounder is snagged by Orlando Cabrera who checks Stewart back to third and throws Mondesi out by several steps. Delgado then grounds out and the game remains tied going into the bottom of the 9th.

Cue Kelvim Escobar. The Blue Jays closer has been on the bench for almost a week and is now called upon to face the heart of Montreal's order: Guerrero and the resurgent Troy O'Leary.

Guerrero watches a pancake pitch flutter over the plate for a strike then pops out weakly to the infield. Escobar induces Troy O'Leary to lunge forward and tap a light fly ball into centerfield, and all seems secure.

Bad luck follows this Blue Jays team wherever it goes, though. Vernon Wells, brought into the game as a defensive replacement, misjudges the ball and can't recover in time to charge forward and catch the soft pop-up. Having run in to adjust for his own mistake, Wells allows the ball to jump over his head and has to race back towards the wall after the bouncing ball.

O'Leary ends up with a double. Naturally, the very next batter, utility infielder Mike Mordecai, hits a single up the middle directly at Vernon Wells. O'Leary heads for home as Wells throws the ball into the stands. The Expos win 6–5.

Montreal moves back within striking distance of the National League East lead. Toronto falls 16 games behind Boston in the American League East.

When all is said and done, 35,500 fans turn out to watch the series at Olympic Stadium. Not too bad. The Blue Jays will hope to do better in a couple of weeks when the teams hook up in Toronto for a series over Canada Day weekend.

As the teams temporarily go their separate ways, Expos manager Frank Robinson learns that he's been selected to the National League coaching staff for the All-Star game. The decision amounts to a symbolic tip of the commissioner's cap to a man who accepted the least wanted job in baseball.

For Robinson, it will be an opportunity to enjoy his rightful congratulations. The Expos have not been an embarrassment and this has allowed the league to focus its attention on other embarrassments instead.

Baseball has officially been stung by a breakdown in stadium security. The threat of terrorism still looms in America. Though SkyDome and Olympic Stadium remain disturbingly accessible to lunatics, the first truly jarring incident of the summer occurs in the United States and appears to have been carried out by idiots with nothing but idle time on their hands.

In the 9th inning of an interleague game between the Philadelphia Phillies and Cleveland Indians, an explosive device is dropped from the upper deck of picturesque Jacobs Field. There are no serious injuries in the explosion.

A woman leaving the stadium is burned on the legs. A stadium employee is burned on the chest. The homemade explosive was not packed with bolts or nails. It didn't set off a panic in the stands. The bums are caught in the act and held by police.

Three men in their early 20s are detained. By all accounts, the device was not especially powerful and was probably not designed to kill anyone, just scare a lot of people. As such, it is unlikely that they will be charged with anything more serious than arson or assault. These are serious crimes but they fail to capture the sudden horror that this incident has introduced, not only in the stands but also in the dugouts of major league baseball.

Players and fans are wide-open targets. At least, in Cleveland, the bombers were captured and will be prosecuted. This fact surely has as much to do with a poorly planned escape than with the safeguards at Jacobs Field. If these buffoons had been smarter, they could have been home watching the whole thing play out on TV.

That the plight of the Expos can be ignored in the midst of these horrible distractions is part of the reason that Robinson has been rewarded with his All-Star appointment. Most managers receive their laurels for bringing teams into the spotlight. It's just one more slice of absurdity playing out in Montreal that Robinson receives his for accomplishing the opposite.

Blue Jays manager Carlos Tosca has not been on the job long enough to be considered for a position on the All-Star coaching staff but all agree that his team is playing much better since he took over. If there's any justice in the selection process, Toronto will still be represented by Roy Halladay.

The Blue Jays roster doesn't feature many players putting up All-Star caliber numbers. Even Carlos Delgado, a legitimate triple-crown threat at his best, is hitting a meager .256. Halladay, on the other hand, continues to be one of the most effective pitchers in the American League.

In Los Angeles, where the Blue Jays continue their interleague schedule against the Dodgers, Halladay faces Andy Ashby. With ace Kevin Brown injured, Ashby is key to the Dodgers pitching staff as his team competes with the Arizona Diamondbacks for the top spot in the National League West.

Against Toronto, Ashby is at his best. He pitches 8 innings, giving up just two runs. This would usually be enough for a win. On this night, he is out-gunned by Halladay who throws a complete game and gives up just one run on a Carlos Delgado error.

That's what makes an All-Star pitcher: facing the other team's best and coming out on top. The 25-year-old Halladay improves to 8–3 and snaps another Blue Jays losing streak by himself.

These positive results are mostly lost in the chaotic build-up to All-Star weekend. With negotiations towards averting a strike going nowhere, and the All-Star game taking place in Commissioner Selig's hometown of Milwaukee, there's no turning away from the bad faith that is consuming baseball.

Labor negotiations attract lies and insincerity the same way high art attracts madness and alcoholism. They're part of the process. The key difference is that artists gain credibility the further they slide into addiction and insanity while labor negotiators look every bit like back-stabbing swindlers the more they manipulate circumstances to their advantage.

Baseball fans can be forgiven if they groan every time the commissioner's office or players' union publicizes a move they've made in negotiations. Most recently, the owners offered to lower the luxury tax on big budget teams for a transition period that would allow players and teams to adjust to the new set of rules. According to the owners, this will temporarily delay the full implementation of measures that would, in theory, limit spending. In the very next breath, the owners turn around and blame the players' union for the fact that the payroll limit, above which this new tax would kick in, is so ridiculously high that it couldn't possibly have any real impact.

The dirty secret these owners are keeping is that they need salaries to keep escalating in order to justify their own reckless spending. If other free agents follow Alex Rodriguez' example and sign contracts in the billion dollar range then, over time, Texas' investment will look shrewd.

The owners are doing it to themselves. The players are letting them and have run out of patience for fans who think common sense in baseball should come from their end.

Four-time National League MVP Barry Bonds has a message for fans who think it's absurd for millionaires to go on strike over salaries. He's stated that, since the children of some fans may someday play in the major leagues, he is actually fighting for their families.

Barry Bonds isn't crazy. He's just obviously tired of hearing it from fans and understands better than most that he has become a pure commodity in the business of baseball. He is a product to be bought and sold.

Maybe there was a time when players and fans were not so alienated from one another that something akin to an intimate relationship was possible. Whether this was ever true or not, it isn't any longer. Middle class people don't feel connected to those who earn 200 times their salary. Multi-millionaires are dismissive of those who view them as products. It cuts both ways.

For their decades of struggle against major league owners, this is what the players have achieved. They make more money than could possibly have been imagined back when Curt Flood first challenged the league but are now half-despised by even the most committed fans.

If the players go back on strike in 2002, this is bound to only get worse. If they don't go on strike, it won't necessarily get better. Players are racing owners to the bottom. Both sides have been doing it for so long now that they don't know how to stop.

> "You can't get 26 owners to agree on anything."
> —Commissioner Ueberroth, on accusations of collusion among owners, 1985

Following the split season of 1981, four years of relative calm settled in. The proposed formula for free agent compensation, imposed when the owners' strike insurance ran out, was abandoned and replaced. Neither formula led to the skyrocketing salaries that owners said would drive baseball out of business but accusations of collusion among owners were widespread as the market for free agent talent seemed to spontaneously dry up.

The owners had learned a very valuable lesson from the imposed settlement in 1981. They'd learned that their claims to insolvency were falling on deaf ears and that much more work needed to be done if anyone was going to believe that they were losing money by running America's national pastime.

As a result, in the build up to labor negotiations in 1985, the owners shifted gears. They no longer argued that new measures proposed by the players were liable to run teams out of business in the future. Rather, they argued that baseball owners were already facing outright failure, accounting for the mysterious drop in free agent signings. This shady maneuver would become part of the business of baseball through the new millennium.

On the field, the years between 1981 and 1985 were pivotal for the Toronto Blue Jays. In 1982, the team came tantalizingly close to finishing at .500 and featured standout performances from pitchers Dave Stieb and Jim Clancy. Still, the team struggled at the plate, finishing near the bottom of the league in hits, home runs and runs, generating yet another losing season. Things finally turned around the very next summer.

The year 1983 would be the start of the most successful decade ever seen in Canadian baseball. It set the wheels in motion for Toronto: 10 straight winning seasons, 5 division titles, 2 World Series championships. That year was the springboard, though at the time it merely represented the first winning season in team history. No one could have predicted that it would be the beginning of so much success.

The offensive woes that plagued the Blue Jays in '82 were entirely forgotten in '83 when the team finished second in the American League in hits and home runs. Suddenly, the Blue Jays were a powerhouse. Willie Upshaw had over 100 RBIs. Jesse Barfield hit 27 home runs. Lloyd Moseby hit .315. All the promise in the Blue Jays' lineup finally generated results.

As for pitching, the team still leaned heavily on the young duo of Dave Stieb and Jim Clancy. If the pitching staff had been a little deeper, the '83

Blue Jays might have been able to make a run at the division title. Instead, they happily settled for an 89–73 record.

In 1984, Toronto repeated its success and recorded an identical record. In 1985, with the team on the cusp of unprecedented success, Major League Baseball's labor troubles intervened, threatening to spoil all the fun.

Unlike in 1981, the owners had not insured themselves against a prolonged strike. This did not stop them from proposing significant changes to the existing system that allowed players to seek salary arbitration after two years of service. Owners claimed that this was adding to their financial woes and recommended that players be required to play for three seasons before going to arbitration. Furthermore, the owners proposed that a maximum 100 percent increase be placed on such decisions.

On August 6, the players went on strike again. It lasted one day. On August 7, the players agreed to a three-year minimum for arbitration eligibility and the owners consented to having no limit to the salary increase that an arbitrator could award.

The agreement prevented any significant interruption in the 1985 schedule. Fans breathed a sigh of relief. The season had been salvaged.

In Toronto, this meant that the Blue Jays were barely impacted by the strike at all, save for having an extra day off in early August. The team's hitters continued to post some of the league's best numbers and its pitching staff, with the additions of Doyle Alexander and Jimmy Key, led the league in wins. The Blue Jays would win 99 games in 1985, good enough for their first division title.

Whereas the strike in '81 delivered a controversial title and devastating playoff disappointment to the Montreal Expos, the strike in '85 came and went without any impact on the rise of the Toronto Blue Jays. As major league owners and players continued to clash over salaries, free agents and claims of bankruptcy, the Expos stammered through years of unfulfilled potential while the Blue Jays transformed themselves into rising stars. The two franchises appeared to have deflected onto different paths.

In 2002, those paths briefly overlap as the second interleague series between the Blue Jays and Expos approaches. Prior to this resumption of competitive hostilities over Canada Day weekend, both teams make history.

For the first time in five dismal seasons, the Montreal Expos are in a position to win seven games in a row. To keep a winning streak like this going, it is sometimes necessary to win cheap. Not every game can be a textbook display of crisp, clean baseball. Every once in a while, winning teams have to play ugly.

The Expos are still capable of either striking at the leaders atop the National League East or sinking to the bottom of the standings. Montreal has lingered in second place long enough to seriously contemplate making another run at the division lead next month when they play 20 plus games against divisional opponents. Before that, they have to contend with Kansas City.

Against the Royals, Expos hitters build a 3–0 lead before their pitchers, in relief of starter Masato Yoshii, get into a world of trouble. The Expos send three different pitchers to the mound in the 7th inning alone and, with two outs, those pitchers spoil the lead by putting Kansas City ahead 4–3. Only a 9th inning home run by Fernando Tatis sends the game into extra innings. That's lucky.

Vladimir Guerrero hits an infield single in the bottom of the 11th then advances into scoring position when the Royals' second baseman throws the ball away in desperation. That's ugly.

The next batter attempts to sacrifice-bunt Guerrero over to third base. Utility infielder Jose Macias successfully lays down an adequate bunt, moving Guerrero over, but when the Royals' pitcher turns to throw Macias out he accidentally skips the ball off the turf. The errant ball careens straight back into the charging Macias who is more than happy to kick it out towards the Expos' bullpen. Very ugly.

Guerrero sees the ball roll into foul territory and scores easily to end the game. The Expos win 5–4, sweep the Kansas City Royals and extend their winning streak to a five-year best.

For their part, facing the Tampa Bay Devil Rays, the Blue Jays do something their franchise hasn't accomplished in over 20 years. They score 20 runs.

Carlos Delgado, Vernon Wells and Jose Cruz Jr. combine for 15 RBIs. This offensive explosion couldn't come at a better time. Pitcher Esteban Loaiza, who started well after coming back from injury, lasts only into the 4th inning and gives up seven runs. The slugfest is on.

For once, the heart of the Blue Jays' batting order gets the job done on a night when their starting pitcher falters. The Blue Jays have displayed this type of offensive venom far too rarely in 2002. The 20–11 win is a historic result.

Less encouraging is the glum mood that descends on some Blue Jays players after this big win in Tampa. Carlos Tosca's honeymoon is officially over. After beginning his tenure with a series of wins, and receiving accolades for showing that extensive coaching experience could translate into immediate major league results, Tosca now finds himself in the middle of a controversy.

"He only has two weeks being a manager in the big leagues.... It's stupid." —*Raul Mondesi, 2002*

Raul Mondesi has reacted very publicly to being benched as a punishment for arriving late to a pre-game meeting. In his own defense, Mondesi points out that he'd missed the previous game with an illness and, as a result, had not been aware of the scheduled meeting. Tosca said there was no excuse and that all players carry the same responsibility. Be on time, or else.

Or else, in this case, meant that Mondesi missed out on the offensive gluttony of Toronto's 20–11 win. His outburst cost him another game on the bench as Tosca left him out of the lineup the next night, too. All are not happy in the Blue Jays' dugout.

General Manager J.P. Ricciardi was already trying to find a team on which to unload the enormously overpaid Mondesi. Now he is proving to not only be a mediocre player but also a serious distraction. Teams are no more likely to trade for him now than they were back when he was merely the league's worst investment.

Such is the state of Canada's teams as they meet in Toronto. One is a doomed franchise still lingering near the top of its division while the other is perceived as a stable franchise despite massive financial losses as it wallows near the bottom of the standings. The stage is set.

On Friday night, both teams look to rebound from recent disappointments. The Expos' winning streak came to an abrupt end against Pittsburgh. The Blue Jays come home after losing a pair of games in Tampa Bay to follow up their promising 20-run explosion.

When the Blue Jays and Expos met at Olympic Stadium earlier this month, Montreal was fortunate not to have faced Toronto ace Roy Halladay. They are not so lucky this time around, drawing Halladay in the series' first game. The Blue Jays draw the bottom of the Expo pitching rotation beginning with Tony Armas, Jr.

To their credit, both Halladay and Armas bring their best and the teams are locked in a pitchers' duel until the bottom of the 5th inning. After Blue Jays shortstop Felipe Lopez leads off with a triple, rookie third baseman Eric Hinske continues to display his uncanny knack for getting big hits at key moments by knocking a single up the middle to open the scoring.

In the very next inning, the Expos respond. Shortstop Orlando Cabrera legs out a double, moves over to third on a sacrifice bunt and then scores on a fielder's choice. It isn't spectacular but it ties the game.

Spectacular comes in the 7th inning when Fernando Tatis, facing Halladay with two outs and nobody onbase, tags the young ace for a solo home run that puts Montreal ahead. From that point, the bullpens take over.

Both starting pitchers leave the game with nothing to hang their heads about. In the end, only Felipe Lopez's lunging catch, halting Vladimir Guerrero's hitting streak at 20 games, provides a brief moment of offensive excitement over the final innings. There is no more scoring. The Expos win 2–1.

On Saturday afternoon, the roof is open at SkyDome. Toronto sends converted reliever Pete Walker to the mound for just the fourth start of his career. Blue Jays manager Carlos Tosca continues to search for anyone who can consistently follow Roy Halladay and Walker is as good a choice as anyone at this stage.

Over the first 5 innings, he shows the occasional lapses in concentration that characterize promising but inexperienced pitchers. He does well, striking out six batters while walking none. He clearly has all his pitches under control. Time and again, however, he throws the wrong pitch at the wrong time to the wrong batter.

In the 2nd inning, Vladimir Guerrero takes him out of SkyDome. In the 3rd inning, Jose Macias goes deep as well. In the 5th inning, Michael Barrett hits a long, long blast that is a sure home run from the moment it leaves his bat. These recurring mistakes put the Blue Jays behind 4–0.

Montreal starter Masato Yoshii cruises through those same 5 innings, completely shutting down the Blue Jays' offense. In the 7th, he is replaced by reliever Joey Eischen as Expos manager Frank Robinson turns the game over to his bullpen, which has not surrendered a run to opposition hitters in the team's last eight games.

The Blue Jays show immediate signs of life after the pitching change. Eric Hinske opens the 7th inning with a single, moving to third base when Raul Mondesi is generously awarded a double on a grounder that hops out of Fernando Tatis' glove. Carlos Delgado then cashes Hinske in with an RBI ground out that finally puts Toronto on the board.

The game moves into the 9th inning with Montreal still ahead 4–1. Toronto closer Kelvim Escobar nearly sells the Blue Jays out again by pitching himself into a bases loaded jam but eventually escapes without giving up any runs. In the bottom of the 9th, the Blue Jays come to life and the Expos fall on their faces.

Raul Mondesi draws a walk. Carlos Delgado singles. Mondesi scores on a ground out. After an Expos error, allowing Vernon Wells to reach base, Felipe Lopez completes the remarkable rally by cashing in both runs with a single to right field. The game goes to extra innings, tied 4–4.

Again, the Expos press Escobar, moving runners into scoring position in the 10th. Again, Escobar escapes on the strength of his strikeout power. Montreal is unable to tag the inconsistent closer and the game remains tied.

Of all the Blue Jays' hitters, Eric Hinske is the last batter that the Expos want to see at the plate with the game on the line. He is the biggest threat in the Jays' lineup and, with one swing, he sets the fireworks ablaze at SkyDome. Hinske's walk-off home run gives Toronto a 5–4 win.

The Expos' bitter disappointment obscures the excitement of a stunning development after the game. Montreal general manager Omar Minaya shocks the baseball world by completing a huge trade that leaves no doubt he is trying to make the Expos a contender this season.

Throughout 2002, there have been whispers that the Minaya's moves have had more to do with seeding the rest of the league with Expos talent rather than improving his own team. Most observers have disregarded such theories as pure fiction given the sincere efforts that Minaya has been making to improve his pitching staff, shifting prospects and looking for a diamond in the rough. This strategy hasn't worked, as evidenced by Minaya's recent abandonment of Bruce Chen.

Minaya never abandoned the Expos, though. Instead, he shifted gears and decided that if he couldn't improve his staff with young talent then he'd go out and find a legitimate star.

Minaya clearly recognizes that the next month will make or break the 2002 Expos. His team plays almost all of July against divisional opponents. The team needs answers to its most pressing problems immediately if it is going to have a shot at the playoffs. His solution: trade Lee Stevens and a handful of first-rate prospects to the Cleveland Indians for established ace Bartolo Colon.

Colon is having an All-Star season. He is 10–4 with a sparkling 2.55 ERA. Of late, he has been complaining about pain in his right side but is expected to be healthy for the rest of the summer.

In Cleveland, Colon was the uncontested ace on a team that had fallen far out of the pennant race. Now that he's in Montreal, he has a chance to turn a doomed team into one of the most sensational stories in all of baseball.

"I hope it sends a message ... we are trying to make the playoffs."
— *Omar Minaya, following his trade for Bartolo Colon, 2002*

July

"Certainly."
—*Stadium promoter, asked to bet his life that SkyDome would be on budget, 1985*

Baseball stadiums are not engines of urban revival. This is most obvious in abandoned cities with problems that run far deeper than any retro ballpark can reach. It is a dangerous reality for healthy cities, too. Vibrant, dynamic cities carry greater risks when buying into these schemes because they have much more to lose.

In 1982, municipal official Paul Godfrey got behind a proposal through which the federal, provincial and municipal governments would have jointly built a $75 million domed stadium in Toronto. This was partly a response to ugly weather at Exhibition Stadium during a football game that same year. Linking civic pride with dry bleachers, Godfrey and fellow proponents convinced themselves that Toronto needed a new facility.

Ottawa dismissed the idea, never seriously contemplating it due in part to ongoing commitments to a massive redevelopment along the Toronto waterfront. This project was already giving federal officials a huge headache. They weren't interested in talking about domed sports facilities.

At the time, Toronto's real estate market couldn't support the stadium initiative through private investment alone. Projects of that magnitude depend on the willingness of lending institutions to carry major risks. In 1982, Toronto's market was in the tank. Banks had basically imposed a moratorium. If the public sector couldn't do it, the stadium wasn't going to get done.

Over the next couple of years, circumstances changed. Federal and provincial governments, eager to cut costs wherever possible, promoted a wave of public-private partnerships while, in Toronto, the cyclical real estate market boomed. This encouraged lending institutions to re-open the development industry for business. The intersection of these phenomena cleared a path for the dormant stadium idea.

In 1985, Paul Godfrey promoted a new vision. The stadium would be constructed as a partnership. The province and city were expected to put up $30 million apiece while a consortium of private investors picked up the slack on a $150 million project.

Trevor Eyton, a prominent local financier and government insider, was recruited to craft the partnership and make the project happen. When CN, a federal crown corporation, committed vacant downtown land to the project, all the pieces started coming together.

The proposal called for a state-of-the-art retractable roof stadium to be located next to the flagship CN Tower. Unlike in cities such as Detroit, the vision in Toronto did not include promises of downtown revitalization.

Toronto was already an attractive destination for businesses, residents and tourists. Still, the suggestion that broad economic benefits would extend from the stadium itself was an important component of Godfrey and Eyton's pitch to the government.

It was important because, at the very same time, Olympic Stadium in Montreal was undergoing a $120 million renovation. Ten years after construction of Olympic Stadium began, Montreal was still on the hook for a roof that was expected to cost nearly as much as Toronto's entire ballpark.

The timing sent a clear message: don't build another hulking money pit that taxpayers will have to keep afloat in perpetuity. This message fell on deaf ears.

Both the province and the city were responsible for putting $30 million forward but the partnership framework didn't include any mechanism for either government to recover its investment. The province was responsible for covering operating losses and providing loan guarantees to ensure that debt financing could be secured. Each private investor put $5 million forward, had a significant stake in potential profits generated by the facility but no share of the risk. It was a lopsided partnership, to say the least.

Nine months later, once construction got underway, the price estimate for the facility jumped from $150 to $225 million. By 1987, after it was decided that a hotel and health club should be added, the price tag rose to $328 million. The following summer, taking a page of out the Montreal handbook, a construction strike added another $50 million.

In the end, SkyDome cost $600 million, a breathtaking 300 percent increase from the original plan. In accordance with the partnership framework, this crushing debt was hoisted on the province alone.

SkyDome was not a bigger disaster than Olympic Stadium, which cost more, was hastily finished and never hosted a champion. Still, SkyDome and Olympic Stadium both tell similar stories.

Montreal's stadium was conceived as a grand public project during the 1970s. Toronto's stadium was conceived as a bold public-private partnership during the 1980s. These are mere cosmetic differences. Major League Baseball

SkyDome was regarded, for a time, as the greatest sports facility on earth despite the financial framework that turned it into a major public liability (Canadian Baseball Hall of Fame and Museum).

in Canada is founded upon grand ideas that turned into permanent public liabilities.

There's no shame in admitting these things. SkyDome is a reminder of World Series glory while the flame outside Olympic Stadium is still lit every four years as a gesture of camaraderie between Montreal and all other Olympic cities. Taxpayers across North America are being swindled into funding facilities that are just as fiscally irresponsible but may never approach the heights that Canada's ballparks have enjoyed.

The real shame of what took place in Toronto is that the vitality of its downtown core, and the revival of a development industry that had fallen idle, contributed to a $600 million debt for the governments of Ontario and, ultimately, Toronto. It's one thing for a dying city to scramble in desperation. It's another for officials in a healthy city to saddle themselves with such an albatross.

SkyDome is still a stunning building. It is at its best when the roof is open, the sun is shining and people can forget about the expensive write-off it eventually became for taxpayers in Toronto. It's at its cavernous worst when, like on Canada Day 2002, it is completely empty.

Though the second interleague series between the Blue Jays and Expos was billed as a Canada Day match-up, both teams fly out of town prior to July 1. Fans don't have the chance to get drunk and dance around for the Jumbotron. Instead, they sit at home reading the sports pages, learning that the Blue Jays are dumping overpriced talent and the Expos are betting the farm on an All-Star pitcher.

In a move that the Blue Jays were desperate to make, General Manager J.P. Ricciardi has sent awful outfielder Raul Mondesi to the New York Yankees. There are two aspects about this trade that must make Blue Jays management cringe.

The first is that Mondesi came to Toronto in a blockbuster deal that sent budding superstar Shawn Greene to Los Angeles. Now that Mondesi has been shipped to New York, this means that the Blue Jays turned Greene into a minor leaguer. Second, Toronto still has to pay half of Mondesi's salary next season. The Blue Jays will pay him to play for the Yankees. That hurts.

As for the Expos, they have a new star on their pitching staff as they head into a key series against the Braves in Atlanta. Montreal has dropped 8 1/2 games behind Atlanta atop the National League East and Bartolo Colon is supposed to help bridge this gap.

Colon is a workhorse, a bona-fide ace. He has already racked up 10 wins this season with Cleveland. Whether the Expos have any real hope of making the playoffs, with or without Colon, is an open question. Even if he gives them five extra wins down the stretch, many suspect that this will do little other than put them 15 instead of 20 games off the pace.

This series is touted as a contest of pitchers but the first game goes in a completely different direction. Perennial Cy Young candidate Tom Glavine opens for the Braves against Montreal's Javier Vazquez. Both receive rude awakenings by giving up solo home runs in the 1st inning.

By the 3rd, it becomes clear that something is physically wrong with Glavine. He gives up a double to Jose Macias and a walk to Vladimir Guerrero, both unusual in that Glavine does not normally leave his pitches high enough for a player like Macias to get extra bases and almost never pitches around any hitter. Glavine then gives up a three-run home run to Fernando Tatis and has to be replaced.

Despite this promising burst, Javier Vazquez is not able to turn a 4–1 lead into a desperately needed win. After a two-base error in the Expos outfield, he surrenders a walk and a base hit then faces veteran slugger Julio Franco with the bases loaded in the 7th inning. Franco drives a liner over Vladimir Guerrero's head for his first career grand slam, giving Atlanta a 5–4 lead. It is the beginning of the end. Atlanta eventually wins 7–5.

This couldn't come at a worse time. July is crucial to Montreal as the team essentially plays the entire month against divisional opponents. Losses at this stage will seriously jeopardize the Expos' playoff aspirations.

With this sobering reality as a backdrop, Bartolo Colon makes his Expos debut. Colon has no margin for error, especially as the team's defense self-destructs around him.

Vladimir Guerrero loses track of a line drive, runs past the ball in mid-air

July

and has to chase it back towards the outfield wall. Gold Glove shortstop Orlando Cabrera launches a routine throw beyond the Expos' dugout, forcing Colon to race over in an effort to collect the errant ball while Braves runners spin round the bases. These errors put Montreal behind 2–0.

From that point forward, Colon takes matters into his own hands, pitching fastballs in the high 90s and keeping the Braves off the scoreboard through the 6th. Finally, he sees the Expos attack at its best.

Catcher Michael Barrett starts the Expos rally with a solo home run to left field. Jose Macias then hits a single, as does Vladimir Guerrero. Wil Cordero draws a walk. Fernando Tatis then brings everyone home by drilling a grand slam that just barely carries over the wall in right field. For the second night in a row, a grand slam makes the difference as Montreal downs Atlanta 5–2.

This, however, is precisely why some are so negative about the Expos' decision to trade for Colon. His outstanding performance puts the Expos 8 1/2 games back. If the Braves keep winning at anywhere near their current pace, the Expos will need an entire staff of Bartolo Colons to catch them.

Expos general manager Omar Minaya is not shrinking away from this challenge. He is angling for other deals instead, now reportedly negotiating with the Florida Marlins towards bringing Cliff Floyd and Canadian pitcher Ryan Dempster to Montreal.

He is behaving as if the Expos' pennant race has already begun and, with much ground to make up but little time to do it, the future is now. It's been a long time since Montreal had this type of general manager.

"They're doing what they have to do to try to win this thing."
—*Cliff Floyd, on the prospect of being traded back to Montreal, 2002*

The Blue Jays are leaving the acquisition of star talent to the Expos this summer but sports boosters in Toronto are aiming as high as ever. The city is making a bid to host the 2008 Olympics and the future of Toronto's waterfront hangs in the balance.

This is not a case of one city striving to replicate the experience of another. Organizers have vowed that the mistakes of the 1976 Olympics in Montreal will not be revisited by Toronto.

For one thing, the Olympics will allow Ottawa to follow through on a 30-year-old commitment to revitalize Toronto's waterfront. The Games will transform this district, long the source of failed public efforts to create a vibrant mixed-use neighborhood, into the core of the world's most hyped sporting event. The flagship Olympic Stadium is planned for this site. Transportation services and pedestrian access will also establish new links between this isolated district and downtown Toronto.

The motley crew of private firms and public agencies that own these waterfront sites have all been drawn to the Olympic glitz. They all want to have their names on the project. The prime minister, premier of Ontario and mayor of Toronto recently convened for a photo op promoting the bid. Only the Olympics could bring these adversaries together.

Toronto's Olympic experience is unique in another way as well. Montreal never had to deal with the embarrassment of insulting key members of the International Olympic Committee (IOC) or the sickly disgust of a public works shutdown prior to the final selection of a host city. Toronto has been the first to introduce these variables.

The city is overflowing with garbage. A municipal strike has halted the city's trash removal service. Over Canada Day weekend, the impact of this public sector dispute became overbearing.

The heat was oppressive. Thousands of visitors had flocked to the city for Canada Day and Gay Pride parties. Restaurants, bars and dance clubs were running at full tilt, generating more waste than usual. In the aftermath, the city's parks, sidewalks and parking lots became mass garbage dumps. Toronto besieged itself.

Mayor Mel Lastman is totally outraged. He has accused the union of deliberately targeting the summer months for the strike because it allows the union to withdraw services when kids are out of school, seniors are overheating and the garbage is guaranteed to decompose under the sun. He's right, of course. This is exactly why the union is striking over the summer. It's no good to strike if no one's going to notice. The mayor is trying to turn that strategic decision into a crime against human decency.

With this approach, he is failing to deliver the one message that might help his constituency survive: make less garbage! Torontonians, like all big-city North Americans, are garbage hysterics. They can't control themselves, lashing out in fits of outrage as it piles up around them only to go home and make more. The mayor might ask these people to compost, recycle and make less waste while he hammers out a contract in 24-hour bargaining sessions. Instead, he asserts the crisis is the union's fault, walks away from negotiations and delegates the problem up to the province.

Mountains of rotting garbage represent a legitimate health hazard so it's likely that the province will eventually step in and force the striking union to move some of the tonnage out to city dumps. Under the Canadian constitution, health and urban affairs are the ultimate responsibility of provincial governments.

In this case, provincial officials will eventually be forced into action for simple lack of being able to delegate further upwards. With the entire city suffocating in the grips of this massive public-sector strike, the best the mayor can do is play this tired political game and hope that he, personally, isn't too dirty when the whole mess finally gets resolved.

By digging in his heels when residents most need him to find a creative, immediate solution, Lastman is following through on the kind of leadership he recently showed on the Olympic front as well. Prior to the final IOC vote to determine the host city for the 2008 Olympic Games, he stunned the world by announcing that he was concerned about visiting African nations for fear of being boiled alive and eaten by cannibals. The comment is regarded as having all but sunk Toronto's slim hopes for hosting the Games since most IOC swing-votes are in the hands of African delegates.

If Lastman's career in municipal politics doesn't work out, he may have a future in baseball. His approach to union negotiations and uncanny knack for turning a marquee event into a major embarrassment could make him a good candidate for commissioner.

The current commissioner is doing much the same for this summer's All-Star game in Milwaukee. Bud Selig opens the weekend of festivities by reaffirming his commitment to contraction and ends by absorbing a shower of boos from his own fans.

In the otherwise jovial atmosphere of All-Star weekend, Selig has made two things very clear insofar as the Montreal Expos are concerned. First, under no circumstances will the team be allowed to increase its payroll. Forget about trading with Florida for Cliff Floyd and Ryan Dempster. Expos general manager Omar Minaya is going to have to make all salaries even out, as he did in the Bartolo Colon deal, if he's going to pick up any new players. Second, by whatever means necessary, the Expos will be contracted.

The sour announcement detracts from a fine showing by Expos representatives. Jose Vidro makes a stellar diving catch to rob the American League of a sure hit. Vladimir Guerrero collects a hit and scores a run.

Blue Jays fans watch Roy Halladay pitch the 3rd inning and yield a line-drive home run to Barry Bonds. It's no embarrassment. That's what happens when the other team's batting order is stacked with the game's best hitters. Halladay has no reason to hang his head.

The game is a seesaw affair that comes to rest at 7–7 in the 8th. It stretches into extra innings where both teams eventually run out of pitchers. In the 11th, managers Joe Torre and Bob Brenly mutually agree that they can't force the one remaining pitcher on both sides to pitch forever so they inform Bud Selig that the game has to be declared a tie.

Selig agrees, advises the umpires and hears it from the crowd. It is a poignant moment. Bud Selig is ushered away under the protection of security as fans at his home field curse him in front of millions watching on television.

In his own way, Selig sets everything straight on this night. He's made sure that there's nothing to get excited about with the Expos playing their best baseball in years. He's confirmed that the plight of struggling teams will be addressed through outright dissolution. He's let fans around the world know that, in a tight spot, it doesn't make a damned bit of difference whether or not they want to see baseball.

> "I'd like to apologize to the fans."
> —*Bud Selig following the All-Star game, 2002*

Immediately after the All-Star tie in Milwaukee everyone goes back to work. Players' union and ownership negotiators pursue their war of words through the media.

Commissioner Selig signals that this war is back on immediately after the All-Star break, proclaiming that the financial condition of some major league teams is so dire that one team is likely to go bankrupt before the end of the season and, within a week, another will not be able to pay its players or staff. Selig, recognizing that he just put a measurable timeframe on the owners' vague claims to insolvency, immediately backpedals. Forget he said anything.

Reigning home run king Barry Bonds announces that he uses creatine, which is the same supplement that Mark McGwire and Sammy Sosa were on when they chased down Roger Maris' home run record in 1998. Though creatine is not an anabolic steroid, its main benefit is that it allows muscles to recover more quickly from workouts and the daily grind of a long baseball schedule. The best use creatine to be at their best.

In Minnesota, a county judge orders the state athletics commission to destroy documents detailing Major League Baseball's finances and contraction plan. The documents had originally been provided as part of a lawsuit intended to block the league's attempt to contract the Twins. Since then, the Minnesota state government has agreed to build them a new stadium so the lawsuit has been dropped.

As a result, the documents will be shredded instead of being released under legislation that requires all material passing through a public agency, such as the athletics commission, to be made available. The judge did not offer any explanation for his ruling.

Baseball is back. Bad faith negotiations are underway. Steroid use has come back to the forefront. Public documents are shredded without explanation. This is the challenge of modern baseball: to concentrate on competing while so many dark clouds collide in a perfect storm overhead. For the Toronto Blue Jays and Montreal Expos, the regular season resumes with visits from high-flying division rivals.

At SkyDome, the 34–52 Blue Jays face a Red Sox team that recently completed a rare five-game sweep when the two teams played in Boston. At Olympic Stadium, the 46–41 Expos welcome the division-leading Atlanta Braves aiming to put an immediate halt to all the talk about Montreal's playoff run.

This is the real business of baseball but the lines that divide the playing field, courtroom and political arena have never been so blurry. The suffocating mess harkens back to an era when the real business of both these cities came to be permanently tangled in the posturing and scandal through which power was exchanged in the Canadian capital.

> "[The] policy will be attacked ... [as] an imperial policy ... [and] a separatist measure. But the object will be the same ... destruction of the government." — *Prime Minister Wilfred Laurier, 1910*

With Wilfred Laurier and Joseph Tarte holding power, the port of Montreal strengthened its position as the hub of international shipping in North America. When Tarte came into the picture, he found a facility that was already in a class by itself, was under the control of the federal government and represented a low-risk target for high-profile investment.

Installed as minister of public works in 1896, he transformed the port. Old wooden walls were replaced with stone. New piers were planned. A small offshore island was removed and massive grain elevators were constructed. When these upgrades were complete, the port became the platform from which worldwide goods were distributed throughout the continent.

By contrast, Tarte left the commercial port of Toronto entirely in the hands of private landowners who saw little benefit in carrying the huge financial

The Port of Montreal (1891) greatly benefited from Tarte's decision to spend public funds on its modernization (Dominion Illustrated / Library and Archives Canada / C-005016).

burden of such upgrades. Wharves were allowed to decay. No effort was made to maintain, let alone expand, their capacity. Little more than repeated dredging, to skim floating islands of pollution from the water, was ever undertaken.

As it had always been, Toronto was a city with no shortage of entrepreneurial zeal and had long since grown accustomed to losing public projects to Montreal. What one industry lacked in public investment another made up in pure acumen. Montreal would have its port. It would even continue to capture the attention of the government, intent on retaining votes in Quebec. No problem. Toronto would find a way.

Responding to the promise of a massive upswing in trade to the west, industrialists collectively decided that bigger was indeed better. Small factories dispersed throughout the expanding urban region shut down, relocated and expanded into bigger facilities more centrally located in Toronto proper. By the 1890s, large-scale factories accounted for most products being manufactured in the city and distributed across the country.

There were difficult periods to be sure. Trade slowed periodically, forcing many enterprises out of business, and labor disputes became more and more common. Unmoved by these phenomena, Toronto's diverse business community continued to ensure that the manufacturing sector adapted to changing market conditions and expanded even during lean years.

In the absence of significant federal investment in facilities such as the commercial port, business in Toronto (1915) turned on issues like free trade (Merrilees Collection / Library and Archives Canada / PA-136356).

The Toronto economy was extremely resilient. As a consequence, or perhaps as a cause, of this resilience, its most influential capitalists were also becoming more defiant, particularly in the face of measures imposed by Ottawa that impacted their capacity to conduct business.

In this environment, the issue of free trade with the United States remained a central topic of debate. Tariffs intended to protect local markets from foreign goods were perceived, by some, as a burden. Others continued to perceive the tariffs as a necessary measure ensuring that the Canadian market could be sustained even during slow periods in international commerce. Conflicts of opinion extended into an election in 1911, challenging both the influence of the federal government and the leadership of Wilfred Laurier himself.

The Laurier government was founded on the appearance and exploitation of public scandal. In order to take advantage of these conditions, Laurier relied heavily on his trusted strategist, Joseph Tarte. Laurier could not have risen to power without him.

Joseph Tarte resigned from his position as minister of public works in 1902. Though he distributed the benefits of his public budget to the same advantage of friends and supporters as his deposed predecessors, he was not forced to resign amid a patronage scandal. Tarte was too clever to ever let that happen. Rather, he resigned in protest over the issue of import tariffs.

It's unclear whether Joseph Tarte was really committed to the concept of higher tariffs or whether he simply seized on this idea as a leadership issue when Wilfred Laurier became ill and nearly retired in 1902. One way or another, Tarte gave speeches that focused on the need for greater government intervention against foreign imports, which was a clear departure from the policy that Laurier himself endorsed. The rift proved irreconcilable and Tarte resigned to become a thorn in Laurier's side in Quebec.

For all the trouble it caused him, Wilfred Laurier thought he had settled the issue of import tariffs for good in 1910. Laurier's finance minister traveled to Washington to conduct trade talks that few expected would generate any significant announcements, then promptly returned to Ottawa with news that the United States had agreed to a deal allowing Canada to retain its protective tariffs on manufactured goods but trade freely in natural resources.

Such terms would allow Canadian exporters open access to growing markets in America without sacrificing Canada's control over its own markets. Few believed that the United States would ever agree to terms that, on their collective face, seemed so favorable to Canada. This development was initially regarded as a political coup, pulled off by Laurier when he was most in need of a shot in the arm.

Laurier's time in the capital had not been without its share of dark clouds. In 1906, his government was rocked by a sensational sex scandal. In 1910, Laurier created a nationwide controversy by introducing the Naval Service Act, which mandated the federal government to build a military fleet for the purpose of assisting the British against the Germans.

Critics in Ontario opposed the act because it did not provide direct emergency assistance to Britain. Critics in Quebec opposed the legislation because it committed public resources to the defense of an empire that was no longer relevant. Laurier was under attack from both sides.

In this climate, the free trade announcement offered an opportunity to show that his shaky administration could get the job done. It was an important can-do moment. That is, until statements suggesting that all of North America would eventually come under the control of the United States drifted up from the House of Representatives.

Canadians became suspicious that the proposed trade agreement would effectively merge the American and Canadian economies into one, and that the United States would gradually wrestle control away from Canada's own government. Though terms of the proposed trade agreement were clearly in Canada's favor, many Canadians recognized an ulterior motive in these generous provisions. They recognized a desire for greater integration as a first step towards eventual assimilation.

Imperialists felt this was a threat to the British crown. French Quebecers saw an American empire as no more attractive than the British empire. Prime Minister Laurier faced the rare convergence of Ontario and Quebec interests on the same issue.

These divergent agendas, which Laurier and Tarte had so effectively manipulated over a decade earlier, now threatened to derail the prime minister's trade pact. The opposition was relentless.

The furor eventually forced Laurier to call a general election. In 1911, with the Naval Service Act and the free trade pact clearly in the public eye, Wilfred Laurier was chased out of power.

Imperialists in Ontario, under Robert Borden, voted him down partly to ensure that Canada would continue to have a place in the British empire. Anti-imperialists in Quebec voted him down because the empire had entirely lost its relevance. Rivalry among these regions, jockeying for greater influence in the capital, had helped Laurier win power but their shared opposition allowed Robert Borden to succeed him.

For Borden, this makeshift alliance was a mixed blessing. The rare overlap allowed him to win the election but he took over a country in which the role of the federal government was changing.

Its power, and the authority it wielded in Canada's largest cities, was beginning to diminish in the face of provincial influence over both natural resources and urban development. During the Borden era, the influence of the federal government in Toronto and Montreal would be challenged.

Robert Borden governed through World War I, which created the need for federal intervention to ensure that industry supported the war machine's ravenous appetite, but the imposition of this federal agenda actually underscored the growing importance of provincial and even municipal governments. These tensions would be aggravated by the policies of a prime minister who came to be more concerned with Canada's status in international affairs than its internal disharmony.

> "The American flag will float over every square foot [of North America]." —*Champ Clark, speaker of the U.S. House of Representatives, 1911*

Barring a strike, there are still 70 games left in the 2002 season. This may leave Montreal enough time to move back within reach of the Braves. Time is on the Expos' side but, if they are going to make a move, the best place to start is with the upcoming showdown against Atlanta at Olympic Stadium.

Prior to this series, Montreal is again in the spotlight because of moves made by General Manager Omar Minaya. The trade that brought ace pitcher Bartolo Colon to Montreal was a sensation. Now, Minaya has acquired the key player he wanted from Florida as well. Cliff Floyd is returning to Montreal bringing his .287 batting average, 18 home runs and 57 RBIs along with him.

Great for the Expos. Still, since Selig has confirmed that no new salary will be added in Montreal, and since Minaya traded away the team's last remaining over-inflated salary in Graeme Lloyd to make room for Floyd, this is likely the last move Montreal will be able to make. The team is in place. Now it has to start winning.

With Atlanta in town, the Expos send Tony Armas Jr. to the mound. Armas has been good of late, posting a 3–0 record in the past month, but a young pitcher on a modest winning streak does not impress the Braves. Atlanta jumps all over Armas. Centerfielder Andruw Jones pounds a three-run home run in the 1st inning, giving the Braves a 4–0 lead.

Montreal cuts the lead in half with solo home runs by Brian Schneider and Vladimir Guerrero. The resurgence doesn't last.

Manager Frank Robinson is guilty of having too much faith in the young Armas, who shuts Atlanta out through the 5th inning but, sent back out to pitch in the 6th, falls apart. Gary Sheffield blasts another three-run homer and the Expos are cooked. Atlanta wins 8–5.

The Expos badly need a win. Losing to Atlanta has dropped them 11½ games off the division lead. Appropriately, the Expos send Bartolo Colon out to stop the bleeding against Tom Glavine.

It is Colon's first start at Olympic Stadium and, thanks to a $1 hot dog promotion, a decent crowd turns out for his debut. In response, he gives them a truly dominating performance.

The teams are deadlocked at 2–2 in the 6th inning. It is typical of two ace pitchers going at one another. All the runs are scored on base hits, sacrifice flies or fielder's choices. Neither team can get their big bats booming. That is, until Tom Glavine gives up the golden goose to rookie center fielder Brad Wilkerson who drives a solo home run out of the Big O on a two-strike pitch. Vladimir Guerrero then drills another home run and, on the very next pitch, newly acquired Cliff Floyd sends the crowd into a frenzy with a homer of his own. Glavine is done.

Bartolo Colon, on the other hand, looks more and more comfortable as the game wears on. He surrenders a solo home run to Chipper Jones in the 8th inning but never gets into the kind of trouble that could put his team's lead in jeopardy. Still throwing menacing fastballs late in the game, Colon comfortably closes his own win.

It is his second straight since joining the Expos and, more importantly, his second straight against the Braves. Colon is doing exactly what the Expos need him to do. He is keeping them on the post-season radar screen.

The Atlanta Braves have been so hot that it's been a full month since they've dropped two games in a row. Twenty-five thousand fans are at Olympic Stadium on Sunday afternoon to see Javier Vazquez put a dent in that record.

For those fans, a multitude by Montreal standards, the game starts with disappointment. Newly acquired outfielder Cliff Floyd, drawn out for a curtain call after his home run the night before, is left on the bench and replaced by Wil Cordero in left field.

Manager Frank Robinson chooses to give Floyd a rest because the Braves are throwing pitcher Damian Moss, who is especially tough on left-handed batters. Robinson figures that the right-handed Cordero will have better luck and his reasoning pays off in a big way.

Moss flirts with disaster early on. He puts the leadoff batter on base in each of the first two innings, balks a runner into scoring position and generally gets himself into trouble. In the 3rd inning his luck runs out. He gives up a single to Brad Wilkerson and gets robbed on a close call as Jose Vidro legs-out an infield single. After giving up a walk to Vladimir Guerrero to load the bases, he gets ahead of Wil Cordero with two quick strikes. He has Cordero right where he wants him until Cordero tags a devastating grand slam.

Like Floyd one game earlier, Cordero reluctantly comes out of the dugout to acknowledge the cheering crowd. The Expos lead 4–0.

Javier Vazquez does not have his best outing but he battles through 7 innings and the Braves don't have enough moxie to climb back into the game. Atlanta pitchers give up 11 walks, offering countless chances for Montreal to run up the score. The Expos happily accept their invitation. The 10–3 win gives Montreal a series split.

These Expos are fighting for their very survival. The team is on the fringes of the playoff picture while the franchise is on the brink of total collapse. On the field, they have reinforcements in the form of Bartolo Colon and Cliff

Floyd. Off the field, new allies have suddenly surfaced in the form of old owners banished to Florida.

Bud Selig and Jeffrey Loria will pay for the deal that left the Expos under the control of Major League Baseball. They'll pay, so long as a $100 million lawsuit filed this week succeeds in proving that the deal amounted to Selig and Loria defrauding the other minority owners out of their controlling interest in the team.

It is an extremely ambitious lawsuit. The rise and fall of Jeffrey Loria in Montreal is either a story of good intentions gone wrong or a story of the premeditated scuttling of a major league franchise. Almost no one thinks that Loria could have pre-planned the demise of the Expos. That's one of the things that makes this lawsuit interesting. It suggests that Loria worked with Bud Selig to make this happen, artificially raising the cost of Montreal's proposed downtown stadium beyond the level that the government was willing to support while issuing constant cash-calls to the other minority owners until control of the franchise was snatched away.

In the end, Loria turned his modest investment in the Expos into a generous buyout from the league. In the process, the former owners in Montreal went from having a controlling interest in the Expos to holding a 6 percent interest in the Marlins.

Most agree that Loria couldn't have done this on his own. But Loria and Selig? Selig, who swapped owners between Montreal and Florida to facilitate the sale of the Boston Red Sox before announcing that the Expos would be contracted? His presence is what makes the whole theory seem plausible. The challenge: how to prove it?

The business of baseball is about as transparent as a cataract but there may be a way to make this lawsuit work. One of the plaintiffs in the case is investment firm CEO Jacques Menard.

Menard was the Expos chairman who negotiated the deal that brought Jeffrey Loria to Montreal. The fact that Menard is involved in this case is significant because he will be able to testify as to the commitments baseball made to the Montreal Expos at the time that Loria came in as the new owner. Menard is a dangerous foe for baseball because he may very well have material evidence pointing to the deliberate swindle that Selig and Loria pulled off.

Time will tell what evidence the group intends to bring forward in support of its claims. Two things are certain in this scenario. First, the timing couldn't be worse for Bud Selig, who is already dealing with a possible strike by players. Second, a little over $100 million is just about enough to buy back the Expos from the league.

That outcome is very unlikely. The Expos have had too many saviors already. These corporate cavaliers are likely trying to lever the team's failure into a payday for themselves. Brochu did it. Loria did it. Now the former owners want their piece of the pie.

Such are the antics upon which Montreal's razor-thin hope of retaining a major league franchise is now pinned. Assuming the former minority owners win their lawsuit and use the cash to re-purchase the Expos from Bud Selig, they still have to figure out how to field a competitive team despite huge financial disadvantages and build a new downtown stadium. Not cause for great optimism.

In a subtler way, the Blue Jays also face a challenge to the long-term viability of the franchise in Toronto. As always, this has not generated much attention in the face of Montreal's more imminent collapse but the ramifications are nonetheless clear. Toronto has failed in its bid to host the 2008 Olympics.

Beijing will be the first nation in the developing world to carry this burden and honor. For Toronto, it means there will be no ambitious redevelopment of the waterfront. For the Blue Jays, it means there will be no new stadium waiting for a tenant following the Games.

If Toronto's bid had been a success, the Olympic Stadium would have become available in the summer of 2009, perfectly timed to offer a replacement as SkyDome approached the end of its life cycle. Now that the Olympic project has failed, baseball fans must once again seek security in the idea that SkyDome is a state-of-the-art facility that the league will not soon expect to be replaced or rehabilitated.

Montrealers wait for the outcome of a fanciful lawsuit sponsored by former owners. Torontonians are reeling from the disappointment of having lost to China in their Olympic endeavor.

The Expos and Blue Jays are both bound to these outcomes as they seek a balance between so much legal and political wrangling and the talent upon which success is supposed to depend. Cold comfort to baseball fans in Canada, but such has always been the case.

"The Pearson Cup ... was often taken something less than seriously."
— *Craig Burley, writer,* Hardball Times,
on the failed exhibition series, 2002

The Pearson Cup was as an exhibition game, intended to raise money for youth baseball. It pitted the Blue Jays and Expos against each other on off-days during the regular season. In 1986, the final Pearson Cup was played in Toronto.

After drawing over 20,000 fans for the first game in 1978, attendance dwindled rapidly. Just two years after its debut the game drew under 7,000. In '86, the event descended into pure absurdity and was subsequently scrapped altogether.

To their credit, the Blue Jays did their part to make the game interesting that year. Pitching prospect David Wells was sent to the mound for Toronto. He pitched four shutout innings and would eventually be credited with the meaningless win.

The Expos, on the other hand, were not so well prepared. Montreal ran out of pitchers late in the game. As a result, manager Buck Rogers called upon pitching coach Joe Kerrigan to take over. The game became a huge joke. It was the end for Pearson.

Hardly anyone mourned the passing of the annual exhibition. Too much else was happening. Ground was being broken in Toronto for the Blue Jays' new domed facility, which was primarily a provincial initiative. Ottawa was still too focused on another high-profile project.

Since 1972, when Pierre Trudeau committed his government to redeveloping Toronto's aged harbor, Ottawa had had its hands full trying to follow through on this campaign promise. By the time Toronto's new stadium was being devised, the federal government had long since assembled enough of the properties on the waterfront to put its plan into action. Trouble was, the basic design principles and performance targets for the project were in a constant state of flux. What had once been envisioned as a low-rise neighborhood with a series of interconnected parks quickly turned into a condo development. Furthermore, the project's overall budget called for all federal funding to be cut off by 1980, which created a certain urgency around bringing private investment into the development.

The result was a spotty high-rise district with many undeveloped industrial sites abutting newly laid park areas and public spaces. What had been a rosy campaign promise, carried forward with the best of intentions, became a controversial half-finished project that tried to please everyone but seemed to please no one.

When Toronto's real estate market went into recession, it brought the harborfront project to a standstill. With this patchy, unloved and incomplete project on its plate, there was little appetite in Ottawa for jumping into a stadium development next door.

This was consistent with the general mood in Ottawa. In 1981, the federal government was trying to get out of such projects while also reconsidering the financial powers of provinces. In 1982, changes in federal accounting practice significantly decreased the amount of personal and corporate income tax that each province was able to collect. By the late '80s, the Canadian government had cut its own spending and prevented the provinces from generating new revenue.

This dynamic would be central to federal-provincial relations for the next 20 years. Though it seems to point to a diminishment of Ottawa's influence over cities like Toronto and Montreal, it would actually lay the groundwork for federal leaders to play a more important role than ever.

These maneuvers didn't immediately impact the Blue Jays and Expos.

The stadium project in Toronto moved forward despite the absence of federal funds. The fact that Olympic Stadium was gaining a reputation as an unwelcoming facility with no prospect of public re-investment wasn't yet a major problem. Still, money at the provincial and municipal levels was drying up while the federal government withdrew from local initiatives.

These kinds of financial constraints, imposed on the provinces, would come to influence the prospects of the Blue Jays and Expos in subsequent decades. At the time, however, these larger trends were easy to ignore because the greatest days of Canadian baseball were just around the corner.

"I didn't just switch to the Blue Jays.... The Expos were beginning to be a very frustrating team." — Greg, former Expos fan, on the disappointment of the "Team of the '80s," 2002

In 1986, the follow-up to the Toronto Blue Jays' first division title was a disappointment. Twenty-five-year-old Jimmy Key posted 14 wins but the rest of the staff struggled. Dave Stieb, in particular, took a giant step backward and was relegated to relief pitching duties. At the plate, the Jays were still a dangerous team. They were young, too. Jesse Barfield, George Bell and Lloyd Moseby were each 26 years old, giving Toronto one of the youngest and most menacing outfields in baseball.

The dynamic Jays were near the top of the league in hits, runs and home runs. If their pitching had been a bit better, the team would have done much better than 86–76.

The excitement of winning the division a year earlier and the buzz created by the new stadium project kept fans pouring into Exhibition Stadium. The Jays drew 2.5 million fans in 1986.

The following season, Toronto led the American League in attendance. The team's hitters took a step forward as well. George Bell hit 47 home runs and had a breathtaking 137 RBIs. Along with Lloyd Moseby and Jesse Barfield, the team added 23-year-old Fred McGriff who hit 20 home runs in just over a half season. The Blue Jays could get the job done from just about any spot in their lineup.

On the mound, things turned around completely. Jimmy Key won 17 games and posted a 2.76 ERA. Dave Stieb bounced back with 13 wins and veteran Jim Clancy won 15. In the bullpen, the Jays were finally giving closer Tom Henke a sizeable workload and he responded with 34 saves. This pitching renaissance was the biggest reason the team fared so much better, finishing with a 96–66 record.

Attendance figures and team performance would slip somewhat in 1988 but with a new stadium nearing completion and one of the most exciting teams in all of baseball no one in Toronto seemed to mind. The Blue Jays were a team to watch.

In Montreal, things were not going anywhere near as well. The so-called "Team of the '80s" never put the kind of season together that its fans desperately hoped to see. The team still included all-time Expos such as Andre Dawson, Tim Raines and Tim Wallach. Among these future legends, only Raines put a decent season together in '86 hitting .334 and stealing 70 bases.

This mediocrity extended onto the pitching mound. Only Floyd Youmans and Bryn Smith managed 10 or more wins, and the Expos wasted a fairly strong bullpen that still included Jeff Reardon. All told, the Expos were a hard team to get excited about and the fans let them know. Montreal finished second to last in attendance.

In '87, things got somewhat better. Though Andre Dawson had left during the off-season, the Expos' offense actually improved. Tim Raines still led the team with a .330 average while others picked up their share of the slack. Tim Wallach led the team in hits, home runs and RBIs. Young first baseman Andres Galarraga posted a solid .305 batting average.

Veteran pitcher Dennis Martinez improved to 11 wins and Pascual Perez thrilled fans with a 7–0 record in just 10 appearances. Tim Burke ably replaced Jeff Reardon, registering a minuscule 1.19 ERA as the team's closer. The Expos' record improved to 91–71 and attendance climbed to near 2 million.

Like the Jays, the Expos stumbled in 1988. They were ordinary with an uninspiring 81–81 record. Predictably, they fell to near the bottom of the league in attendance again.

The year 1988 was forgettable for both the Jays and Expos. The difference was that Toronto had a young team on the rise with a provincially funded stadium around the corner while the Expos were perennial underachievers playing in a 10-year-old stadium with such poor turf that Andre Dawson left for fear of destroying his knees. Montreal was ho-hum, wondering where all that talent had gone wrong. Toronto was electric with anticipation.

In 2002, these sentiments are back. Montreal is faltering in its desperate attempt to catch Atlanta. The new talent is not generating results. For Toronto, there is excitement in the air. The Blue Jays are turning heads and manager Carlos Tosca is no longer the target of angry outbursts from underachieving malcontents.

The Tampa Bay Devil Rays are the most recent team to visit SkyDome and discover that the Blue Jays have remembered how to hit. Toronto scores 23 runs in two games against Tampa. Their pitching still isn't the best but the offense is coming back around.

J.P. Ricciardi's house cleaning has been worrying and unsettling but is starting to show benefits. He has dumped useless baggage and retained players that are beginning to make real contributions. The biggest question now facing Ricciardi and, in fact, the entire franchise is what to do about Carlos Delgado.

Delgado is a mega-star. He is also an agreeable man, by all accounts, and is a fan favorite. When Delgado signed his current $17 million a year contract, briefly becoming the highest paid player in baseball, he seemed to signal that the Blue Jays would continue to be big-money spenders.

The Canadian dollar, municipal taxes and dwindling fan support have since taken their toll and it has sometimes seemed like only a matter of time before Delgado agrees to a trade out of town. Ricciardi is not in the business of paying $17 million for a player on pace to hit .250 with 30 home runs and 110 RBIs.

Those are good numbers and Ricciardi would surely love to keep Delgado. Any team would want him in their lineup. But the Jays do not have the luxury of paying so much, even for their best. Furthermore, moving Delgado may provide Ricciardi with the leeway to sign young stars like Eric Hinske and Roy Halladay to more permanent contracts.

To some, Carlos Delgado has become something no one ever imagined he'd be in Toronto: an obstacle to long-term success. Delgado is still the heart of Toronto's offense, which is currently the best thing the team has going. All the same, his salary is the team's biggest outstanding burden. This is a critical issue for the rookie general manager.

The Toronto Blue Jays and Montreal Expos both sit in fourth place in their respective divisions. There was a time, just a couple of weeks ago, when it seemed the Expos could be dark horse playoff candidates and the Blue Jays were coming apart at the seams. Montreal's acquisitions might have put them over the top while Toronto's salary dump seemed to signal a long rebuilding process. It hasn't worked out that way.

The teams are still headed in different directions but fortunes have turned very quickly. The Blue Jays have won eight of their last eleven. The Expos have dropped eight of their last eleven and have gone 20 plus innings without scoring at all. It has been a flop in Montreal and a resurgence in Toronto.

The Blue Jays keep moving in the right direction against Baltimore. Roy Halladay, who has been very vocal in his support of J.P. Ricciardi's overall vision, finds a way to pitch out of a bases-loaded jam in the bottom of the 9th inning. Along with Halladay's hot hand, the Blue Jays continue to enjoy big hitting from their pared-down lineup.

Outfielder Vernon Wells hits two home runs and Carlos Delgado delivers a clutch three-run homer to pace Toronto to its 6–3 victory. Delgado is now the only player other than Joe Carter to hit at least 20 home runs in seven consecutive seasons for Toronto.

The Expos roll into New York hoping to gain some ground against the Mets, who've waltzed past Montreal into second place. The team gets a decent pitching performance from Tohmo Ohka but the offense and defense continue to disappoint.

Of all players, lumbering Mo Vaughn challenges Vladimir Guerrero's arm on a lazy fly ball, advancing from second to third on a tag-up that draws a wild throw. Guerrero's reputation alone used to prevent runners from trying to advance. No longer.

A communication breakdown in centerfield then leads to a Keystone Cops routine as neither Brad Wilkerson nor Cliff Floyd corral an errant pop fly. Finally, Floyd slides in to catch the sinking ball but it skips off the heel of his glove.

These foibles account for three runs. Following a solo home run from Mo Vaughn, the Expos are finished. The best Montreal's offense can muster is a meaningless blast from catcher Michael Barrett, the first runs the Expos have scored in a long while. The Expos lose 5–2.

As if to underscore the desperation of the Expos, Yankees owner George Steinbrenner chooses this moment to speak his mind. Steinbrenner, who once set off impromptu celebrations in his own stadium when it was announced that he'd been banned from baseball, has lashed out. To those who feel that the Yankees are hurting baseball by carrying a huge payroll and bidding up the price of free agents, Steinbrenner has this to say: you've got it backwards.

According to the Yankees boss, baseball's problems cannot be addressed by creating a salary cap. Instead, the appropriate course of action is to create a salary floor. Steinbrenner believes that the problem is not that some owners are spending too much but, rather, that most owners spend too little. It is the sort of proposal that perfectly captures the state of baseball in 2002.

While Steinbrenner's proposal seems ludicrous, it may actually reflect the position of the commissioner, who seems determined to turn small markets into big markets by levering hundreds of millions of dollars in public subsidies. Maybe this is why Bud Selig's much-ballyhooed luxury tax would allow teams to carry $100 million payrolls without penalty. Maybe the Steinbrenner model of ownership is what baseball ultimately wants.

It's enough to make a Canadian baseball fan yearn for days of old. A hundred years ago there was cholera in the streets and pro sports was still a con game, but Canadian cities were at least a factor.

Near the turn of the 20th century, the sports scenes in Toronto and Montreal were evolving. Lacrosse was still immensely popular. Masses in the growing urban cores of both cities enjoyed taking time out of their days to watch the exploits of strongmen such as legendary Louis Cyr in Montreal, as well as the wrestling and boxing melees of Tommy Harrison in Toronto. Amidst these established sports and contests, newer activities were also gaining popularity.

A Canadian hybrid of football and rugby generated clashes between rival clubs. Horse racing at Woodbine in Toronto drew large crowds. Of course, the curiosity of the Canadian people had also begun to turn towards a peculiarly fast-paced winter sport becoming all the rage at outdoor skating rinks. Included along with these comparatively new spectator sports was baseball, which distinguished itself from many of the others by the sheer number of people who regularly came out to watch the game being played.

In 1886, the Toronto Baseball Grounds was home to the freakishly named Toronto Torontos, which competed in the upstart International League. This hybrid circuit, an amalgam of three former leagues, introduced professional baseball as an integrated North American business. Canada, home to one of the first organized baseball games in history, was formally incorporated into what had become America's game.

The club in Toronto had fewer problems retaining the interest of city residents than the International League had just staying alive. The Toronto Baseball Grounds, which became known as Sunlight Park not because of its natural beauty but because of its proximity to a soap factory, was regularly full and crowds in the tens of thousands were not unusual for important games.

The late 1880s and early 1890s, however, were a turbulent period for professional baseball in the United States. Rival leagues pillaged one another for talent and openly conspired to corner the market on America's growing love affair with the game. As a result of this interleague espionage, and in response to the problem of travel expenses for many of the league's franchises, the International League dropped some teams, added others, and even dissolved altogether for a brief period.

Caught up in so much turmoil and uncertainty, and offering little talent for fans to get behind, the International League franchise in Buffalo opened the 1890 season in front of just 1000 fans and could not reliably generate enough revenue to carry the basic costs of staying in the league. The franchise was relocated to Montreal.

The woeful team didn't fare much better in Montreal and was quickly shifted to yet another city. That same season, the franchise in Hamilton experienced similar struggles and was itself relocated to Montreal on an interim basis. Shortly thereafter, the league completely collapsed.

By the very next summer, the International League was up and running once again. Party due to a lingering economic depression, it couldn't shake its problem with teams folding. By 1896, the league finally stabilized. Then a fire broke out in Rochester and destroyed the local ballpark. With nowhere for the team to play, the International League turned to its most reliable short-term solution. Rochester's team moved north to Montreal with the understanding that, one season later, it would return to America.

Funny thing, though. Montrealers had taken to the game in a big way and when the time came for the team to return to Rochester its promoters simply refused. The game had taken root. There hadn't ever been a franchise in the city, just loaners from other cities that couldn't support the game, but Montrealers discovered that they loved baseball. Buoyed by popular support among local fans, the franchise stayed.

Toronto's team, eventually renamed the Maple Leafs, was a pioneer in the fledgling International League. Montreal's franchise, on the other hand, was created by accident. Professional baseball would be a part of both cities for the next 100 years.

Toronto's successful minor league franchise would be renamed and moved from the Baseball Grounds to Maple Leaf Stadium, acclaimed as one of the finest facilities of its era (Canada Department of Interior / Library and Archives Canada / PA-043709).

In the long history of baseball in Canada, few players have represented both cities. Catcher Darrin Fletcher is one of those players. Fletcher is paid just under $4 million per season in his current contract with the Blue Jays, which comes to an end following the 2002 season. When he hasn't been injured, he's compiled a .220 batting average, well below his modest career average of .269. Fletcher is becoming a liability.

He is not the only player to have spent his career in Canada, splitting time between the Montreal Expos and Toronto Blue Jays, but he is the only one to play in both cities as Canada's status in the major leagues crumbled. There should be a spot for him in the Canadian Baseball hall of Fame. His career numbers aren't terribly impressive but the Hall in Canada isn't always about stats.

Players like pitcher Reggie Cleveland, who won just 14 games in his best major league season, have been inducted based on pure longevity. Jack Graney seems to have been inducted based on the fact that he was the first major league batter to face Babe Ruth on the pitcher's mound. Paul Beeston was a top executive with the Toronto Blue Jays until taking a position as chief executive officer with Major League Baseball. In that position, he reportedly lobbied in favor of contraction and Commissioner Bud Selig has stated that he might not have considered contracting the Expos if not for Beeston. If Paul

Beeston is in the Canadian Baseball Hall of Fame then there must be room for Darrin Fletcher.

Whatever his long-term legacy, Fletcher will always be remembered as the backstop to the most unlucky team in the history of the Expos, and as having withdrawn from the Toronto Blue Jays with his self-respect intact. He has just made General Manager J.P. Ricciardi's job a little easier by announcing his retirement.

The Blue Jays shave another $4 million from their payroll, paring down but still seeming to get better as the season progresses. This is exactly the kind of trick that Ricciardi was hired to turn.

He was also hired to transform the Blue Jays into a playoff team. He is still a long way from accomplishing that goal. This is underscored as the Blue Jays enter a series against the Minnesota Twins, a team that has turned a contraction death sentence into a stranglehold on the American League Central.

The Minnesota Twins used to be the Montreal Expos of the American League. While the Expos have faded from playoff contention, the Twins have continued to surge. They currently lead their division by 14 games.

The government of Minnesota also committed to a public investment in a new stadium, which has kick-started talks aimed at saving the team. The Twins are not the Expos of the AL any longer. They are a division leading team with a lifeline from the state government.

The Blue Jays roll into Minnesota on a tear of their own. In fact, the Blue Jays-Twins series is a showdown between the hottest teams in baseball. For Toronto, it is an opportunity to signal to the league's best that they are for real. Minnesota gives the Blue Jays something to aspire to by showing them just how well a talented, motivated young ball club is capable of playing.

The Twins win the series' first two games then send 23-year-old Johan Santana to the mound in search of a sweep. Santana has shown plenty of promise but, like all young pitchers, has struggled with consistency.

This month he gave up a single run against Oakland, then got chased out of a game against Anaheim, then shutout Detroit and finally got shelled against Chicago. He's young. The Twins figure he'll learn. The Blue Jays find out just how much he's learned already.

Sometimes a pitcher turns the very idea of offense and defense on its head by relentlessly going on the attack. The very best pitchers do this all the time. Curt Schilling. Pedro Martinez. A young pitcher only flirts with this sort of thing in fits and starts. It takes unwavering confidence.

Johan Santana finds that confidence against Toronto. He blows them away, striking out 13 batters. Though Toronto pitcher Esteban Loaiza is tagged with the loss, the real problem is Toronto's inability to hit anything Santana has to offer. The Twins win 4–0 and sweep Toronto under the dome in Minneapolis.

Toronto's deflating failure against the Twins is not reflective of the team's improved play since the All-Star fiasco in Milwaukee. Prior to the now infamous tie, the Blue Jays were playing baseball in a repetitive pattern: lackluster, lackluster, Roy Halladay, lackluster, lackluster, etc. Of late, this has changed.

The relative health of the pitching staff now provides capable backup for Halladay and the Blue Jays offense has been cranking out enough runs to make up for any pitching struggles. Toronto baseball has suddenly reached symbiotic balance. On nights when the pitchers struggle, the bats are there to clean up the mess. On nights when the bats fall asleep, the pitchers keep them in the game.

Coming at the worst possible time, the Montreal Expos have found their way into the same rut that the Blue Jays vacated. When Bartolo Colon pitches, the Expos look like a team with something to prove. With Colon on the bench, they look like a team waiting for the one terrible inning.

Montreal starters are chased from games early, leaving relief pitchers tired and overworked, making the team vulnerable to long opposition rallies. The Expos continue to have a formidable offense but, on most nights, it's not enough.

Bartolo Colon has been the Expos' stopper. All three of his wins since the trade have come immediately after Montreal losses and two of those wins have ended multi-game losing streaks. This pitching staff, which was supposed to be bolstered by Colon, has been leaning on him from the start. It's a pattern that holds true against the visiting Florida Marlins.

With the Marlins and Expos now tied, each 15 games out of first place in the division, the Expos need Colon to earn them a series split and keep them ahead of Florida overall. Colon doesn't get any help early on.

In the 1st inning, he gives up a double to outfielder Eric Owens who then immediately tries to steal third base. Brian Schneider, playing in place of regular catcher Michael Barrett, cocks his arm back to throw but, seeing third baseman Fernando Tatis out of position, tries to stop halfway. The ball slips out of his hand and rolls idly into play. Owens scores easily. Bartolo Colon shakes his head and proceeds to give up just one more hit for the rest of the game.

The Expos scrape a lead together on the strength of solo home runs from Jose Vidro and Fernando Tatis along with a pair of hits from Orlando Cabrera. It's no offensive explosion but it's enough with Colon at his best. The ace pitches another complete game. Great stuff. The better Colon gets, the more it underscores how badly the Expos need wins from pitchers like Javier Vazquez and Tony Armas Jr.

The Expos have not slipped out of the playoff picture altogether. They are on the fringes. July was a make-or-break month and, though it's probably a bit harsh to say that the season is over, this is not where the team needed to be after the acquisitions of Bartolo Colon and Cliff Floyd. Not by a long shot.

With these unrealized expectations as a backdrop, General Manager Omar Minaya confronts the ominous trade deadline. July 31. It is a whirling dervish of rumor and speculation as teams prepare for one final opportunity to add impact players or trim payrolls before season's end.

The Expos have been gunshy about deadline deals since dumping pitcher Randy Johnson in exchange for Mark Langston in 1989. Despite this history, the Expos have been very active in 2002 and continue this trend at the deadline.

They are the first team to announce a significant move. Montreal announces the outright abandonment of a player that just three weeks ago seemed to signal a serious push for the postseason.

After trading a handful of prospects to the Florida Marlins in exchange for outfielder Cliff Floyd, the Expos have dealt Floyd to the Boston Red Sox in exchange for a handful of prospects. Floyd has not been a catalyst since coming over from Florida. He has hit just .207.

The optics are bad. The Florida Marlins under Jeffrey Loria, the Montreal Expos under Commissioner Bud Selig, and the Boston Red Sox under John Henry have passed the star slugger around between them by sliding prospects in and out of the Expos' system. Ugly. Beyond these mere optics, the move also calls all of the Expos' playoff aspirations into question.

> "When we acquired Cliff Floyd, we didn't have five teams in front of us." —*Expos general manager Omar Minaya, commenting on the Floyd trade, 2002*

August

"Money. Canadians ... can think of nothing else."
—*Roger Taillibert, Olympic Stadium architect, 1972*

Legacy building and envy are terrible reasons to spend public money. It doesn't matter whether that money is spent building libraries or stadiums. If the decision is motivated by ego or a vain desire to match the excesses of other cities, a disaster is in the works. Of all the reasons taxpayers in Montreal have to bemoan Olympic Stadium, the fact that it was driven by a man who spent too much time admiring other cities and too little time worrying about fiscal responsibility is surely the biggest.

In 1970, Mayor Jean Drapeau led a delegation of boosters to Amsterdam in support of Montreal's bid to host the 1976 Olympics. Montreal faced stiff competition from Los Angeles and Moscow. Drapeau, who had feverishly toured the capitals of Europe in a promotional blitz unmatched by other bidders, was confident he would carry the day.

Members of the International Olympic Committee (IOC) questioned the capacity of each prospective host to bear the financial burden of the event. Representatives from Los Angeles and Moscow guaranteed that their respective governments would absorb the expense. Mayor Drapeau had already pledged that his Olympics would not cost taxpayers a penny. He had no strong financial guarantee.

Drapeau could only remind the IOC that Moscow had pulled out of its commitment to host Expo '67 and Montreal had graciously stepped in at the last minute. He could also point to a tireless preoccupation with bid financing through which the Los Angeles team had waged a war of words against the globetrotting mayor himself. These were Drapeau's trump cards and he played them aggressively, emphasizing that Montreal would build a frugal Olympic park requiring no heavy-handed guarantees.

IOC votes were split but Drapeau's commitment to a modest Olympics won Montreal the honor of hosting the Games. No sooner did he get home from Amsterdam than the frugal Olympics were dumped in favor of a flashier vision more in line with what had been realized at Expo.

Expo '67 was a last-minute undertaking. Tight deadlines called for snap decisions and mass expenditures. Whenever the project seemed to be running off course, and organizers running out of money, Drapeau went straight to Prime Minister Lester Pearson for more cash.

The process worked well. Pearson was anxious to ensure that Expo did not become a national embarrassment on the country's 100th birthday so money kept flowing. Facing timeframes no one thought he could meet, Drapeau delivered Expo '67 on schedule.

Upon his return to Montreal, victorious in his effort to win the '76 Olympic bid, Drapeau reasoned that he could again implement a bold vision on a tight timeline and uncertain budget. If trouble arose he could strong-arm Ottawa. The no-frills concept didn't suit him anymore. Instead, he embraced the idea that Montreal's Olympics would leave a physical legacy to rival monuments in the great cities of Europe.

To get the ball rolling, Jean Drapeau issued contracts to members of an exclusive social club where he was a prominent figure. He released vague budgets upon which the cost of Olympic development could not be accurately projected, and ignored repeated appeals from Ottawa to account for financial statements that made it impossible to plan the federal government's contribution. For the first time in modern Olympic history, a foreign architect was selected to design the Olympic Stadium without an open competition. Mayor Drapeau also selected east-end green space for the Olympic park without seeking the consent of his own urban planning director, a move that created open dissent among city councilors who felt the site was much too far from downtown. Those councilors were subsequently thrown out of Drapeau's political party.

This is how the Olympic project unraveled in Montreal. Contractors flagrantly milked the city, eventually leading to a lengthy criminal investigation. Costs ran completely out of control and, since Prime Minister Pierre Trudeau wasn't intimidated by the fiery Drapeau, organizers quickly realized they had no financial safety net. Costs escalated from $200 million into the billion dollar range, producing an unfinished stadium deep in the city's east end. Expo '67 it was not.

It's no accident that Olympic Stadium gained a reputation as a somber place where bold ideas go to die. If it's possible for such a thing as a personality to be built into a structure, this is the personality that the Big O adopted from its creators.

In August 1989, for example, San Francisco pitcher Dave Dravecky made a miraculous comeback from cancer in his throwing arm. It was the good news story of the summer until Dravecky came to Olympic Stadium where the sound of his arm snapping in mid-delivery could be heard, even in the bleachers. Such is the building's legacy.

In August 2002, the Big O welcomes another visiting pitcher striving for a lofty goal. Arizona Diamondbacks pitcher Curt Schilling is making waves, putting up stats that are raising the prospect of a rare 30-win season.

In the first week of August, Schilling sits at 18 wins. To have so many at the beginning of August is freakish. His other numbers are just as impressive. For every batter Curt Schilling walks, he strikes out 12. He has not lost a game to a National League opponent since April and has been his best against Arizona's closest playoff rivals.

This is the story as Arizona arrives to face the Expos. Montreal has played so poorly since the All-Star break that many have written them off for dead. Schilling's inflated win total is an important sub-plot as he tries to victimize the struggling Expos lineup.

Through 7 innings, Schilling casts his typical spell. He yields just a single run while striking out seven and walking none. Despite this classic performance, the game is tied because young Expos pitcher Tohmo Ohka matches Schilling every step of the way.

In the 8th, Schilling pitches his way out of a jam. The Expos put a runner in scoring position and the bind is tight enough to draw a visit to the mound from Arizona's pitching coach. Schilling, yet to throw a hundred pitches in the game, convinces the coaching staff to leave him in. Escaping without giving up a run, he seems fine.

It's unclear whether or not the prospect of giving Schilling a chance to earn his 19th win, keeping the dream of 30 alive, is part of Arizona manager Bob Brenly's decision to let him pitch the 9th. Maybe not. Given the score, Schilling has to pitch at least two more innings to record a win. For whatever reason, with the game tied, Brenly lets him continue.

In the 9th inning, Schilling faces Vladimir Guerrero with one out and nobody on base. He has been able to contain Guerrero so far with a cutting fastball that dives off the inside of the plate. Guerrero has seen the pitch in every at-bat and has failed to record a hit. Schilling decides to stick with what's working but inadvertently leaves the ball too high in the strike zone. Guerrero stings it so hard that it barely arcs in the air at all before slamming into the bleachers. The Expos win 2–1.

It is a dramatic victory, a walk-off home run that keeps Montreal's slender playoff dreams alive. Guerrero carries the Expos to a win at home but the result is primarily reported as a sad blow to Schilling's bid for 30 wins. These are the minor insults that swirl around the Expos. Even when there isn't any doom-and-gloom at Olympic Stadium, stories are still spun that way. It's almost satire.

"If Major League Baseball owns Montreal and they get [Floyd] and trade him to our biggest competitor.... What's that say?"
—*Yankees owner George Steinbrenner, 2002*

The New York Yankees have had their eyes on outfielder Cliff Floyd all season. They wanted him and, more importantly, wanted to ensure that the Red Sox didn't get him. When the Expos succeeded in bringing him to Montreal then the Red Sox brought him to Boston for a handful of prospects, Steinbrenner went off.

To him, the transactions are evidence of a conspiracy to thwart the New York Yankees. Ignoring the fact that the entire league is risking a crippling strike in order to support the Yankees' $100 million model, Steinbrenner sees writing on the wall. The tirade is downright loopy.

It's also badly timed. By most accounts, there is less than a month to go before the players' union walks away from negotiations and baseball grinds to a halt. This is not the best time for Steinbrenner to be pointing fingers, postulating about zany schemes to bring down the sport's most powerful franchise.

In truth, there's plenty of time to save the season because little negotiating actually needs to be done. The players don't like contraction but the spending sprees and financial madness that created the idea of contraction in the first place are making players rich beyond their wildest fantasies. Owners are refinancing their franchises through public subsidies and Bud Selig's luxury tax will only impact teams with $100 million payrolls. This won't threaten player salaries in any meaningful way. There's no reason for the two sides not to come to an agreement.

Still, driven to a panic by the prospect of a strike, some prominent Hall of Famers including Stan Musial and Sandy Koufax have issued a letter to the owners and players' union. They, like many others, think the strike is the problem instead of the inevitable product of problems that none have seriously proposed to address.

> "To protect the game we all love ... we suggest you agree to a qualified mediator that will allow you to ... avoid a work stoppage."
> —*Joint statement issued by Hall of Famers, 2002*

Amidst these distractions, the Toronto Blue Jays continue to make waves. They have become a dangerous offensive team and at the core of the renewed attack is a player who looked like the odd man out back when General Manager J.P. Ricciardi began putting this team together in the spring. It wasn't clear whether outfielder Shannon Stewart would accept the role of designated hitter. After speaking out against the idea, it seemed like his days in Toronto were numbered.

Stewart has since become the team's best hitter and, for reasons ranging from the Mondesi trade to Jose Cruz' lackluster play, has taken a regular turn in the outfield. For much of the season, Stewart and rookie third baseman Eric

Hinske shared the team lead in batting average. Stewart now stands alone as the best hitter on a team that is rebuilding faster than anyone expected.

In the second week of August, Toronto kicks off Alumni Week at Sky-Dome, dedicated to players and coaches who brought the franchise its first World Series championship ten years ago. Former manager Cito Gaston throws out a ceremonial first pitch. Former ace Jack Morris is in the stands while sparkplug outfielder Candy Maldonado makes a cameo appearance in the broadcast booth.

Against the visiting Seattle Mariners, this is supposed to be about remembering past glory. Instead, it turns into a nerve-racking celebration of the future this team may soon enjoy.

Seattle is a playoff caliber team. The Blue Jays don't show them much respect. With Roy Halladay pitching, the young Jays tear a swath through the Mariners and blow the game wide open by the 6th inning. Rookie Josh Phelps drives in a run. Rookie Orlando Hudson goes four for four. Shannon Stewart and Eric Hinske hit back-to-back triples. Toronto kicks the Mariners pitching staff all over SkyDome, establishing a 13–2 lead.

Holding an 11-run cushion, not even Toronto's sketchy bullpen can blow it. At least, that's what manager Carlos Tosca must be thinking as he turns the game over to Mark Hendrickson, who is making his major league debut. After striking out the first batter he faces, things look good. Without recording another out, Hendrickson eventually leaves the game with an incredible 135.00 ERA.

Three more Blue Jays pitchers try to shut down the Mariners but the team still finds itself defending a two-run lead in the 9th, facing the potential winning run at the plate with Kelvim Escobar on the mound. As he has much of the season, Escobar looks uncertain as to what pitch he should throw and, worse, seems more surprised about where those pitches end up than the hitters. Mercifully, Escobar escapes without giving up the lead. The Jays win 14–12.

The Blue Jays' resurgence, uncertain as it seems against Seattle, has created a perfect atmosphere for Alumni Week. Former players have filtered into town to bask in the glow of World Series victories in 1992 and 1993. Baseball fans everywhere should be so lucky as to celebrate the brightest stars of their team's history as the entire league staggers towards a possible strike.

Perhaps more than any other sport, baseball has a way of turning the accomplishments of former players into superhuman feats. In the case of the Blue Jays, certain moments need little embellishment.

Joe Carter's home run to win the World Series in 1993 was an all-time moment. No one needs to pump it up.

On the other hand, Devon White's over-the-shoulder catch in 1992, which some have called the greatest catch ever, was an excellent grab only turned into mythology by the bumble-footed base running of the Atlanta Braves.

Sometimes, fans try too hard to convince themselves that baseball is more than just a great game.

In this environment, it's surprising that more attention isn't paid to the opinions of those same players when it comes to things like labor negotiations and the future of the game. During Alumni Week, legendary players have been eager to tell reporters that another baseball strike would be disastrous and unnecessary. These former greats have the experience to speak intelligently about how to cure a sick business. Instead, they smile for the cameras and send helpless letters to those who are ruining the game they spent their careers building.

Alumni Week could be about more than just celebrating Toronto's past glories. It could be about tapping into the collective wisdom of those who've seen Canadian baseball at its best. It might be about these things, if not for the fact that Toronto has an enormous amount of success to look back on, leaving little time for the other stuff. Maybe that's the way it should be.

"This is like ... do you believe in miracles?"
—*Blue Jays outfielder Joe Carter, 1993*

By the turn of the 1990s, baseball in Canada was reaching its peak. Founded upon a partnership that would eventually drive the building into bankruptcy, SkyDome was a sensation. The Blue Jays became the first team to host 4 million spectators in a single season. In 1989, the Blue Jays served notice that the nucleus of a championship team was coming together when, replacing manager Jimy Williams with Cito Gaston, they challenged for a spot in the World Series.

Up and down, the Toronto lineup featured a combination of youth and experience. Dave Stieb and Jimmy Key combined for 30 wins. Twenty-four-year-old Todd Stottlemyre and 26-year-old David Wells competed for jobs in the starting rotation while 25-year-old Duane Ward shared duties as closer along with the dominating Tom Henke. The mix of established performers and rising stars offered a solid foundation for coming years.

The same was true of Toronto's offense. Twenty-five-year-old slugger Fred McGriff led the team with 36 home runs. At 29, George Bell was already an established star, the franchise's flashiest and most outspoken player. The Blue Jays finished near the top of the league in home runs and runs scored. All of the 25- to 29-year-olds were contributing.

The Jays won 89 games in '89, good enough to send them to the American League championship against the Oakland A's. Unfortunately, facing the A's at that point meant facing Rickey Henderson in his prime. Over the course of five games, Henderson hit .400, drew seven walks, stole eight bases and tagged two home runs. He was unstoppable.

The Blue Jays had a nice balance of youth and experience but couldn't match Oakland's one overwhelming offensive personality. Over the course of a full season, balanced pitching and hitting get the job done. In a winner-take-all playoff series, it often takes one player to step forward and be the difference.

Oakland relied heavily on pitchers such as Dave Stewart and Dennis Eckersley, and also featured Jose Canseco and Mark McGwire at the plate, but it was Rickey Henderson who beat the Blue Jays. It was a lesson learned.

The following year Toronto slipped back out of the playoff picture. Kelly Gruber joined McGriff and Bell at the heart of the team's offense while David Wells and Todd Stottlemyre both recorded over 10 wins apiece to join Steib and Key on the pitching staff. The Blue Jays were trying to take an enormous step into baseball's elite but couldn't quite put it together.

To a lesser extent, the same dynamic was also at play in Montreal. Fan favorites Tim Wallach and Tim Raines were at the core of a team that also included youngsters like Larry Walker, Delino Deshields and Marquis Grissom. The foundation for a winning ball club was clearly coming together.

In 1990, when the Blue Jays won 86 games and were looking to advance to the next level, the Expos won 85 games but did not seem to have the same lofty ambitions. Though the teams were remarkably similar in their shared composition of young and established talent, they were heading in radically different directions.

Expo attendance was sliding and the team's ownership group was reluctant to respond by investing money in players. Conversely, the Blue Jays were leading the league in attendance and the team's owners used this largesse to make the team even stronger. In the winter that preceded the '91 season, the Blue Jays made a move that put them over the top while the Expos began taking on the posture of a problem franchise.

If one solitary moment can be singled out for having set Canada's two franchises on such seemingly different courses, it has to be the moment that the Toronto Blue Jays acquired Joe Carter and Roberto Alomar. That was the touchstone. From that point forward, the Blue Jays were for real. The Expos weren't even in the picture.

Toronto immediately jumped back into the playoffs. In addition to Carter, a virtual lock for 30 home runs and 100 RBIs every season, and Alomar, who had some observers talking about Hall of Fame potential in his 20s, the Jays also added fleet-footed centerfielder Devon White. Between them, they led the team in every significant offensive category. Add Kelly Gruber and 22-year-old John Olerud to the mix and Toronto was still every bit the up-and-coming team.

Veteran starter Dave Stieb was limited to just nine appearances that season. The balanced corps of young and old pitchers on the rest of Toronto's pitching staff more than picked up the slack. Jimmy Key established himself as the staff ace with 16 wins while Todd Stottlemyre and David Wells each added 15. As if this wasn't enough, sensational youngster Juan Guzman thrilled local fans by winning 10 consecutive decisions. With Tom Henke and Duane Ward in the bullpen, the pitching was in good hands. Ninety-one wins later, the Blue Jays took another shot at the World Series.

As they had in '89, Toronto discovered that in the playoffs a balanced lineup doesn't always go as far as a stalwart individual. Whereas the Jays had previously been sunk by offensive heroics against the A's, they could not handle the pitching of Minnesota ace Jack Morris.

In 1991, it seemed that Morris could pitch every day if necessary. Against Toronto, he was the difference. Morris won both games he started and, once again, the Jays fell victim to a dominant personality they could not overcome.

Minnesota went on to meet the Atlanta Braves in the World Series, a contest between teams that had both gone from worst to first in their respective divisions. Jack Morris paced Minnesota to a seven-game series. Atlanta's arrival signaled the beginning of that franchise's decade-long mastery of the National League East.

The Expos were nowhere to be found that summer. With just 71 wins, they were basement dwellers, last in their division and last in attendance. It was a brutal season and the team's owners, crying poor and blaming fans for not supporting a team that was both too young and too old at the same time, did nothing to make the team any better. This situation began to draw serious attention from the league's front office.

The only bright spot for Montreal in 1991 came on July 28 when pitcher Dennis Martinez brought the entire league to a standstill by pitching a perfect game against the Los Angeles Dodgers. Typical of Expos karma, the game took place on the West Coast so few local fans had a chance to enjoy Martinez' historic gem. The story in Montreal continued to be that of a franchise falling to pieces.

In 1992, the Expos turned a corner of sorts. Young players like Larry Walker and Marquis Grissom started realizing their potential. Young Ken Hill joined aging Dennis Martinez, each recording 16 wins to lead a pitching staff that included fireball closer John Wetteland. Gary Carter even came back to Montreal to close out his career in 1992, hitting a game breaking double in his final at-bat. Most significantly, the Expos replaced Tom Runnells with Felipe Alou as manager, introducing Montreal to the man who would become by far the city's most beloved baseball personality.

The Expos won 87 games and, if not for the Atlanta Braves, could have been a playoff team. Attendance at Olympic Stadium doubled from the year before. Nineteen ninety-two might have been big for the Expos but nothing happening in Montreal could match the phenomenon that Blue Jays baseball had become at the very same time.

Toronto learned its lessons. Sunk by Jack Morris in the American League championship the season before, Toronto acquired Jack Morris for 1992.

Problem identified. Problem solved. Morris was every bit the workhorse that Toronto hoped he'd be, logging a team-high 241 innings on his way to winning 21 games.

Behind Morris, Toronto leaned heavily on young Juan Guzman as well as veterans Jimmy Key and Dave Stieb. The rotation was so good that David Wells pitched primarily out of the bullpen where Duane Ward and Tom Henke continued to be an awesome duo. This was largely the same pitching staff that had led the Jays into the playoffs in '89 and '91. The only differences were more experience and the acquisition of one key performer in Morris.

It was the same story on offense. Joe Carter surprised no one by hitting 34 home runs and driving in 119 runs. Roberto Alomar hit .310 and swiped 49 bases. As with the pitching staff, the attack was supplemented by one key addition intended to push the whole group to a new level. That addition was 40-year-old slugger Dave Winfield who finished second to Joe Carter with 26 home runs and 108 RBIs.

Toronto responded to previous playoff disappointments by addressing the crucial weakness that had sunk them on both occasions: a dominant starter and a sparkplug hitter. In 1992, the Jays cruised into the playoffs with 96 wins, picked up pitcher David Cone for added depth at the trade deadline and faced the Oakland A's in a rematch of the '89 AL championship.

Though Toronto had picked up Morris and Cone for clutch playoff pitching, Toronto carried the series because of long-time Blue Jays Duane Ward and Tom Henke. Late in several games, when Oakland could turn to Dennis Eckerseley in the bullpen, the Jays could turn to both Ward and Henke.

In Game 4, which lasted 11 innings and gave the Blue Jays a stranglehold, the difference was that Toronto had two star relievers ready to go. Two games later, back at SkyDome, the Jays pounded Oakland 9–2 and advanced to the World Series.

The Blue Jays then faced Atlanta. As it had been against Oakland, it was two long-standing Blue Jays who made the difference. Pitcher Jimmy Key, who'd been the team's ace through struggle and heartbreak, beat Tom Glavine in Game 4 and recorded another win in extra innings of Game 6, giving up just one earned run over both appearances. On offense, with all the firepower that Toronto had cultivated and acquired, it was catcher Pat Borders who hit .450.

With the Blue Jays leading 4–3 in the 9th inning of Game 6, Joe Carter stepped on first base to put out speedy Otis Nixon, who'd attempted a desperation bunt, then leapt up and down in an endearing display of honest joy. Carter could jump around all he wanted. The Jays were the champs.

The Blue Jays followed up a glorious '92 season by turning into absolute monsters in '93. Dave Winfield was replaced with veteran Paul Molitor. Former Oakland A's starter Dave Stewart replaced David Cone. As if to add a final punctuation mark, the Blue Jays added former rival Rickey Henderson.

In '92, the Blue Jays had succeeded in part by adding some of the same key performers that other teams had employed to defeat them in past playoffs. These moves paid off so well that the team did the exact same thing in '93. Rickey Henderson and Dave Stewart helped sink the Jays in '89. Toronto acquired them both. The '93 Blue Jays were the best Canadian baseball team ever.

How else can a team that had each of the American League's top three hitters be described? The Jays were a terror on the rest of the league. John Olerud hit .363. Paul Molitor hit .332. Roberto Alomar hit .326. Add Joe Carter's requisite 33 home runs and 121 RBIs, and its starts becoming clear that the '93 Jays were a powerhouse.

The pitching staff lost David Cone, David Wells and Tom Henke but didn't miss a step. Duane Ward responded by recording 45 saves. Pat Hentgen emerged as the surprise ace on a staff that, true to the Toronto model established in the late '80s, was a mix of young upstarts and established performers.

The Blue Jays won 95 games in 1993 and, after dispatching the Chicago White Sox in the AL championship, faced the Philadelphia Phillies in the World Series. The Phillies were an ugly team, proud of their collective reputation as sandlot ruffians.

Lenny Dykstra proudly claimed that he tried to avoid reading. John Kruk reveled in his stature as the most out-of-shape athlete in pro sports. The enormous Darren Daulton looked more like Jack Nicholson in *The Shining* than a major league catcher. These were the bad boys of baseball, pitted against the clean-cut Blue Jays.

The first four games were slugfests, reaching a wild crescendo in Philadelphia when Toronto pounded a receiving line of pitchers including Philadelphia closer Mitch "Wild Thing" Williams to win a come-from-behind offensive orgy 15–14. The teams combined for 32 hits and runs were scored all night long but Williams' collapse was singled out as the key factor in Toronto taking a 3–1 series lead.

In Game 5, Curt Schilling put his inevitable stamp on the binge by shutting out the Blue Jays in a complete-game Philadelphia victory. This sent the World Series back to Toronto and laid the foundation for Canada's all-time classic baseball moment.

It was fitting, the way the '93 Series ended. The wild games and inflated scores cast an intense and, at times, malevolent spotlight on Philadelphia closer Mitch Williams, who had built a reputation for flirting with disaster but pulling through in the clutch. Against Toronto, he seemed like a risk not worth taking for the Phillies.

Part of the reason his team faced elimination at SkyDome was Williams' inability to hold a massive lead in Game 4. What would happen if the World Series were on the line, and Williams had to be called upon? Maybe it was inevitable that, pushing the Blue Jays to the brink of a seventh and deciding game, the Phillies should face this very question.

In front of 52,000 fans in Toronto, Philadelphia looked like a team that had done enough to send the Series to the limit. In the 7th inning, the Phillies erased a four-run deficit by bringing five runs home and establishing a precarious lead. After cruising through the bottom halves of the 7th and 8th innings, Philadelphia manager Jim Fregosi faced his most crucial decision. What to do about Williams?

In fairness, Fregosi is guilty only of having done the right thing. He didn't ask a starter like Curt Schilling to pitch in relief. He didn't trick himself into thinking that relievers who hadn't been good enough to close all season long would suddenly be transformed with the World Series on the line. Williams had recorded 43 saves that summer. He had been Fregosi's go-to guy straight through the playoffs. The Phillies were built upon brashness and ugliness and risk. Fregosi really had no choice. He brought Williams in and watched the World Series blow up in his face.

Rickey Henderson, long a pariah in Toronto from his days with the A's, opened the 9th inning by manipulating the shaky Williams for a walk. Henderson had a ridiculously small strike zone and a way of collapsing that zone even further as a pitch was delivered. To sneak a strike past Henderson, a pitcher had to be perfect. "Wild Thing" did not make his money being perfect.

With Henderson on base, Williams looked as though maybe he'd set himself straight by registering an out against Devon White. Paul Molitor then slashed a single through the infield, bringing Joe Carter to the plate.

At that point, Fregosi might have taken Williams out but the power versus power match-up against Carter was actually more in Williams' favor than it had been against Henderson or Molitor. Carter may have been the only bat in Toronto's lineup that Fregosi was confident Williams could handle. Again, Fregosi was guilty of making the right call. He ruined Mitch Williams' life by leaving him in the game.

In the aftermath, Williams would join Bill Buckner among the ranks of those so badly haunted by baseball failure that they had to leave their homes and seek refuge in anonymity. Williams' house would be vandalized. He would receive numerous death threats. The World Series would break him.

With Joe Carter stepping to the plate, before any of that came to pass, Williams must have felt that this was the out he had been born to register. If he got lucky and heavy-footed Carter hit into a double play, it would have been gold. Williams got two strikes on Carter then reeled back to deliver the knock out punch.

Carter took him over the left field fence and in one breathless moment, before the Blue Jays slugger even left the batter's box, it was all over. Carter blasted a walk-off home run to win the World Series.

For the second year in a row, all cameras were on him. He jumped into the air and pumped his fists as he rounded the bases. He honestly looked like he couldn't believe it. The Blue Jays had done it again.

If any hint of a dark cloud can be cast over the accomplishments of the awesome '93 Blue Jays it is this: Toronto's success shone an awful light on an Expos team brimming with talent but facing terrible problems. The Blue Jays turned 95 wins into a second consecutive World Series title. The same summer, the Expos turned 94 wins into serious questions about the very sustainability of the franchise.

Toronto's success seemed to highlight Montreal's problems and, with 1994 looming, the collective bargaining agreement between players and owners came to an end. The Jays snuck a World Series in just before a possible strike season.

The 2002 Blue Jays are once again looking to the success of the Oakland A's for lessons on the long road to championship form. In the 1980s, Oakland taught Toronto that playoff success turns on dominant performers who drive an otherwise balanced attack. This summer, the A's remind the Blue Jays that youth can lead a team back to the postseason. Oakland illustrates this lesson by ripping Toronto.

The Blue Jays are especially vulnerable coming into Oakland because Carlos Delgado is on the disabled list. It is the first time in almost three seasons that Delgado has been out of the lineup due to injury. He has already missed a week with a spasming back and it looks like the lingering problem is going to cost him and his team more than originally expected.

Delgado has not been the perennial triple-crown threat that most expect him to be every year. Nonetheless, Delgado continues to be one of Toronto's most gifted players and contributes a veteran presence on an increasingly inexperienced team. Now out of the lineup, it leaves a huge hole in the team's offense.

Against Oakland, this problem is magnified. The A's are not a team that anyone would choose to face with its best player on the mend. Star hitters such as Miguel Tejada and Eric Chavez, complemented by veterans Ray Durham and David Justice, put constant pressure on the opposition to score runs while pitchers like Tim Hudson and Barry Zito make short work of a depleted lineup. Making matters worse for Toronto, the A's also have former Blue Jays closer Billy Koch in the bullpen.

General Manager J.P. Ricciardi shipped Koch to Oakland before this season, acquiring third baseman Eric Hinske who is now approaching the team record for doubles by a rookie. These are the kinds of results that the Jays expect out of Ricciardi. He is proving that a full-scale rebuilding process doesn't necessarily need to take more than a few months. Buy low, sell high. They are obviously thrilled with how Hinkse has worked out but Billy Koch recorded 30 plus saves in each of his three seasons with the Jays.

Toronto faces Koch, once described as unhittable by his teammates, on consecutive nights in Oakland. In the first of these appearances, Koch looks vulnerable. Toronto's offense has been on fire and any pitcher in the American League is likely to look vulnerable against this lineup. Koch looks especially shaky and is lucky to hold on for the save.

The following night, Koch shows Toronto exactly what it's been missing since making Kelvim Escobar their closer. Using just 12 pitches, he mows down Toronto's last three hitters.

Such are the dangers of starting from scratch. Every once in a while a loss hurts that much worse because it comes at the hands of a former player. As the Jays walk off the field following consecutive losses against Oakland, they're still on the outside looking in. Lesson learned.

All told, Major League Baseball is stumbling through August. Pennant races are taking shape. Barry Bonds has joined the exclusive 600 home run club. Ruining it all, the players may announce a strike on August 30 and the current labor conflict seems to have more to do with snatching at money already changing hands rather than examining the basic needs of an ailing business. In this environment, the only vehicle for addressing truly fundamental issues now seems to be legal wrangling among the owners themselves.

The former minority owners of the Expos are still suing Commissioner Bud Selig and Marlins owner Jeffrey Loria. More recently, the co-owner of the New York Mets has sued the league for artificially undervaluing his franchise. The lawsuit claims that, as part of Bud Selig's effort to undervalue baseball franchises to support his claims to financial insolvency, a biased appraiser set the value of the Mets well below its full market price.

This is no joke. The co-owner of the New York Mets has accused Major League Baseball of pursuing a campaign to undervalue its own teams and misrepresent the financial state of the league. Those are serious allegations.

Nonetheless, baseball is not easing off its claims to financial instability. League officials recently reported net operating losses across Major League Baseball at over $450 million, nearly twice as much as the contested estimate Bud Selig already provided to the U.S. government. According to Selig's numbers, the Boston Red Sox should be worth about $300 million. They sold this year for $700 million. This is how people end up in court.

Baseball's front office calls the sudden wave of lawsuits "nonsense." As time moves on, these are the conflicts that will shape the future of baseball. The owners are turning on each other. Before long it won't be labor disputes that challenge the stability of the league, it will be court cases.

Through it all, games are being played. The Blue Jays measure their future potential against the A's. On the other side of the continent, the Montreal Expos fight to stay in the hunt for a playoff spot this very summer.

The Los Angeles Dodgers are at Olympic Stadium, offering the Expos a golden opportunity to make up ground against one of the many teams they have to overcome in order to earn the wild card. Like the Blue Jays in Oakland, Montreal faces one of its own with the Dodgers in town. Hometown boy Eric Gagne makes his first appearance in Montreal since becoming one of the most overpowering closers in the league.

For Gagne, this is more than just a homecoming; it's a downright triumphant homecoming. He has recorded 39 of 41 save opportunities this summer. Major League Baseball recently released a television commercial promoting the diversity of cultures in the game by featuring *Take Me Out to the Ball Game* sung in a hodge-podge of different languages. Eric Gagne sung in French. The prodigal Quebecois returns.

Against the Expos, Gagne has an opportunity to show off in front of fans who rarely get to cheer their own. More importantly, there are playoff implications to the Expos-Dodgers series. No team has yet run away with the wild card.

As such, with the Dodgers carrying a 3–2 lead into the 8th inning, the 14,000 fans at Olympic Stadium all know what's coming. Vladimir Guerrero draws a walk against Dodgers starter Andy Ashby, chasing him from the game. Fans rise to their feet. Eric Gagne walks in from the bullpen.

The crowd cheers through his warm-up, and cheers while Expos outfielder Troy O'Leary digs into the batters' box. The crowd isn't quite as sure what to do when O'Leary drives Gagne's first pitch over the right field wall to give Montreal a sudden 4–3 lead. There's a moment of disbelief then the cheering starts again.

The Dodgers threaten to score in the 9th but Expos closer Scott Stewart ends the game with a strikeout to give Montreal fans what they want. Eric Gagne got his standing ovation and the Expos still draw within a half dozen games of the final playoff spot.

Around the league, no one bats an eye when this type of scenario unfolds. Fans like to see local players make good in the big time and there is usually a raucous cheer reserved for any player coming home. In Canada, people view this phenomenon as something unnatural when it happens in Quebec. It speaks to Canada's deep insecurity that people think this has something to do with separatism.

There is a disconnection between the Canadian people and the broad brushstrokes of their history. It's hard for most Canadians to understand that not only was separatism created by the Maritimes and Ontario as well as Quebec but that at the crucial moment when it became a phenomenon peculiar to Quebec on its own, the rest of Canada was pushing the province away just as much as it was claiming its status as a separate entity.

The rivalry between Toronto and Montreal was never really about the English-French thing. That basic reality was lost, or forgotten, when the fear and passion of war took over. Though Ottawa's overt interventions would return as a significant influence after the war, the perceived link between sovereignty and language became permanent.

> "Quebec would ... accept the breaking of the Confederation."
> —*Joseph-Napoléon Francoeur, motion to Legislature of Quebec, 1918*

As everywhere, politics in Canada breed incestuous clans of insiders. This is the enduring legacy of people like Charles Tupper. He tricked Nova Scotia into joining the confederation, was prime minister for a brief period after John Macdonald's death and continued to have an influence over Canadian government long after his retirement by encouraging one of his son's friends to move into professional politics. That friend was Robert Borden.

Borden became prime minister in 1911 by focusing his election campaign on the supposed threat to Canadian sovereignty posed by the United States which, he suggested, was poised to use free trade as a vehicle to rob the Canadian people of their freedom. Silly idea, really.

Back in 1812, the U.S. invaded Canada. At that time, the presence of European imperial powers as well as First Nations warriors prevented Canada from being overtaken. Once the imperial militaries moved away and the First Nations became unwilling to fight for a country actively trying to destroy their respective cultures, it was clear that the United States could take Canada whenever it pleased. This planted the seeds of a deep-rooted paranoia in the Canadian psyche. Robert Borden exploited that paranoia.

No sooner did he succeed Wilfred Laurier than he was down in New York reassuring American counterparts that he believed it was Canada's duty to establish a bond between the once adversarial interests of the U.S. republic and the British empire. Borden beat the drums of nationalism then hurried down to America to make sure no one paid too much attention.

This would characterize Borden's tenure as prime minister. He became something of a champion of Canadian independence on the international stage while his own policies helped pull Canada apart from within.

The balance Borden had struck between the interests of Quebecers and Ontarians did not last. The old rivals soon turned on each other again, creating serious domestic unrest at a time when the Borden government was coming to terms with international burdens that all Canadians were expected to shoulder.

In 1912, the Ontario government introduced a regulation requiring that the first three years of a child's education be in English only. This infamous regulation threatened to leave thousands of francophone schoolchildren without access to basic education. The measure did not sit well with Quebecers. A subsequent decision of the Quebec government to allow its municipalities to donate money as compensation to Ontario children going without an education was itself just the sort of reaction required to turn the situation into a full-blown national crisis.

Such was the state of the Canadian union when news of an assassination on the streets of Sarajevo turned the entire western world's attention to the threat of war. Germany, Austria-Hungary and Italy were poised to square off against England, France and Russia in open military conflict.

In Canada, still a part of the British Empire, the prospect of war raised the obvious question of whether Canadians would be called upon to kill and die in Europe. Prime Minister Robert Borden answered in no uncertain terms.

Canada would participate in the defense of the empire. When war was declared, thousands of people are reported to have thrown their hats into the air in Toronto. In Montreal, archbishops spoke of a sacred duty to assist. Canadians thought it would be a quick war, a bit of fun in the Old World.

Canada's military was a joke: 3,000 regular soldiers and one factory dedicated to producing the crappy Ross rifle. To make matters worse, only gung-ho volunteers could be counted upon to swell the ranks of the armed forces.

The federal government couldn't force citizens to fight. Prime Minister Borden was nonetheless determined that Canada should play an important role in the war effort. The first thing he did was use the brief period of solidarity among politicians to push the War Measures Act through Parliament, thereby offering the government extensive powers to curtail the rights of Canadian citizens in times of war. He also encouraged the provinces to send supplies to Europe and to promote military enlistment.

Recruitment rallies were held across Canada. The province of Ontario accounted for the most volunteers. The province of Quebec accounted for the fewest. This disparity aggravated lingering tensions. The issue of language rights became hopelessly entangled in the rhetoric and passion of war.

Prime Minister Borden traveled to Europe in 1915. What he saw was a snapshot of horror and death. The experience convinced him of two things. First, Canada had an obligation to provide substantial reinforcements to back up the men who'd already suffered. Second, if Canada was going sacrifice so many men it ought to speak and be heard as an independent voice on the international stage. These convictions would directly impact the course of Canada's history.

In Ontario, the slogan "equalization of sacrifice" had taken root and was intended as a rallying cry to shame Quebec into putting more people forward for the war. In Quebec, the token presence of French-speaking officers and the implied imperial commitment of fighting in support of Britain were taking a heavy toll on enlistment.

Stories were filtering back from the front. People knew what they were getting into. Fewer were standing up to join the dwindling ranks.

Quebec's lukewarm support for fighting in the trenches turned cold as ice when Prime Minister Borden started speaking seriously about the idea of conscription. The federal government had failed to generate substantial new recruits for the front and, by 1917, it was starting to look like Canada's war effort might fail.

In response, Borden put the idea of conscription forward and it split Canada in two. There was an election. Borden and his supporters carried the day. The key issue was conscription and, though Borden won, he lost Quebec entirely.

In the aftermath, the province of Quebec was left completely unrepresented in Borden's cabinet. Quebec had no voice in Ottawa and no friends in the government. The prime minister lost Quebec for himself, his party and the whole country.

In the spring of 1918, most of Canada perceived conscription as a necessary measure. In Quebec City, there were riots in the streets. Prime Minister Borden sent the military from Toronto to calm angry crowds. Anxious soldiers shot into the masses at random. Four people, not even participating in demonstrations, were killed. Canada had mobilized its military to move into Quebec and force the French to fight for Britain. Canadian union was totally fractured.

Wartime policies divided the nation and, though no participants died during this anti-conscription rally in Montreal (1917), the domestic unrest was sometimes fatal (Canada Department of the Secretary of State / Library and Archives Canada / C-006859).

That same year, the government of Quebec briefly debated a motion suggesting that the province consider separating from Canada since the interests of the two no longer fit together. The motion was not seriously considered but it was the beginning of a new era in Canadian history. Separation would eventually come to be regarded as a uniquely French-Quebec phenomenon.

Thankfully, the war in Europe did not last long after the introduction of conscription. For all the potentially irreparable harm it did to the country as a whole, conscription itself generated 80,000 soldiers, few of which actually made it to the trenches before the end of fighting in 1918.

Prime Minister Borden spent the immediate post-war years arguing that Canada's enormous sacrifice required that it be treated as a sovereign nation, not just a member of the British Empire. This push for greater Canadian independence in the world community would be Borden's legacy even though his domestic policies aggravated deep fissures widening within the Canadian union.

Along with the political isolation of Quebec, Borden's wartime decisions enhanced the power of the federal government at a time when its relevance to Canadians living in the country's expanding cities was coming into question. At confederation, one of the provisions that made nationhood attractive to leaders of what would eventually become the country's provinces was the concept of direct taxation. Provinces were granted exclusive authority to generate revenue by taxing the incomes and assets of its citizens.

During the war, Borden became gravely worried about the cost of the military effort. As a result, he introduced the federal income tax as a temporary measure intended to generate funds for the war.

This was a hugely significant decision not just because the federal income tax quickly became a permanent fixture in federal budgeting but also because it redirected essential resources away from Canada's provinces, which had total jurisdiction over the affairs of cities like Toronto and Montreal.

In a speech to the directors of a major commercial exhibition in Toronto in 1918, Prime Minister Borden himself underscored the rise of provincial power by highlighting the importance of urban affairs and natural resources to the success of post-war Canada. The thing about urban affairs and natural resources is that they fall under the exclusive jurisdiction of provincial governments. Borden recognized that matters over which the prime minister had no constitutional jurisdiction had become central to the country's success and, as such, wanted to make sure he wasn't cut out of the picture.

The relative importance of the federal government in domestic affairs was slipping away. The strain of the war effort had created the conditions necessary for Robert Borden to start reeling control back towards Ottawa by redirecting taxes and keying in on areas of provincial jurisdiction. This strategy would have lasting impacts on Toronto and Montreal. Prime Minister Borden was making moves to ensure that Ottawa's power in these cities was not lost.

In the years that followed, provincial governments scrambled to generate new revenue streams through such things as the control of alcohol sales and gas taxes. Though federal tax revenues gradually dropped throughout the 1920s, the financial burden on both provincial and municipal governments only increased with the national economy constantly teetering on the brink of collapse.

By the Great Depression, provincial control over urban affairs, natural resources and the provision of crucial social services created an unmanageable burden. In most of Canada, getting as much assistance as possible out of Ottawa became an obsession. In Quebec, getting out altogether started sounding better and better.

From the very onset of Canadian nationhood it was clear that cozying up to federal politicians was key to securing a fair deal. This is the line of reasoning through which Nova Scotia was swindled into the union. It is the reality that industrialists in Toronto and Montreal employed to engender Canada's classic urban rivalry.

In the Borden era, it became that much more important because the prime minister captured much of the provinces' power over taxation and waded into territory previously restricted by the constitution. In Quebec, where the otherness of its people was constantly reinforced by the rhetoric of radicals and the vitriol of its neighbors, this deal no longer seemed worth the trouble.

When the ordeal of scrambling after the favor of central authority outweighs the benefit of succeeding, people stop trying. This isn't restricted to national politics. It can happen on a much smaller scale as well. For the most part, it explains how people in Montreal came to give up on the Expos.

In 2002, it has become clear that no amount of fan loyalty is going to save the Expos. There are no attendance figures high enough to make this happen. Take away that hope and support is hard to raise.

Baseball players will be in a position to walk away on August 30. If that happens, the strike will begin just before the Montreal Expos return to Olympic Stadium to face the Atlanta Braves. Given the very real possibility that this strike could wipe out the rest of the 2002 season, and the fact that Major League Baseball is still committed to doing away with the Expos, it's conceivable that the Expos will never return from the road to face Atlanta. In this scenario, a home game against the San Diego Padres stands out as potentially the last ever to be played in Montreal.

This is old news. The Expos and their fans have heard the death knell before.

Still, the fact remains that certain stars in the baseball galaxy are aligning against Montreal's survival. It's undeniable. This year, perhaps more than any other, the Expos are staring down the barrel.

Just over 8,000 fans make the trek out to Olympic Stadium to catch what might be the team's last home game. Too bad. Colon has been the only real standout in the weeks that have seen them slide out of the playoff picture, and he takes the mound to face San Diego.

Against the Padres, Colon delivers more of the same. After Vladimir Guerrero tags his 33rd home run of the year, extending Montreal's lead to 4–0 in the 3rd inning, Colon mows down San Diego hitters in extremely short order. The game takes less than two hours from start to finish. In that time, Colon pitches a complete game shutout, allowing only four Padres to reach base. The win lifts the Expos' record back to .500 at 62–62.

With the Expos facing an unceremonious end in Montreal, the Blue Jays continue their road trip with a visit to Texas where they come face to face with the very heart of baseball's biggest problem. Against the Rangers, Toronto encounters a player who, through his talent and charisma, received a flabbergasting contract that has come to represent the irresponsibility that is killing the entire league.

How much baseball player can an owner buy for $250 million? A lot, that's how much. Shortstop Alex Rodriguez is an outrageously good ballplayer but when a team spends that much money on one player it doesn't leave much in the bank to pay all the others. The Rangers have got Rodriguez, a few aging and injured once-All-Stars and not much else.

Over 162 games, there's only so much that one player can do to elevate the play of an entire team. In baseball, it takes much more, especially from a team's pitching staff, in order to be successful.

Rodriguez already has close to 40 home runs and 100 RBIs in August. Despite this awesome contribution, the Texas Rangers are last in the American League West. Against the Blue Jays, Alex Rodriguez displays the drama and panache that dazzle owners into making such terrible, terrible decisions.

The Blue Jays send Roy Halladay out to face the Rangers in the series opener. As he's apt to do, Halladay pitches six strong innings and gives up just three runs. He yields two of those runs to Alex Rodriguez but hands the game over to his bullpen with Toronto in front. Halladay then watches from the sidelines as closer Kelvim Escobar comes in to pitch the 9th.

With the game tied, Escobar faces Rodriguez. Moments later, the game is over and Rodriguez is walking off the field after hitting a home run that gives him four hits and three RBIs on the game. The Rangers win 6–5.

Rodriguez is good in the first game. The next night he explodes, tagging Toronto starter Steve Parris for a pair of home runs and adding another homer against the Blue Jays' relief corps. He is the difference in a 9–5 Texas victory.

In the series' final game, Rodriguez gets historic. He pounds out two more home runs and becomes one of a handful of players to ever hit six in three games. The Rangers' pitching staff holds off a desperate 9th inning rally to preserve a 10–7 win and seal the series sweep. Two hundred fifty million dollars may not buy any World Series rings but it will occasionally buy a record-setting night.

This summer, the plight of the Texas Rangers and the embarrassing excess of Alex Rodriguez' salary not only highlight the dangers of big-money free agency but also the nature of the true dilemma facing baseball as a whole. Much time is spent discussing systemic changes and financial models that will help fix the ailing business of professional baseball. The rhetoric surrounding a possible players' strike next week often turns on these types of analyses. Rodriguez' contract helps illustrate that much of the talk about these systems and models is misguided in an industry that most needs common sense and fiscal restraint to prevail.

The trouble with baseball is the mismanagement of resources. No team should be paying any player a quarter of a billion dollars. If owners were more sensible in their spending, none of the present trouble would even exist. Maybe Rodriguez makes $10 million per season, a nauseatingly huge sum. That even this level of restraint is unlikely is the real problem in baseball.

With mere days to go before an ominous strike deadline, it's easy to point an accusing finger at both players and owners. People like Bud Selig and players' union representative Donald Fehr have so little credibility on which to fall back that they are the easiest targets of all.

The unfortunate truth is, these people and all their minions are simply expanding on themes that were established decades ago. If the labor dispute of 2002 becomes the most damaging and divisive on record it will be quite a feat. The bar has been set very high by the bickering mobs who've come before.

"We should have gone all the way. Or, could have."
—*Larry Walker, on the 1994 Expos*

When the 1994 baseball season got underway, there was no agreement in place between the players and owners. Perhaps as a sign that good faith negotiations could be conducted over the course of the summer, but more likely to run the stakes higher by allowing a season to commence before threatening a strike or lockout, both sides assumed their familiar postures. The trench war had resumed.

Serious people with an honest desire to come to terms on divisive issues don't need an artificial deadline to initiate meaningful discussions. The jokers who run both the players' union and the major league front office are not serious in this way. They are serious in the way that punks on the street can be serious. They want bullied respect and the presumption of being dangerous to other people. For this reason, the summer of 1994 progressed with only sporadic meetings and featured a series of insincere proposals that amounted to little more than constant reiterations of tired positions.

The owners wanted to introduce a salary cap, to do away with salary arbitration and to lower the percentage of revenues shared with players to 50 percent. The players rejected any notion of capping salaries, wanted to make salary arbitration more readily available and sought to maintain their existing 58 percent share of revenues. The positions proved to be totally irreconcilable.

By August, the prospect of a strike threatened to bring an artificial end to some exciting individual and team performances. On August 11, Tony Gwynn, among the finest hitters of his generation, took a page from John Olerud's book by making a run at .400. On the 11th, Gwynn was hitting an incredible .394. Almost as exciting as this one player's electrifying pace was the baseball renaissance taking place in Montreal.

Like Gwynn, the Expos seemed to be following up on a standard of excellence that had already been established in Toronto. The Expos were a revelation, recording a stellar 74–40 record.

Better yet, the Expos were playing an infectious kind of baseball. They were near the bottom of the league in home runs with only Moises Alou, son of much loved manager Felipe, registering more than 20. They were not heavy hitters. Instead, they were all over the base paths, league leaders in stolen bases, doubles and batting average.

The strength of the offense was its collective speed. Every hitter in the order, with the exception of catcher Darrin Fletcher and Moises Alou, was a threat to steal. The ball tended to stay in the park but the Expos were constantly rounding the bases. It was exciting baseball and fans were beginning to respond.

The Expos were still near the bottom of the National League in attendance due primarily to the habitual skepticism of fans in the early stages of the summer. Conventional baseball wisdom has it that a franchise can expect a serious attendance spike the season following its rise to the ranks of contenders. The fact that Montreal hadn't fully embraced the Expos over the first few months of the season was totally consistent with this truism.

By mid-August, it was not unusual to see 30,000 fans at the Big O, an enormous draw for baseball in Montreal. The Expos had their eyes set on the playoffs and their long-term hopes pinned on filling their home field to capacity in the coming seasons. On August 11, they had the best record in baseball.

On August 12, it was all over. The players walked away and the owners closed shop. The rest of the season shelved and the World Series was cancelled. Teams leading their divisions at the start of the work stoppage were awarded the meaningless titles of division champions while the title of world champion was left empty.

In some circles, inhabited primarily by stats junkies on the Internet, mock playoffs were run based on comparative statistics. This is as close as the Expos would ever come to competing in the World Series. It was a depressing time for all of baseball, a crippling time for the Expos.

As if the league hadn't already done enough to squash a baseball revival in Montreal, it cited so-called political instability as a problem in Quebec as well. Over the summer of 1994, the Parti Quebecois, traditional political party of pro-sovereignty supporters, had been campaigning in advance of a fall election. The PQ was asking the electorate to prepare itself for another referendum to determine Quebec's status as a potentially independent nation. By the time the 1994 World Series was cancelled, the PQ was in power, building support and momentum for a vote on Quebec's independence.

While Canada braced itself for a debate over sovereignty in Quebec, Americans watched as their government jumped into the baseball dispute with both feet. President Clinton lobbied for a settlement to the strike, which extended through the winter. A mediator was appointed to push proposals forward. These efforts all failed and, as spring training rolled around, there was still little hope of a settlement.

In a show of outright disdain for the union, owners prepared to enter the 1995 season with replacement players, telling the scabs that they'd get a shot at a spot on the regular rosters no matter what happened with the strike. Plenty of players took the gamble. Some got pulled off day jobs. Some simply took the de facto promotion from the minors. They all stepped into the crosshairs of a furious players' union otherwise content to just wait and wait.

This development was generally regarded as an abomination. With the support of President Clinton, the ongoing dispute went to the courts where an injunction against the owners forcibly reinstated the work rules established under the expired collective agreement.

This effectively turned back the clock by validating the free agent and revenue sharing provisions that, through their expiration, had initiated the whole messy situation. With this injunction in place, the players and owners mutually agreed to play the 1995 season under the old rules. Most of the replacement players were sent home, some returned to the minor leagues and many would forever be blacklisted from the major leagues due to their participation in the cynical experiment.

The strike of 1994 accomplished absolutely nothing. It would be three years before another agreement would be reached between the players and owners. The strike had only two lasting impacts. First, it jaded an entire generation of would-be baseball fans who came to understand that all the talk about the integrity and tradition of baseball was bunk. Second, it completely destroyed the Montreal Expos.

It did not help that, just when the franchise seemed at its weakest, the talk of creating an independent nation within Quebec's borders had become most serious. In 1995, the question of separation was put to a vote that was so close all of Canada held its breath hoping that there would be enough federalist support from Montreal itself to keep the country together.

In that desperate summer, there may have been only one person thanking his lucky stars that the strike took place at all. Pitcher Matt Herges was one of the players who crossed union picket lines as a replacement. He spent seven long summers paying his dues in the minor leagues and must not have felt very good about his chances of ever making the L.A. lineup through the front door because when he got the chance to walk in through the back door he wandered right in.

His gamble paid off. Herges stuck with the Dodgers and, raising the ire of his teammates and the union he challenged, became a major leaguer. In theory, there's some person out there presently toiling in the minor leagues or at a buck-an-hour job because Herges is taking his place on a major league roster.

In 2002, Matt Herges now finds himself in the unique position of having to decide whether or not to vote in favor of the same strike that he defied back in '94. He is also a member of the Montreal Expos pitching staff, which puts him in the even more unique position of having to decide whether to vote in favor of a strike that turns, in part, on the contraction of his own team.

Ultimately, the decision is taken out of his hands. At the end of August, the players' union and owners jointly announce that a deal has been reached. Once finalized and ratified, this will stabilize labor relations in baseball until 2007. The strike has been called off. Everyone takes a moment to breath a sigh of relief.

When that moment passes, most will look at the actual terms of the agreement itself and sigh again at the solution it proposes to baseball's biggest problems. Faced with the enormous divide between teams spending $100 plus million on payrolls and those spending closer to $30 million, negotiators have effectively decided to tell the small market clubs that their financial problems are a result of their not spending enough money.

This has been George Steinbrenner's argument all along. The deal sets a luxury tax limit so high ($117 million–$137 million) that almost no team will be penalized or encouraged to curb their spending. It also introduces a revenue sharing model ($155 million–$258 million) through which small market teams will be expected to make massive payroll increases, living off scraps from the tables of teams that will still outbid them for top talent.

In the first year of this deal, the total amount of league revenue sharing is actually $12 million less than the amount Commissioner Selig claims was shared between the big and small market teams in 2001. Even at its peak, which will take four years to be phased in and will last only one season, the deal will see the total amount of money shared among all teams equal just twice as much as top teams are allowed to spend on their payroll in a single year.

As for contraction, the plan to eliminate two teams has been called off until 2007 at which point the players' union has agreed not to intervene. So the owners are closer to contraction than they've been all year long.

In fact, now they can take their time and make sure all the court cases are out of the way before absorbing franchises, digesting the up-front cost then regurgitating the franchise licenses to new markets. This will create enormous profits based on the difference between what they will pay for their own undervalued franchises and what they will receive from new owners and cities making the suckers' investment in baseball. It's been smoke and mirrors all summer and this deal is the final illusion, the big showstopper.

Across North America, headlines trumpet a great day for baseball. Moving forward, it's hard to see how this agreement could possibly give any of the small market teams the tools necessary to compete. Looking back, it's clear that the players never had any problems with the terms being proposed by owners. The sides have been arguing the same points back and forth, and now congratulate one another for a deal that changes nothing.

"All streaks come to an end, and this was one that was overdue."
—*Players' negotiator Donald Fehr, on settling before the strike deadline, 2002*

September

> "We're happy to be able to do this for New York."
> —*George Steinbrenner, on plans to build the Yankees a new stadium, 2001*

In September 2001, New York's Yankee Stadium hosted a remembrance service for the victims of the 9/11 terrorist attacks as well as for the firefighters and police officers who sacrificed themselves saving innocent people from the smoldering World Trade Center towers prior to their collapse. Planes weren't allowed to fly overhead and roses were handed out at the gates, a far and fitting cry from the LaGuardia bound jets and bobblehead dolls that otherwise greet people flowing into the hallowed facility.

That afternoon, New Yorkers were desperate for a reprieve from the horror and panic that gripped all of America following an outrage that left thousands dead and countless more in mourning. The "House that Ruth Built" was a treasure and benefit to those people. Less than three months later, it was scheduled for abandonment.

In December 2001, Mayor Rudolph Giuliani agreed to finance a new stadium for the Yankees. The plan had percolated for years and the mayor's love of baseball was public knowledge so the announcement came as no shock.

Against the backdrop of an enormous public debt brought on by the terrorist attacks, it left a bad taste in many mouths. Against the backdrop of the most powerful sports empire in the world, it exposed the fact that Major League Baseball's push for public stadium financing has nothing to do with the sustainability of local markets.

The government of New York has been in the baseball business since 1971 when it built Shea Stadium and purchased Yankee Stadium thereby becoming landlord to both the Mets and Yankees. This established a relationship that made Giuliani's stunning financial commitment possible. It also overturned a half-century of private enterprise.

Yankee Stadium was conceived as a solution to the Babe Ruth phenomenon. This is baseball lore and, for all intents and purposes, is true. When Ruth exploded onto the scene, routinely registering more homers than other entire teams, attendance at Yankees games doubled. Building the stadium was a supply and demand decision. Across the Harlem River, in a borough known as the Bronx, Yankees bosses found land upon which a stadium of the unprecedented magnitude being contemplated could be built.

The Bronx was growing in leaps and bounds during that period. The town on which it was founded had been established by a group of rich families back in the 1650s, was devastated by fighting during the Revolution and drew mass numbers of immigrants in the early 1800s. This growth put enormous pressure on the town for services and infrastructure. Most assumed that it would be annexed by the city of New York.

At the turn of the 20th century, this is exactly what happened and, as a result, the Bronx received subway and train service connecting it to New York. Many of these new lines extended into areas that had not been fully developed and builders jumped all over the opportunity. The Bronx quickly became a destination of choice for working class families looking to move away from the tenement lifestyle offered by crowded New York City.

Prior to the depression that brought all this growth crashing to a halt, the Bronx was an up-and-coming neighborhood where builders of all sorts were undertaking major projects. The New York Yankees jumped in with the rest, paying $3 million for the property and stadium, which was completed in 1923.

Yankee Stadium was an ambitious project undertaken by a private business that had market demand on its side. It was a sound investment, facilitated by public expenditure on transit links that opened new areas for mass development. The stadium was an extension of the city's financial commitment to the Bronx as a whole.

The Great Depression put an end to this boom and then, following World War II, close to 200,000 people were displaced in a slum clearance campaign that sent waves searching for affordable housing. This created whole communities of impoverished people in the south Bronx, which became one of the least desirable places to live in all of New York when insurance fraud and a government policy that gave public housing priority to victims of property fire created a wave of arson. The neighborhood literally went up in flames.

By 2001, a renewal of the original public investment that enabled the boom of the '20s was desperately needed. There was a $2 billion shortfall in public funding necessary to address severe problems in areas such as health, housing, education and transportation in the section of the Bronx where Yankee Stadium stands.

The challenge of meeting this critical shortfall was compounded by the September 11 terrorist attacks as New York faced projected budget deficits of $3.5 billion for each of the years between 2001 and 2004. There was no money for the Bronx. Yet, Mayor Giuliani found $800 million for the Yankees and Mets. No one is under any misconception that this astonishing subsidy will benefit anyone other than team owners.

Yankee Stadium is already one of the busiest facilities in baseball. If the Bronx needs $2 billion as it stands, another stadium is not likely to make that situation any better. There is no danger of the Yankees moving out of New York, the biggest market for professional sports in America. The threat of relocation doesn't even apply. Making this scenario even more difficult to accept are figures that accompany the Yankees' candidacy for public assistance.

The Yankees generated $250 million in 2001 alone. They entered into an exclusive ten-year $95 million endorsement contract with Adidas. They also negotiated a joint promotional contract with the Manchester United soccer club. The Yankees enjoy revenues, endorsements and promotional deals that are shared by no other team while operating in America's largest market. It is by far the most successful franchise in baseball and one of the most powerful sports empires in the world.

The very idea that New York could be investing money it cannot afford to prop up the Yankees is not only offensive to common sense, it is evidence that public stadium financing in Major League Baseball has absolutely nothing to do with the sustainability of local markets. How could it?

In 2002, the Yankees are angling to become yet another recipient of misguided public investment in a sport that has spent the past decade making such subsidization a basic precondition of membership in the major league family. They are also gearing up for another run at the World Series. All is well in their insulated universe and, in the first week of September, the Toronto Blue Jays pass through this fabulous oasis, this oblivious refuge from the harsher realities facing lesser teams.

The Blue Jays meet their division rivals with little to show for the new agreement reached between players and owners. The league has committed to the extension of a currency equalization provision. This will benefit Toronto. Revenue sharing will redirect some resources to the Jays, who started accepting financial handouts earlier this summer. At the face of it, there seems to be an upside.

A closer look will remind fans that currency equalization is nothing new and the Blue Jays' status as have-nots in the league does not translate into good news. In fact, since the league now has the agreement of the players' union to contract teams in 2007, and the Montreal Expos are not likely to be a problem by that point, it's hard to spin the new agreement as something worth getting excited about in Toronto.

The team plays below .500 in an aging, artificial turf stadium in front of a smattering of fans. These things need to turn around entirely for the Jays. If they don't, the agreement is likely to put Toronto on the list of contraction targets in 2007. That's not a step in the right direction.

Thirty-two thousand people turn up at SkyDome to watch the Jays take on New York. Today, folks are happy just to soak up the pleasure of having baseball to watch even if the home team is hopelessly out of contention playing opponents who symbolize an ideal that the Jays will never be able to achieve. Baseball, it seems, will be enough.

Roy Halladay goes after his 15th win against David Wells, the Yankees pitcher who has twice left the Blue Jays organization after blasting Toronto management and fans. It's a nice match-up. Halladay, the young ace who pitched in the minors last season, against Wells, the outspoken star who'll do anything to stay in New York.

The Yankees gain an upper hand in the game's first half by chipping away at Halladay. It is typical Yankees baseball. In the 1st and 3rd innings, they score on base hits that bring Derek Jeter home. In both cases, Jeter reached base by drawing a walk from Halladay. Walk a Yankees, give up a run. Showcasing the power that runs up and down this batting order, the Yankees also add a solo home run in the 4th and take a 3–0 lead.

All seems secure for New York until two of Toronto's promising youngsters put Wells through the grinder. Josh Phelps is the 24-year-old designated hitter who many expect will replace Carlos Delgado if general manager J.P. Ricciardi is able to get fair value in a trade for Toronto's last remaining big-name star. Orlando Hudson is the 25-year-old second baseman whose .300 average has made him an instant favorite among fans and media alike.

Between them, they have 300 major league at-bats to go against David Wells' 2500 innings pitched. Nonetheless, Phelps and Hudson both collect RBI hits in the 6th inning, chasing the Yankees pitcher to the showers.

This rookie rally leads to an eventual 7–6 win, a promising display of what the Blue Jays' young lineup is capable of accomplishing. Still, following the game, Toronto's own manager cannot help but include a sobering qualifier to the win.

"The Yankees are the model."
—*Blue Jays manager Carlos Tosca, 2002*

Tosca's grasp of the status quo is not his most valuable quality. Since taking over from Buck Martinez in mid-season, Tosca's ability to coax young players into reaching their potential has been key to the Jays' overall turnaround. In recognition of this yeoman's work, Toronto has extended his contract through 2004. The team is 40–44 under his guidance. Not great, but better.

No such guarded hopefulness surrounds Montreal's clubhouse in the first week of September. The settlement between players and owners brings the Expos back to Olympic Stadium for a series against the Atlanta Braves. That's good news. Many have speculated that, since the agreement formally delays contraction, the team will likely be relocated instead of eliminated. That's not necessarily a bad thing. Some even hold out hope that the ongoing lawsuit between former Expos owners and the league itself will provide a vehicle for saving the team. Most have long since abandoned this idea and will be pleased if anything positive at all comes out of this summer.

Two thousand two started slipping away from the Expos right after the All-Star break. The Dodgers and Giants are now running away with the National League wild-card race and the Expos are playing out the string.

Expos fans just want to see a respectable .500 finish and maybe see the team take a bite out of the league's remaining contenders. The would-be spoilers get their first chance in this diminished role, welcoming the Braves to town for a series that might have been important had the Expos not already tumbled out of postseason contention.

Kevin Millwood takes the mound for Atlanta. He has really come into his own this summer. Though a serious arm injury cost him a good portion of last season, he has 14 wins in 2002 and has struck out three times as many batters as he's walked. Against the Expos, however, Millwood has uncharacteristic control problems, walking four hitters and having to be replaced in the 6th inning.

To Atlanta's delight, this erratic performance pales in comparison to the total meltdown of Montreal relievers in subsequent innings. In the 8th, Britt Reames walks the bases loaded before walking in a run. In the 9th inning, Dan Smith uncorks a wild pitch, allowing another Braves' runner to score. In the end, Atlanta wins by that margin, 6–4. For Expos fans hoping to watch their team finish at .500, it is a blow.

This time of year, teams that have fallen out of the running count on a sentimental connection with their fans to keep stadium seats full. In some cities, like Chicago, this isn't a problem. It doesn't matter how badly the Cubs play, people still flock to Wrigley.

In Montreal, fall arrives with much gloom. If Chicago is at one extreme, Montreal is at the other.

After the Braves leave town, just 3,000 people show up for a game against the Phillies. Looking over the crowd, there's a tangible sense that it could be worse. There could be fewer.

The next night, the Expos close out their home stand with a dispiriting loss. The official gate tally is 2,100 but the stadium very much looks like it holds less than 1000 at game time. For a team that's had more than its share of lows in the past decade, it's hard to reach rock bottom. The Expos have done it.

Montreal is not the only city facing attendance problems in September. Many non-contenders see crowds dwindle. Slightly more out of the ordinary are attendance problems brought on by the opposite circumstance. Whereas teams like Montreal have trouble drawing at the gate by virtue of their lack of success, there are others, like Atlanta, which struggle because they've been too successful.

After a lonely series against Philadelphia, the Expos travel to Atlanta where no one cares about anything but the World Series. So luxurious has been the Braves' success that their fans wake up only when the Yankees are in town and the astonishingly racist "Tomahawk Chop" starts ringing through the stadium. The sight of empty seats at Turner Field during the playoffs is as conspicuous as the sight of an empty stadium in Montreal during the regular season.

With Bartolo Colon facing Tom Glavine in an ace pitching duel, and the Braves one win away from clinching the division title, Atlanta draws half its stadium's capacity. Still, the change of scenery does the Expos good.

Colon is too much for the Braves while Montreal jumps all over Glavine. Vladimir Guerrero and Jose Vidro, the only Expos batting over .300, combine for five hits as the Expos slam the Braves 7–0. Atlanta has to wait one more day for its division title and two more months for its fans to notice.

In baseball, some transitions take longer than others. It doesn't take long for Expos fans to give up on a lost season. It takes quite a while for Braves fans to break out the war paint. Other transitions take all summer.

Two thousand two began with Bud Selig massaging the sale of the Boston Red Sox, facilitating a plan to contract the Expos. As the months muddled along, the threat of a strike created drama and distraction. With the season winding down it's become clear that there was never much of a dispute. Selig has approved a deal that actually decreases revenue sharing, and can now focus on lawsuits being pursued by the league's smallest and largest teams. That's a lot to cram into one summer.

Bud Selig can handle a tight schedule. The commissioner sets as many fires as he puts out and, in the process, the league has ceased to be an amalgam of competing franchises. It has become a centrally planned monopoly.

Tracking the story of where Toronto's rivalry with Montreal came from, and trying to understand where this shared history is taking the cities and teams, has made this dynamic very familiar. Canadians know all about individuals who catch a whiff of power and decide to turn free enterprise into privileged monopoly. This is where the rivalry came from, after all.

It's also where the rivalry ended. Wartime created conditions in which the federal government curtailed provincial power and secured its influence over the affairs of Toronto and Montreal. War would come again, of course. With it, the artificial struggle in which these two cities had been engaged since the earliest days of Canadian nationhood would forever be settled.

"Business today is being operated largely for the benefit of the government."—*Clarence Howe, minister of munitions and supply, 1940*

Following World War I, Prime Minister Robert Borden made the mistake of assuming that his rivals would balk at the sour prospect of using the immense sacrifice of war as a lever against the government. Opportunism, however, has an iron stomach.

Borden soon discovered that his stature as the defender of Canadian solidarity in world affairs, hard won on the backs of dead soldiers and at the expense of his credibility in Quebec, had left him open to criticism. Even before the war claimed its final young lives, certain politicians recognized that Borden had exposed himself to broadside attack.

Mackenzie King, for example, aligned himself with former Prime Minister Wilfred Laurier, first in opposition to conscription and then in an open challenge to the legitimacy of the Borden government itself. When Laurier passed away, King stepped right into his place.

No sooner was the war over than Mackenzie King questioned whether the Borden government, cobbled together in haste, had a mandate during peacetime. King drew public attention back to questionable contracts awarded by the Borden administration, observing that the old business of federal patronage was alive and well. These were bitter criticisms that rang true, particularly in Quebec where voters were eager to inflict pain on Borden's government.

In 1921, these attacks brought Borden down. King was elected prime minister and, acutely aware of the damage that controversial decisions could do to an administration, immediately adopted a strategy of doing nothing wrong by doing nothing at all.

This had two results. First, it cost King his own seat in Parliament in the election of 1925, though his party held onto power. Second, it inspired some civil servants in his administration to do whatever they wanted. They decided to smuggle booze into the United States in exchange for cars they brought to Canada at enormous profit. When the press got hold of this, the prime minister was in big trouble.

King resigned, throwing Parliament into utter turmoil. His successor, in turn, managed to create such a mess that Parliament actually had to be dissolved altogether, prompting a snap election. King swept straight back into power in 1926.

In all the fuss and controversy, King learned that he couldn't just sit back and let his bureaucrats run the country. If the federal government wanted to get its shady dealings right, the prime minister would have to take care of them himself.

Just as it had when Robert Borden was in power, the relative importance of federal programs was dwindling compared to those of the provinces and cities. Control over urban affairs, in a country whose cities continued to grow, and natural resources, at the core of the national economy, were of paramount importance. That control was in the hands of provincial officials.

For King to play a more active role in shaping the fortunes of his friends he had to wade further into areas of provincial interest. He soon figured out a way to do just that and, true to his political nature, it hardly involved his doing anything.

All King had to do was turn a blind eye while political fundraisers padded his party's accounts with massive contributions from a Montreal businessman named Bob Sweezey who had his sights set on developing a hydroelectric power station along the St. Lawrence River. This Sweezey knew how to make the political establishment jump.

The feds had jurisdiction over navigable rivers. The province of Quebec had jurisdiction over resource development. The province of Ontario was the most likely purchaser of the power Sweezey intended to generate. Sweezey paid them all, except for Quebec, which was eager to promote any economic development projects in the wake of the international depression that took hold in 1929.

Sweezey got his project approval and Prime Minister King benefited by staying out of the way. It all would have gone off without a hitch if it hadn't been for the fact that this palm-greasing had become so common that Sweezey didn't know to keep his mouth shut.

When his competitors got wind of the scheme they went to the press and, for a brief period, succeeded in turning the whole affair into a national scandal. Federal leaders had benefited financially from allowing a massive public contract to be awarded to a Montreal businessman who then built infrastructure extending directly into Toronto.

Back when John Macdonald was pulling this sort of scam he tried to hide the dirty dealing under the auspices of a crucial railway network. The deal was just a bad part of a supposedly grand federal initiative. When Mackenzie King thrust his hands into the age-old cookie jar, there was no such bold national vision to hide behind and, making matters worse, he was influence peddling in an area of provincial jurisdiction. Everyone was in bed together, though, so the story was allowed to quietly go away.

Actually, the hydro scandal may have helped Mackenzie King. He turned the controversy into a reputation as a go-getter who knew how to make big things happen. This is King, remember. He did everything he could to avoid taking committed action and the hydro scandal itself was a case of him benefiting by doing nothing. Nonetheless, in the panic of the Great Depression, it made him look like a player.

If the Great Depression taught Canadians anything it was that, when the chips are down, they shouldn't turn to Ottawa. Sure, the federal government scrambled to conjure some make-work projects, lifted trade tariffs with the United States and introduced welfare reforms. These were not irrelevant measures but, in the end, it was still the provinces and the cities that bore the brunt of serving a population suddenly cast down into poverty.

Cities like Toronto and Montreal were focal points for the desperation of their people. The cities delivered services. The cities endured riots. The feds took the credit when an economic cycle entirely beyond their control turned back around and things brightened up near the end of the 1930s.

In a way, it's fitting that Mackenzie King was prime minister during those years. He ably contributed to that long tradition through which people in Toronto and Montreal came to see each other as rivals. Through the Great Depression, the cities were again in competition for scarce public resources siphoned from Ottawa.

It was also fitting that Mackenzie King happened to be prime minister during this period because, with war once again brewing in Europe, it was precisely the kind of hands-off approach that King himself preferred at home that allowed Adolf Hitler to drive the western world back into military conflict overseas. King actually met with Hitler before war broke out in earnest. The prime minister judged him to be a harmless simpleton, and supported the appeasement of Germany.

War was not an issue that Mackenzie King was prepared to face. He knew what impact it could have on a government and its leader. He had, after all, used the war and conscription crises to claim power 18 years earlier. It was not in his make-up to wade back into those waters now that his head was the one that would end up on the political chopping block.

Of course, it's hard to know what Mackenzie King's make-up actually entailed. He was a bit of a kook, known to have trusted mystics. It's hard to pin down the precise nature of a man who believed he could speak to the dead. Whatever his motives, Prime Minister King was re-elected in 1940.

Canada would inevitably be drawn into World War II and would suffer huge losses from the very first moment its troops scrambled up the beaches of Normandy. Much to the prime minister's dismay, Canada's formal declaration of war almost immediately thrust the very issue that had helped make Mackenzie King's political career back into the national spotlight: conscription.

As always, the prime minister was determined to weather the storm by avoiding it. He introduced a watered-down version of conscription that involved a draft for homeland defense then had the mayor of Montreal arrested for speaking out against it. He even fired his own minister of defense when he pressed the prime minister on his military commitment in Europe. King put off a decision on conscription for so long that by the time he was eventually forced to accept it as a necessary measure, it once again came into effect at the tail end of the war before many conscripted Canadians could be sent to the front.

This is not to say that Mackenzie King succeeded in sidestepping controversial decisions entirely. All it means is that conscription and the English-French tensions it again enflamed weren't at the core of those controversies. In fact, King changed Canada's political and urban history by forever settling a rivalry founded on the relationship between cities and central government.

When Canada first entered World War II, it not only had to face the problem of a badly underfunded military but also a serious gap in industrial capacity left behind by the Great Depression. The county neither had enough soldiers nor enough factories to create the physical machinery of war.

This created a panic that King used to force drastic measures through Parliament, most notably co-opting more resources from the provinces and handing sweeping powers over private industry to the so-called War Supply Board. This board was mandated to ensure that Canadian industry produced enough vehicles, weapons and equipment to fight the war. King appointed a man named Clarence Howe to make this happen.

Howe had been the owner of a construction firm that specialized in massive public works projects before entering politics and becoming the federal minister of transport in 1935. During his years at that post, he developed a reputation for being able to marry the interests of government with the motives of private industry.

Howe figured that the Canadian economy wasn't big enough to support competition and that closely monitored monopolies worked better. When Prime Minister King gave him control of the War Supply Board, Howe became known as the minister of everything.

Howe was not shy about his chosen strategy for mobilizing the Canadian economy. What he did, completely in the open where everyone could see, was call up a thousand of his pals to establish an insider society of businessmen who decided how the enormous wartime budget would be spent.

Over the next five years, Howe created 28 Crown Corporations, manufacturing over 100 airports, 10,000 planes, 600 ships and one half million vehicles to help carry the 85,000 heavy guns and the millions of tons of equipment that the war in Europe necessitated. This nearly tripled the output of the Canadian economy. That's the good news.

The bad news is that the monopolies Clarence Howe helped his friends establish were not compatible with balanced competition among suppliers. Howe thought the Canadian economy worked best when the main producers were free from the burden of competition. When he needed steel he appointed a producer, provided it with the necessary funds to upgrade its operation to meet the huge demand and bought from that producer exclusively.

Through it all, the big winner was Toronto. Aircrafts, automobiles, guns and ammunition would eventually involve two thirds of the city workforce in production for the War Supply Board. Much more importantly, the emphasis that Howe placed on the Great Lakes region as the focal point for wartime production helped establish permanent industrial operations, not just in Toronto, but also in a ring of smaller cities that surrounded the city. This would conclusively turn the tide of Canadian history in favor of Toronto.

In the years that followed World War II, both Toronto and Montreal would go through periods of unprecedented growth with Toronto outpacing

During World War II, Clarence Howe took control of the national economy, establishing Toronto as an unrivaled manufacturing and industrial power in Canada (National Film Board of Canada / Library and Archives Canada / C-068669).

Montreal by a slim margin. At the same time, the satellite cities that surrounded Toronto, whose businesses were all interrelated in one massive industrial juggernaut, were also growing.

This amalgam represented the true Toronto region and grew at a ferocious rate that far outpaced Montreal where no such complementary peripheral development had taken place. Canada's classic urban rivalry was settled.

To be sure, Toronto's success turned not only on the intervention of the federal government but also on the acumen of financiers and business owners capable of taking full advantage of such enormous political good fortune. The story of Toronto is, after all, the story of cavalier merchants capable of turning the smallest advantage into a legup on competitors.

Similarly, the old money and powerful institutions upon which Montreal's claim to power had always turned still came into play in the years that followed. The fundamental character of both cities remained intact. Clarence Howe simply made it impossible to think of any city but Toronto as the hub of national industry and inconceivable that Montreal's economy could ever keep pace.

Central planning creates these types of scenarios. At the level of national economies, winners and losers are measured across broad geographic regions. At the level of individual industries and businesses, winners and losers are measured on a much smaller scale but are nonetheless products of the same dynamic. Where success turns on support from the center, skill and determination will always be supplementary to, or trumped by, decisions made by a more powerful authority.

Baseball, as an industry, is no different in this regard. The prudent management of individual franchises and the achievement of talented performers are necessary preconditions but are, in the face of a dominant central authority, insufficient to guarantee success. There's only so far merit can take an organization under these circumstances.

The Toronto Blue Jays and Montreal Expos operate in this environment in 2002. The model for success that has been endorsed by Major League Baseball is not geared towards either franchise and both are on the outside looking in despite the achievements of managers and players who should be cause for optimism all on their own. This optimism is tempered by the actions of a commissioner who, now more than ever, plays a direct role in deciding which teams succeed and which fail.

The Blue Jays are almost certainly going to finish below .500 while the Expos have a good chance of being a winning team in 2002. Between the Jays and Expos, which team has had a more successful summer? It's hard to pick the Expos.

This is what passes for normal in Major League Baseball. The team striving for a winning season is impossible to regard as a bigger success than the team with no more than a mathematical possibility of doing the same. It is an awkward kind of normal, founded on such overbearing intervention from the league that the meddling itself has become a measure of success. At certain points, any kind of normal will do.

> "I think it's important to play, for the same reason the president said it was important to try to get things back to normal."
> —*Commissioner Bud Selig on the anniversary of the 9/11 attacks, 2002*

September 11, 2002.

A year ago, America was shaken to its foundation. Both towers of the World Trade Center in New York collapsed after a pair of hijacked airplanes crashed into their upper levels. The Pentagon in Washington burst into flames after another hijacked plane slammed into one of its sides. An empty field in Pennsylvania was the site of a third crash, resulting from a passenger revolt on yet another hijacked plane.

Today, America braces for two things. First, the anniversary of that terrible day. Second, the possibility that terrorists could strike again while the country is in mourning.

Across the United States, the catch phrase is "normalcy." Professional sports shut down in the aftermath of the attacks last year, acknowledging their irrelevance in the face of so much rubble. Major League Baseball resumed six days later and offered Americans some familiar comfort to offset the deep sense of insecurity that plagued the nation.

Baseball helped people feel like life could be normal again and there's something to be said for that small contribution. Baseball didn't heal America. America has not healed itself to this day. It was simply there. People took some solace in that fact.

In 2002, baseball does not grind to a halt to commemorate the anniversary. Instead, in the midst of many memorials and vigils, baseball again offers an escape into familiarity. To everyone's relief, there are no attacks against America. All is quiet. The only incidents marring the day actually help to underscore the normalcy of it all.

In New York, it is revealed that Yankees pitcher David Wells lost two teeth in a brawl with a disgruntled fan. In Milwaukee, Commissioner Bud Selig is involved in a minor traffic accident on his way to a fast food joint. Neither are seriously hurt, which is good news. David Wells got into a fight because he encountered a nut and because he's kind of mouthy. Bud Selig was in a traffic accident because he was in a hurry to chow down. No terrorist agendas. Mouthy people sometimes get punched and hurried people sometimes drive off the road. It's all normal.

Things that count as normal in baseball have, in certain cases, remained unchanged for a hundred years. The role of league intervention in creating an atmosphere of impermanence in Montreal is a good example. In other cases, they are products of radical and painful departures from the game's early history. The racial integration of Major League Baseball stands out in this respect, unquestionably the source of that same city's finest moment in baseball. Normal is always evolving.

> "We don't believe in operating the league ... for the benefit of a couple of clubs who will make money."
> — Sam Lichtenhein, Montreal Royals co-owner, 1917

Montreal's first professional baseball teams came into being because other cities failed to provide appropriate facilities or fan support. Baseball was a tease.

In the 1890s, franchises from Buffalo, Hamilton and Rochester each came to town. In one case, a more desirable location was quickly identified. In another, the league itself had to be shut down. In the case of Rochester, the team only came to Montreal with the understanding that it would shortly be moved to another city. It was harsh treatment for local fans who showed a sincere interest in the game even during uncompetitive seasons.

This resilience earned Montreal a measure of permanence when the Rochester franchise stayed. Professional baseball became a true Montreal institution in the early 1900s when this team, renamed the Royals, was purchased by local investors.

These investors understood that the most pressing issue facing the Royals was the suitability of its stadium. The Royals played at Atwater Park on the grounds of a downtown seminary. It had been battered by fire and its main grandstand needed major repairs. Furthermore, as the seminary barred all baseball games on Sundays, the team had to play some of its home games at a separate location.

The new owners had their eyes on a piece of undeveloped land in the city's east end but, before any serious planning took place towards the construction of a new stadium, they accepted a rent decrease offered by the seminary and stayed. Subsequent years featured more fires along with constant repairs and upgrades. The Royals did not have good luck on their side.

Just three years after taking over the team, the consortium of local owners came apart at the seams. The Royals were perpetual underachievers. Pressure to improve the team's play caused a serious rift among the partners, and it seemed the franchise was marked for failure. When another fire ripped through Atwater Park in 1915, the team's prospects looked grim.

The ownership group strained to hold itself together and the pressure to win was beginning to show. Still, the franchise was afloat. It was enduring. What the Royals discovered they could not survive was the conviction of league officials that Montreal ought to be scrapped as a host city.

By 1917, World War I had created a crisis. Travel was expensive and the pool of available players was dwindling so the league's owners convened to decide whether or not play should continue. In the end, they decided to maintain league operations but that certain cities were too far removed from the rest to make travel affordable. One of those cities was Montreal.

Foreshadowing a decision that would be made almost a century later, owners in Toronto voted along with the majority in favor of dropping Montreal. The Royals were contracted.

There was no professional baseball in Montreal over the next decade but the sport grew in popularity among local enthusiasts and Babe Ruth himself came to town for a home run display that drew thousands of spectators. Montreal mirrored a cross-Canada trend towards the adoption of baseball.

In 1927, wartime hardships eased and, feeling that the foundation for professional baseball was still sound, the same person who brokered the original deal that created the Royals returned to Montreal with an eye towards finding new backers willing to give the game another whirl.

A member of the provincial legislature along with a prominent local investment broker spearheaded a new ownership group, establishing separate managing bodies for the team and the development of a new stadium. It was clear to all that Atwater Park was no longer suitable and the same site that the Royals' previous owners had contemplated buying was still available. The total investment of local financiers approached $2 million. For that sizable sum, the new Royals received a lavish facility.

Located at the intersection of busy streets, nestled into the strict rectangular confines of a typical downtown development site, the new stadium was the envy of teams throughout the league. The Royals were back and playing in style.

Style, without question, was the order of the day. The 1920s were a boom period. Montreal and Toronto were growing and changing. Immigration channeled workers into both cities as the economic momentum that accompanied the war's end created a boundless sense of optimism.

This manifested itself in many ways. Middle class families sunk their savings in stock markets. Confidence in Canada's growth was so strong that people with no trading experience whatsoever fell over themselves trying to secure risky investments. The general optimism was also evident in the physical transformation of the cities and, as always, the federal government was implicated throughout.

In 1923, the Canadian National Railway was established, absorbing almost every other railway into a single entity under federal control. This led to the

Opposite: Bustling St. James Street in Montreal (1920) before a continental Depression stunned the national economy and ruined thousands of families (Rice Studios / Library and Archives Canada / PA-030615).

centralization of all their offices into one facility in Montreal. As a result, two plans came into effect. The first was to build a new Central Station. The second was to redevelop the sites made obsolete by the consolidation of the rail lines.

Together, these plans completely changed the face of downtown Montreal. In fact, the current skyline of the city core owes much of its character to buildings that were eventually erected on these sites.

Though planning and construction would not be completed for over twenty years, Place Ville Marie, the Queen Elizabeth Hotel, the CIL Tower, the Stock Exchange and CIBC Building were all erected on sites made available by federal consolidation of the rail industry. These are Montreal landmarks that introduced the multi-purpose, high-rise character of Montreal's downtown core and moved the city's business district away from the old commercial port.

Not that the port was any less essential to Montreal's economy or any less a focal point for political attention. During the 1920s, it expanded beyond the historic harbor towards naturally deep waters along the eastern waterfront. Facilities were upgraded to accommodate specialized cargo such as petroleum and coal. The port changed with the times, as much a key to the city's prosperity as ever.

Officials in Ottawa couldn't help but be drawn to port activities. They were part of a grand new vision. Despite the stability of existing activity in Montreal, federal leaders wanted to change the very nature of shipping in Canada by expanding the waterway that connected the Great Lakes to the St. Lawrence River.

This was a dubious proposal in the eyes of Montreal's magnates because it promised to redirect business to Toronto. There was little they could do to prevent the idea from taking shape, however, because the federal government had already taken over the port's managing body.

Similar forces were at play in Toronto. The federal government directed millions of dollars towards the expansion of port facilities along the waterfront. This was generally accepted as necessary to the viability of distribution activities through which Toronto linked eastern and western Canada together. It also supported the broader federal agenda pertaining to the St. Lawrence Seaway.

Changes in downtown Toronto mirrored the transformation in Montreal as well. Less a product of federal decisions and business consolidation, Toronto was clearly taking on the character of a high-rise metropolis.

In 1929, the Canadian Pacific Railway, standing alone as the only such operation not under the direct control of the newly amalgamated federal corporation, built the Royal York Hotel. In 1931, the Bank of Commerce opened its flagship office tower, the tallest such building in the world at the time. Downtown Toronto, moving away from the shops and piers connected to the old harbor, boasted new structures comparable to the most glamorous on earth.

The Royal York Hotel (1930) not only stood as a symbol of Toronto's prosperity, it also signaled the city's growing aspiration to world-class status (Canada Department of Interior / Library and Archives Canada / PA-043864).

Toronto and Montreal were also becoming the hubs of expanding regions. This was a phenomenon for which neither city was especially well prepared.

Both were still organized as amalgams of manufacturing, financial and residential districts around traditional downtown cores. Few resources were committed to planning development beyond the old city. Frequent calls for the creation of plans to manage this growth were not heeded with great seriousness in either case.

Montreal, especially, featured lax development controls. As early as 1909, an organization called the City Improvement League was created to promote the concept of a general plan for the city. The need for such leadership was underscored a year later when a massive tract of north-end land was purchased for the development of railway terminals and a residential enclave that came to be known as the town of Mount Royal.

The town's plan featured winding roads and diagonal avenues slicing through a loose grid of streets radiating out from a large open space. This cut the district off from the rest of Montreal and created a confusing network of odd angles for people trying to move between the two. City officials had little recourse to challenge the plan. The land was sold in good faith and the developer had almost free reign.

In 1921, the charter for the city of Montreal was amended to allow for the establishment of a planning commission to take more direct control over these types of projects. It would be twenty years before an actual planning department was formed. In that time, towns and boroughs surrounding Montreal expanded with little coordination.

The legacy left behind by early efforts at city planning is better in Toronto. Officials made more sincere attempts at controlling development much earlier than their counterparts in Montreal.

Toronto shared many of Montreal's core challenges. Development in outlying areas as well as the city proper was proceeding without comprehensive coordination. The whole city was characterized by problems related to transportation. Streets were too narrow. Streetcars couldn't keep up with the number of passengers. Calls for street widening and a subway system were regularly heard.

As early as 1912, Toronto endorsed measures aimed at bringing this under control. By implementing the City and Suburbs Act, officials put developers under the scrutiny of the provincial government. Any new project located within the boundaries of a specified urban area became subject to the approval of the province. There were few clear guidelines upon which the province could judge such proposals. Few had a clear idea of what city planners ought to do but most agreed that something had to be done.

Such was the state of Canada's two cosmopolitan rivals when the bubble burst. Scrambling to bring unchecked growth under control, they depended on the health of traditional industries to keep themselves afloat and were completely blind-sided by a crash that took down the entire continental economy.

Stock markets are fickle things because at their heart are nervous humans whose livelihoods depend on trends that are in constant flux. When everyone is buying, woe is the trader who misses out. The same is true of a selling spree. Traders whip each other into frenzies. This is what happened in 1929.

Traders started dumping stocks that they felt were overvalued, in part, due to the enormous investment corporations had made in real property that had nothing to do with production capacity. Once this started, the other traders couldn't resist. Sell, sell, sell. The price of stocks fell through the floor. The value of massive corporations disappeared. The savings of whole families were gone. The Great Depression caught everyone by surprise.

For two cities dependent upon the shipping, processing and distribution of goods this was totally crippling. Rail yards and port facilities fell idle. Factories closed their doors. It was a desperate period. Toronto and Montreal both took it on the chin.

A year prior to the crash, the total value of construction activity in Toronto peaked at $50 million, which is significant because municipal revenues were generated primarily through the collection of property taxes. When the Depression took hold, the value of development activity tumbled to just $4 million, leaving the city with almost no revenue at a time when demand for services was at its highest point ever.

Things were no better in Montreal. Though its budget was marginally less dependent upon property taxes, other income came from a form of personal tax that was no more reliable with masses of people out of work. Between 1930 and 1934, the City of Montreal carried a $270 million debt. This drove Montreal into bankruptcy and placed it under the administrative control of the provincial government.

In the midst of so much desperation, some people still made their personal fortunes. Certain personalities always see opportunity in even the bleakest days and those carrying enough capital will always turn money into more money. Such was the case with Jean-Charles Trudeau.

During the Great Depression, one of the few commodities valuable enough to sell at a profit was fuel. Trudeau owned service stations that drew the attention of a massive oil company eager to cut out middlemen. Trudeau sold his holdings for millions, turning the Depression into a family fortune that would eventually pay for his son, Pierre, to become prime minister.

His wealth also allowed Jean-Charles Trudeau to invest in the Montreal Royals at a time when the franchise was, once again, on the verge of collapse. The financiers who'd paid $2 million to bring the franchise back to Montreal and build a lavish new stadium at Lorimier Grounds were no more insulated against the effects of the Depression than other businessmen. The team owed tens of thousands in unpaid taxes and was on the verge of defaulting on its stadium mortgage. The Royals needed cash. In 1933, Trudeau provided some of that cash.

This was the first of two maneuvers that helped keep the Royals afloat. Along with an injection of capital from new investors such as Trudeau, the Royals also negotiated a deal that allowed them to stock the team's lineup with quality young players without having to pay a penny of their salaries.

A formal partnership was established with Major League Baseball's Brooklyn Dodgers. In 1938, the Royals changed their team color to blue and officially became a Dodgers affiliate.

Back on sound footing, the Royals' fortunes started turning around just as the worst years of the Depression subsided. Though it took only a few days to tear the continental economy to shreds, the gradual return to form at the end of the 1930s was a slow process. Businesses were effectively starting over from scratch.

Little wonder that, during the 1940s, Minister of Everything Clarence Howe didn't see much value in free competition while the federal government was preparing to meet its World War II commitment. Confronted with the enormous task of delivering planes, trucks, artillery and supplies to the front by marshalling an economy still putting itself back together, Howe set about remolding Canadian industry into a form that suited his most immediate needs. This, as it turned out, created an indomitable industrial powerhouse out of Toronto.

Toronto and Montreal continued to grow and neither would be prepared for the impact of the automobile, which changed the face of cities following World War II. The stunning success of new neighborhoods like the prototype Don Mills suburb in Toronto forever held cities hostage to the demands of millions of car owners. Despite these shared challenges, the decline of Montreal began during this period.

Happily, Montrealers could not have recognized the status to which their city had been relegated at the time. Instead, Montreal was thrust into the international spotlight by a daring experiment that created a sensation across the entire continent and literally changed the face of professional sports.

World War II was a wake-up call in many ways. The realization, for example, that Nazi Germany had devised and implemented a system aimed at the total extermination of the Jewish people had such a profound impact on European and North American culture that, in philosophical circles, it called the very legitimacy of reason itself into question. On a more concrete level, in America, it contributed to a crisis over the miserable treatment of black people in a country that had sacrificed so many lives in overthrowing the Nazis. The American conscience was challenged by a disconnect between the role of its soldiers in opposing cruelty and oppression overseas, and the tradition of cruelty and oppression that still thrived in the United States.

In baseball, this manifested itself in the ongoing prohibition against black players participating in the major leagues. To some, segregation was a small part of the larger system of injustice. To others, it was one of the last remaining traditions through which white and black people were rightly kept separate from one another. America was painfully torn. For one organization in major league baseball, the question had a very practical dimension that couldn't be ignored.

The head of the Brooklyn Dodgers, a man named Branch Rickey, championed the idea that baseball was turning its back on the largest untapped source of talent available by keeping blacks out of the major leagues. In 1945, Rickey transformed his theory into stunning reality by presenting Jackie Robinson with the awesome challenge of breaking baseball's color barrier.

Citing the need for Robinson to hone his skills in the minor leagues before considering a jump to the Dodgers, but also acknowledging that Robinson's transition might be facilitated by playing in a city where his presence was not likely to create riots in the streets, Rickey sent him to Montreal. The Royals frequently traveled down to the United States so Robinson was not completely insulated against the controversy that his presence generated but Montreal was judged to be a comparatively safe refuge.

This played out during Robinson's first weeks with the Royals. He started the 1946 season on the road where racial slurs and cruel taunting followed him daily. When the team finally returned to Montreal, Lorimier Stadium had a carnival atmosphere. Robinson would later describe it as "love at first sight."

The Royals were a great team in 1946 and Robinson led by example. He was the league's best hitter and thrilled fans with unmatched base stealing ability.

The affection between Montrealers and their adopted team leader ran so deep that, during the playoffs that summer, once the Royals returned home from Louisville where Robinson was cursed at every turn, locals taunted the Louisville side relentlessly in retaliation. The fact that fans in Montreal had come to Robinson's defense inspired him to observe afterwards that he might have been happy to have played his entire career there.

In fact, Branch Rickey had been wrong about the likelihood of Robinson's presence creating riots in Montreal. Following the Royals' championship victory over Louisville, Robinson was called back to the field by fans who'd climbed down from the stands to cheer and sing until he came out.

The jubilant crowd rushed and lifted him into the air. That moment, when fans carried Jackie Robinson on their shoulders around a stadium that had been electrified by his presence, was Montreal's finest in baseball.

> "It was probably the only day in history that a black man ran from a white mob with love instead of lynching on its mind."
> —*Journalist Sam Malton, on Robinson's encounter with Royals' fans, 1946*

It is a long, mournful fall to the waning days of the 2002 season. In the latter half of September, while the Expos struggle to reach .500, they learn that a lease extension has been negotiated at Olympic Stadium and that Commissioner Bud Selig has decided to keep the team in Montreal for one more summer. He cannot make up his mind about where the franchise will be moved.

Washington, capital of the United States, already has a contingency plan in place for the speedy renovation of an aging football stadium to accommodate the Expos on short notice. Portland, on the West Coast, is home to many deep-pocketed Internet entrepreneurs who abandoned their own companies in time to avoid the stock market correction that ruined thousands of investors. The necessary corporate culture is in place to make baseball work.

If either of these cities agrees to pay for a new stadium, the deal will be done. Until then, the Expos will remain in Montreal and local fans will continue to be lambasted for not supporting "their" team.

With attendance at Olympic Stadium falling into the hundreds, fans in Montreal will continue to be derided as the worst in the league despite the fact that it is absurd to ask them to support a franchise run by its competitors who keep it in place only for lack of a clear idea where to send it next. Furthermore, though Olympic Stadium is occasionally close to empty for baseball games, at least the few people who attend Expos games aren't there to cause trouble.

Stadium security has dogged the league since last year's terrorist attacks made everyone in America feel vulnerable. When fans raced onto the field and accosted stars in Boston and New York early this season, eyebrows were raised. When a pipe bomb exploded in the stands of a Cleveland Indians home game later in the summer, security was once again thrust under a microscope.

Fans in Montreal are often told to be more like those in Chicago, where attendance is not a problem for the Cubs. Few give Expos fans their due when Chicago hosts another of baseball's embarrassing security lapses. The incident involves fans of the White Sox, not the Cubs, but offers a jarring reminder of just how thin security is stretched in major league venues.

Tom Gamboa is a base coach for the Kansas City Royals. When the Royals are batting, Gamboa stands behind the foul line, a few feet beyond the playing field. With the Royals beating Chicago 2–1 at Comiskey Park, Gamboa's proximity to the crowd makes him the target of a freakish assault.

Two shirtless buffoons come charging out of the stands and jump Gamboa for absolutely no reason. They are surely either drunk or stoned because they hardly get any clean shots in against the unprepared base coach before the entire Royals team charges out of the dugout to rain blows down on them. Gamboa escapes with just a minor cut on his forehead. The two idiots are pounded into the dirt by a swarm of players.

It might have been much worse. The drunken attackers were on top of Gamboa before anyone knew what was going on and there was talk afterwards of a knife left behind on the field. The most troubling aspect of the attack is the fact that the Kansas City players were first to come to Gamboa's aid. The entire Royals team was pounding down on the assailants before security intervened.

The summer of 2002 has been unsettling in this respect. Fans running amok have eluded police. There has been a bomb. Now, a coach has been attacked. At a time when the general public most needs to feel protected, baseball stadiums most feel like open targets.

This is just as true in the ballparks of America where a military atmosphere still engulfs most major public events as in Canada, which has not adopted as aggressive an approach in response to the 9/11 catastrophe. SkyDome and Olympic Stadium are accessible facilities, soft targets. Nonetheless, they have not suffered the indignity of hosting any of this summer's most unsettling security breaches. What does this say?

On one hand, it says that even in the midst of America's nationwide security crackdown little can be done to ensure that every facility is absolutely safe at every moment. That's the bad news. There is a silver lining. That is, none of what's taken place this summer has had anything to do with terrorism.

Baseball's biggest security dilemma is the malice of its own fans. There's no telling how many psychos dream of blowing up a major league facility as some freakish statement about American policies overseas. Despite this reality, baseball's real challenge is to convince drunken pranksters to stay in their seats. For the time being, baseball has more to fear from shirtless idiots than jihadists. Maybe things aren't so bad after all.

Accepting that certain terrible risks can't be controlled, and allowing that some people will always fail to understand that their antics are just stupid, baseball fans focus on pennants and individual milestones that add relevance to the games of teams that have already fallen by the wayside. Such is the condition of fans in Toronto and Montreal.

Though Blue Jays pitcher Roy Halladay will not get the chance to reach 20 wins this season, he is still putting the finishing touches on an impressive and surprising campaign. With the schedule winding down, Halladay faces the moribund Baltimore Orioles in an effort to win his 18th game and raise the Blue Jays into third place in their division. For a team that started the summer with a pared down lineup that thrust unproven players into the spotlight, such a finish would be gratifying.

Baltimore puts up a fight in the game's early goings by sneaking a cheap run past Halladay on a fielder's choice. Happily, it doesn't take the Blue Jays long to get back on track as the team's best all-around player flexes some muscle.

Immediately after Baltimore takes its meager lead, Carlos Delgado pounds his 30th home run to put the teams back on even footing. Two innings later, Delgado is at it again, hammering another home run to almost the exact same spot, and catapulting the Blue Jays to a 7–1 advantage.

With this pair of blasts, Delgado becomes the first Blue Jay to ever record five consecutive 100 RBI seasons. General Manager J.P. Ricciardi may not like paying Delgado his massive salary but the affable superstar clearly gets the job done.

Staked to a massive lead by the team's marquee slugger, Halladay cruises to victory. He has made 2002 his breakthrough season while giving the Blue Jays an unexpected foundation upon which to build a solid pitching staff. Behind the Yankees and Red Sox, these Blue Jays will take a third place finish.

In Montreal, Expos outfielder Vladimir Guerrero is a single home run shy of 40 and could become just the fourth player in league history to hit 40 homers and steal 40 bases in a season. Against Jeffrey Loria's Florida Marlins, Guerrero fails to tag his historic blast but the Expos still see a personal milestone reached.

Bartolo Colon gets knocked around by the Marlins. He is far from his best and has to be bailed out by Montreal's offense, a rare departure in Colon's brief tenure with the Expos. He has rarely leaned on the rest of his teammates for help.

Holding an early 2–0 lead, Colon walks home a Florida run then gives up a dog's breakfast of cheap hits and squibbers. By the 4th inning, he is behind 4–2. To his relief, before leaving the game, Colon receives emergency run support and wins a 6–5 decision he probably doesn't deserve.

The win is his 10th since coming over from Cleveland, giving him 20 when combined with those he'd already recorded before the trade. A pitcher will take that 20th win no matter how it comes. The rest of the Expos will gratefully take the win as well, as it propels them back over .500.

The Blue Jays and Expos have little other than these individual honors left to pursue. Each team has an impressive core of young players, a manager that has squeezed respectable results out of modest lineups and an aggressive general manager unafraid of risk and controversy. The franchises continue to parallel one another in all but one respect. The Expos are doomed. The Blue Jays are not.

Despite the relentless chastisement of the league's front office and the sarcasm of clever-dick reporters across the continent, this condition is not the product of a sweeping apathy among Montreal fans. This apathy exists but is not the cause of the Expos' failure.

To properly understand how this actually came about, and why the Blue Jays and Expos are perceived as separate cases when they mirror each other at many levels, it is necessary to look back on a risk taken by a man committed to championing Montreal baseball but who ended up sinking the franchise instead.

"What motivated me, was keeping the Expos in Montreal."
—*Claude Brochu, promoting his personal memoirs, 2002*

The Toronto Blue Jays opened the 1995 season as reigning World Series champions. Less than a year after the Montreal Expos had been the class of a troubled league, and two years removed from Toronto's dramatic win over the Phillies, the Blue Jays were baseball's phantom champs while the Expos were, at best, acknowledged as the biggest victims of a strike that accomplished nothing.

The reason Montreal was in such bad shape is that the Expos' managing partner, a man named Claude Brochu, came to believe that the Expos could not afford to compete in an era of skyrocketing baseball salaries. Rather than re-signing Canadian slugger and future MVP Larry Walker or fireball closer John Wetteland, he allowed both to leave without even trying to lock them into deals. Brochu felt that such players would never pay for themselves by stimulating sustained attendance at Olympic Stadium so he cut them loose.

With his hands tied by an ownership consortium trying to minimize losses on the team, Brochu tried to bend the league to the reality in Montreal. This was a big risk. Rather than invest in players in the hopes of drawing back fans who had responded well in 1994, he slashed payroll so dramatically that the league had no choice but to take notice. The gamble did not pay off.

The Expos won only 66 games that season. In the self-fulfilling logic by which Brochu managed his affairs, the team proved him right by once again generating the league's worst attendance.

There were some positives in that summer. Twenty-three-year-old Pedro Martinez led the pitching staff with 14 wins while 23-year-old Rondell White hit .295. This promise helped stimulate some interest in the team when the following summer rolled around.

The 1996 season started with a series of galactic ka-booms as outfielder Henry Rodriguez enjoyed the most productive spring of any Expo in the team's history. Though he would end the summer with more strikeouts than hits, a dubious stat, he still managed to crank out 36 home runs and 103 RBIs. Right behind him was Moises Alou who rebounded from a gruesome ankle injury the year before to hit 21 home runs of his own. It was a team of new faces and much promise.

Montreal won 88 games in 1996, a major improvement from the previous summer. It was not enough to dissuade Claude Brochu. More cuts were on the way.

While the Expos lost what little established talent remained in Montreal, the Blue Jays were buying players and trying to set themselves straight. Carlos Delgado emerged as the unquestioned foundation for the team's future by hitting 25 home runs. He and Shawn Greene made fans forget that the team's collective offense was one of the league's worst, in the same way that Cy Young pitcher Pat Hentgen made them forget that the rest of the pitching staff was usually missing in action. The Jays lost 88 games in '96, the same number of games that the Expos won, but there was still optimism founded primarily on the fact that Blue Jays owners were prepared to spend money.

Toronto coaxed Roger Clemens to come north of the border in 1997. Clemens followed up Pat Hentgen's Cy Young season with one of his own and, if not for the repeated failings of a Blue Jays offense, the team might have been a winner. It was another disappointing summer at SkyDome but fans were still streaming into the stadium to watch stars who were coming rather than going.

Not so, in Montreal. In a way, Expos players were dashing Brochu's plans because so many quality prospects came into their own under manager Felipe Alou that it was difficult to really gut the team.

The Expos were in limbo. They weren't good enough to challenge for pennants. They were nowhere near bad enough to self-destruct completely. The final straw in this backbreaking process was Pedro Martinez.

In 1997, the 25-year-old Martinez was awesome. He recorded 17 wins, which is nothing special. His eye-popping ERA of 1.90, 13 complete games and 300 strikeouts made him the game's most fearsome fastballer.

The Expos featured a quality lineup, with youngsters Vladimir Guerrero and Jose Vidro competing for spots in the lineup and four separate hitters registering 20 or more home runs. Martinez still stole the show. He won the Cy Young award and was immediately shipped to Boston where he would continue to be baseball's most dominating pitcher.

This was Claude Brochu's masterstroke. He jettisoned Martinez so quickly that it left no doubt the Expos would balk at ever spending any money to keep a star player. If they weren't even prepared to try to keep Martinez, who could they be expected to keep?

These tactics were totally incompatible with Major League Baseball moving forward. Owners would continue to spend as much as they wanted, making it affordable for themselves by refinancing the entire league through public stadium subsidies.

In short, the Expos would be expected to spend along with the big boys and replace Olympic Stadium with taxpayer money. Claude Brochu could not respond to either imperative.

By 1998, it was all going wrong. The Expos started bringing up young players too soon because there weren't enough bodies to fill all the roster spots.

Jose Vidro is a good example. Promoted from AAA at the age of 22, the future All-Star struggled just to show he belonged and, if not for the faith that Felipe Alou showed in his potential, might never have established himself.

The Expos were hanging on by the skin of their teeth. A famously deep farm system was stretched to the limit. The entire franchise was worn down to the bone.

This did not go unnoticed by officials at the major league front office. Montreal was becoming a serious problem, an embarrassment. The Expos needed to triple their payroll and figure out a way to build themselves a new ballpark.

How could Brochu have been expected to make this happen? In 1998, he had to convince skeptical governments that funding a downtown stadium was a good public investment. He had no credibility because his whole platform leading up to that point was about telling people that baseball wasn't working in Montreal. Now he had to turn around and argue that it was in the best interests of government to pump $300 million into that business.

The sad part, if history is any guide in such things, is there was no reason to believe politicans would turn their backs on the Expos. Certain pieces were in place for baseball to come out ahead in Montreal.

A former federal property abutting Montreal's downtown core had been tabbed for redevelopment. Ottawa had even commissioned a special subcommittee to study the impact of major sports franchises on local economies that, amazingly, concluded such franchises were good investments. The problem was that Claude Brochu could not turn these positives in his favor. He had spent years trashing his own team. Decision-makers needed a reason to get involved. Brochu could not give them one.

Even this might have worked in the Expos' favor. The provincial government in Quebec almost always takes advantage of an opportunity to show up the federal government by supporting a local initiative that the feds turn down. They love that. If the government of Quebec had seen the Expos as a vehicle through which they could upstage Ottawa, the premier would have signed the checks out of his own bank account. Instead, the Quebec government mimicked the federal government's stance. It would not subsidize millionaires using tax revenues.

Frankly, that's a perfectly responsible position for governments to take given tight budgets and scrutiny. However, public institutions in Canada have always struggled to insulate themselves against the advances of millionaire friends. The wise decision to ignore pleas for stadium financing to rescue the Expos was made possible by the disconnection between Claude Brochu and the political leaders he'd done nothing to molly-coddle.

If Brochu had not put himself in such an impossible position, the stadium could have been built. Claude Brochu told leaders in Ottawa and Quebec that they'd better ante up the cash, or else. In response, they simply called his bluff. "Or else, what?"

The 1998 baseball season saw two opposing initiatives unveiled with respect to the Expos: the re-engineering of Expo ownership to replace Brochu and a plan to relocate the Expos to Washington. By that point, Brochu didn't care which one moved forward. So far as he was concerned, he'd done everything possible to save Montreal baseball and now he was getting out.

On the field, Montreal looked every bit like a team that was waiting for the axe to fall. The Expos generated the fewest hits and runs in the National League while building their 65–97 record and falling to dead last in home attendance. The only bright spots were Dustin Hermanson on the mound and Vladimir Guerrero at the plate. Neither could turn the attention of fans and media away from the sinking ship they were all witnessing.

In Toronto, baseball was being steered in a different direction. The Blue Jays, unafraid to put big league money towards big league talent, turned 20 wins from Roger Clemens into an 88-win season that seemed to be pointing to playoff contention right around the corner. Carlos Delgado and Shawn Greene hit 73 home runs between them and the team acquired Jose Canseco as designated hitter, generating another 46 home runs all on his own. They were a potent long-ball threat, capable of turning any game around with one swing of the bat.

Just as the Blue Jays looked like they were about to achieve something great again, Clemens packed his bags and moved to New York where he would help keep the Blue Jays out of the playoffs for years to come. Over the next two summers, the young talent in Toronto's lineup would continue to develop. The front office paid them like major league stars while trying to make up for the loss of Roger Clemens by bringing in pitchers like David Wells and Joey Hamilton. It didn't work and, by 2000, the Blue Jays were a perennial third place team.

As it became more and more clear that the team could achieve nothing better than mediocrity, attendance at SkyDome started to feel the pinch, falling to near the bottom of the American League. Between 1998 and 2000, the Jays lost approximately $60 million and suddenly found themselves looking for new owners to right the ship.

Still, needing a new owner to address massive financial losses is better than lacking the basic resources necessary to create those losses in the first place. No matter how bad things got in Toronto, they were always worse in Montreal.

The crazy thing is that the Blue Jays and Expos might have been working together at this stage. Though Major League Baseball is a privileged monopoly, it is still a cross-border industry that is supposed to follow the dictates of the North American Free Trade Agreement (NAFTA). Under NAFTA, governments are not allowed to give massive subsidies or tax breaks to domestic businesses, making it impossible for international competitors to get by.

The Blue Jays and Expos might have brought an enormous NAFTA challenge forward against all the American cities and states that had provided their baseball teams with free and tax-free stadiums in the preceding decade. They didn't do anything of the sort.

Finally, a glimmer of hope shone for the Expos. The Quebec government made a major concession on the topic of a downtown stadium project, offering to use funds from its existing tourism budget to cover interest on a stadium loan so long as Claude Brochu could be convinced to accept a buyout. Neither the province nor the feds would have anything to do with Brochu.

The future of the franchise depended on getting him out. He wouldn't go away until the other owners paid him what his portion of the team would be worth if the franchise were sold and moved to Washington. Under these desperate circumstances, the emergence of a potential buyer named Jeffrey Loria was a sensation in Montreal. If Brochu could be broughtout and Loria brought in, maybe the franchise could be saved. At least, that's what people thought.

In truth, the damage had already been done. The fact that Loria ended up being the team's final false savior stands as a sad but mere sidebar.

Such is the story of how the Expos fell to the mercy of Commissioner Selig. It has nothing to do with the sustainability of the local market and everything to do with the relationship between the franchise, the league and the realities of stadium financing in Canada.

On the final day of the 2002 season, there are two stories playing out at Olympic Stadium. Win or lose, the end of this game will mark the first winning season for the Montreal Expos since 1996. They come in at 82–79, guaranteeing a better than .500 record.

Because the winning record is sewn up, the game's second storyline becomes that much more compelling. Vladimir Guerrero still needs one more home run to join Barry Bonds, Alex Rodriguez and Jose Canseco as the only players to hit 40 homers and steal 40 bases in a season.

Last night, Guerrero was teased by baseball history. He lifted a high fly ball into right field and trotted around first base only to see the ball bounce off the very top of the outfield wall and ricochet back into play. He literally came within an inch, maybe less, of clearing the wall. Instead, it was the longest single of his season.

Guerrero is also mocked in his last attempt to hit his big shot as well. After hitting a double and a few fly balls through the first 7 innings, Guerrero comes up for his last at-bat with the Expos comfortably in the lead at 7–2. With no one on base, and the game all but over, Guerrero has nothing but the record to worry about.

For a player who swings at so many pitches that the strike zone becomes irrelevant, it's a rare moment when he bothers to check his swing. In this case, he needs just the right swing on just the right pitch to get the ball out of the park. With this in mind, Guerrero holds off a two-strike offering. The umpire calls him out.

In a game already decided, that has nothing to do with the standings or the playoffs, the umpire shows Guerrero who's boss by calling him out on a check-swing. Olympic Stadium fans litter the field with debris and the game is postponed for several minutes. Guerrero misses the 40–40 club.

Last night, he missed it by an inch. Today, he misses it on a judgment call by an umpire recording one last punch-out before going home for the winter.

The Expos eventually win 7–2 and finish with an 83–79 record, second in the National League East behind the Atlanta Braves. These Expos now face an off-season in limbo. It is unclear whether the team will be moved, the outcome of fraud charges against the league is still unknown and no public stadium plan has emerged in any of the candidate cities trying to lure the franchise.

Even if the team stays in Montreal several Expos are due for salary arbitration, which could raise the team's payroll 10 percent to 20 percent. Since the league has stated that the Expos will not be allowed to increase payroll under any circumstances, this suggests that there could be a fire sale. Par for the course for the Montreal Expos.

One final note on the 2002 regular season. The Montreal Expos finish the year dead last in National League attendance, having drawn 812,545 fans to Olympic Stadium. Second to last are the Florida Marlins, having drawn approximately 500 more fans than Montreal in total. It's a sad state of affairs for Jeffrey Loria's new team.

Even worse, a Florida businessman has admitted to purchasing 15,000 tickets for $1 apiece from Loria himself solely to ensure that the Marlins finished the season with better attendance than the Expos. That's just perfect.

"Where were they?"
—*Phillies manager Larry Bowa, on 10,000 phantom fans in Florida, 2002*

October

"MLB is a good community-building asset ... you can't tell how rich someone is by where they sit ... [except] for the boxes or club seats."
—*Benefits of stadium financing according to the Oregon House Committee, 2001*

One city's failure can be another city's golden opportunity. American towns vying to resuscitate the Expos are banking on this transformation, wagering that the gap between the two extremes can be bridged with public money.

They know what they're getting into. After years of coercing local governments into rash investments, Bud Selig is not giving anything away for free. These baseball hopefuls face a very expensive reality. It's a reality that says a lot about the game's future in Canada because the conditions they are striving to create, the same ones that could save the Montreal Expos today, are conditions through which the Toronto Blue Jays will have to be bailed out in years to come.

Portland wants the Montreal Expos and, since at least 2001, the government of Oregon has debated funneling money into a new stadium to make it happen. This is opposed 10 to 1 by local residents so it's no mystery that a massive "public education" drive is regarded as necessary. One look at what baseball boosters are proposing and it becomes clear why this is so important.

Extraordinarily frank politicians at the state and municipal levels are upfront about conditions that taxpayers will have to accept in order to bring the Expos to Portland. The first is 80 percent public financing for a new stadium.

They fancifully estimate that 80 percent will come to $150 million, meaning the stadium will cost under $190 million. That's impossibly low. Just the same, the other half of their equation is tax-free status for the stadium in perpetuity, which is expected to inject upwards of $50 million into the new team's mid-term operating budget.

They aren't arguing that capital subsidies and property tax exemptions for baseball are good public policy. What they actually say is that such measures are necessary to the competitiveness of a team relocated to their city. This is where the state of Canada's teams becomes an issue.

Canada and the United States are both signatories to the North American Free Trade Agreement (NAFTA), requiring that governments treat foreign businesses only as badly as they treat domestic ones. Baseball gets away with a lot of shady dealing but it can't escape the fact that it is an international industry.

In 1998, the government of Canada convened a sub-committee of Parliament to study the relationship between NAFTA and professional sports. As part of this investigation, the sub-committee was advised that sports franchises stand as investments under chapter 20 of the agreement and that governments may be in violation of NAFTA when they grant subsidies and tax exemptions to local teams.

Political leaders in Toronto, Montreal, Ontario, Quebec and Ottawa could all bring challenges forward and request that U.S. governments either stop doling out this cash or compensate Canadian teams for the bonanza they've been missing. None have intervened. Rather than pursue this kind of trade dispute, they have tested dirty waters.

The government of Ontario has been confronted with the revelation that it willfully covered up a secret agreement with Toronto's hockey, basketball and baseball teams allowing them to avoid millions in taxes each year. Bureaucrats are scrambling to protect high-ranking politicians from the fallout. There's blood on the water. No sooner is this plan exposed than it is hastily withdrawn.

The history of this country has been molded by people adept at making the public believe they want their money to be spent supporting the influential friends of political figureheads. There is really only one piece missing from this age-old puzzle. Baseball is not such a friend.

The league has spent millions lobbying Washington for special regulatory status. It also exerts enormous pressure on local officials to sign stadium deals into law. If a fraction of that investment were directed at finding a new generation of Canadian politicos eager to play the games of America's power elite, baseball could land on solid ground.

These are the unhappy issues that face the Blue Jays and Expos. Billions have already been spent on both teams but Major League Baseball will eventually come looking for more.

SkyDome has a functional life cycle of about 25 years so it's probably got another decade of service left before it needs to be rehabilitated. That is, if team officials don't want to let it run down to the state of Olympic Stadium before making another investment.

Whichever way it goes, Portland's ambitions send a clear message to Canada's incumbents. Short of an enormous NAFTA challenge moving forward, Canadian taxpayers, just like those in Portland, have to learn to accept 80 percent ballpark financing and tax-free status forever. The Expos need it now and the Blue Jays are not far behind.

It's easy to be distracted from these issues as baseball's postseason charges forward. The question of whether the Blue Jays will ever really need the type of lifeline that the Expos are desperate to receive is contentious. Some still think that SkyDome is a modern marvel and that the Blue Jays are many decades away from needing emergency relief, something they already received just three years ago. These questions are obscured by the fleeting excitement of the playoffs' opening games.

"It really got ugly for us."
—*Yankee manager Joe Torre, on defeat at the hands of the Angels, 2002*

Baseball fans have a painful love-hate relationship with the New York Yankees. Most groan at the thought of another free agent signing or lopsided trade working out in the Yankees' favor yet no sooner are the Yankees knocked out of the playoffs than baseball's television ratings drop into the toilet. It's a strange phenomenon.

Some of the horrible ratings that the playoffs generate are tied to broadcast timing. The final innings of most games are played well past midnight and a dedicated fan will routinely be awake into the early hours of the morning. This discourages viewership. Beyond this factor, there are also the Yankees.

In the wild card round, they face a largely unknown Anaheim Angels squad that few expect to advance past the playoff-veteran New York lineup. The Angels are nobody's favorite team. They are not loved as a small budget miracle like the Oakland A's. They are not the chic team-du-jour Minnesota Twins on whose bandwagon many jumped once it became clear they would make the playoffs despite Bud Selig's death sentence. They are every bit the underdog, without any of the romance that comes along with this status.

As such, when the Angels explode for 26 runs over the last three games of their first round series, they do all non-partisan fans a favor by sticking it to the Yanks. For a brief moment, everyone has something positive to say about the Angels. Then they tune out altogether. Once the Yankees are gone, everything else is an anti-climax.

It's unfair to the yeoman-like Angels but television ratings will really fall now that the Yankees are eliminated. Those old enough to stay up won't be bothered, and those so young as to still be on the edge of their seats won't be awake.

"Major League Baseball behaves like Soviets."
—*Sam Minzberg, lawyer for former Expos minority owners, 2002*

The Montreal Expos' margin for error was very slender in 2002. Everything was going to have to go their way if this team hoped to be in the playoffs. Looking back, that margin for error was far too slender.

The heart of the Expos' offense was pumping all year long. Vladimir Guerrero and Jose Vidro hit a combined .325 with 58 home runs and 207 RBIs. Complementing this core, the Expos received solid contributions from some of the supporting cast. Brad Wilkerson, for one, provided a much-needed answer to Montreal's quest for a centerfielder, setting a team record for home runs by a rookie along the way. Unfortunately, the list of hitters who failed to deliver is longer.

Oft-injured third baseman Fernando Tatis hit an underwhelming .225. Shortstop Orlando Cabrera took a step backward. Slowed by injury, catcher Michael Barrett couldn't turn his hot start into anything other than a mediocre year. Cliff Floyd was a total flop. These struggles stalled the momentum created by Guerrero and Vidro. Montreal's offense sputtered when it needed to explode.

It was essential for Expos hitters to explode because the team's pitching never came around. Bartolo Colon was everything the team expected and more. The same holds true for Tohmo Ohka who was not expected to be a key contributor but led the team with 13 wins. As good as that is, Tohmo Ohka cannot lead a team into the playoffs.

Javier Vazquez and Tony Armas Jr. are talented enough to dominate. Together, they won just 22 games. Given a few more wins from these pitchers back when the Expos played a whole month against division rivals, the team might have been in wild card contention. Instead, the combination of good starts scuttled by bad hitting and bad starts at the wrong time for Vazquez and Armas sunk Montreal.

The Expos could be competitive again next season except that several players are eligible for salary arbitration and the team's payroll is going to increase. The Expos are likely to be trimmed.

For their part, the Toronto Blue Jays were just six games under .500 at the close of the season. Few expected them to be so close to breaking even. Once a big-money magnet for free agent talent, the Blue Jays nervously put their fate in the hands of a rookie general manager committed to trimming the fat. That nervousness was transformed into hope for a bright future.

The Blue Jays' offense underwent a transition that the entire organization faced in 2002. Familiar names were shipped out of town, survived by young unknowns and veterans playing on borrowed time. The results were just as mixed.

Carlos Delgado did not have a good year by his standards but those standards are dizzyingly high. He hit .277 with 33 home runs and 108 RBIs. That would be a good season for many players. Raul Mondesi would have sold his soul for those kinds of stats. He was awful prior to being traded to New York, becoming the prototype addition-by-subtraction for Toronto. Jose Cruz should thank his lucky stars that there wasn't a prospect nipping at his heels or he'd have been shipped away too.

Happily, the Blue Jays received enough good news from their core of young prospects that the struggles of over-paid veterans were all but forgotten at season's end. Third baseman Eric Hinske is a good bet to win Rookie of the Year. Centerfielder Vernon Wells became the youngest Jay to record over 100 RBIs. Josh Phelps hit 15 home runs in just three months. Orlando Hudson has already secured his spot at second base. In the short time these players were together, Toronto seemed like a dangerous team again.

The same can't be said for the pitching staff. Far fewer individuals on a retooled staff stepped forward to impress. Needless to say, Roy Halladay did more than his share. His emergence is the single greatest thing to happen since Joe Carter and Roberto Alomar joined the team. He is the hub around which Toronto's pitching staff will turn for years. Beyond Halladay, there are nothing but question marks.

The Jays have the nucleus of a decent club. It remains to be seen how Ricciardi's long-term vision will play out. To most, Toronto looks secure.

Canada's major league teams are both stacked with young talent and saddled with problems on the pitcher's mound. Yet the Expos are in such deep trouble that the league isn't even looking for a local owner while the Blue Jays look to 2003 and beyond with real hope for the future.

The idea that Toronto and Montreal could help each other by supporting a challenge to public subsidies for American franchises under NAFTA does not receive any attention. It is regarded as a concept borne out of the Expos' desperation, having nothing to do with the Blue Jays.

The Expos are not loved enough in Canada to inspire such a showdown. If more people acknowledged that the Blue Jays are one defunct stadium away from joining them, it might be different.

Ten years separate the Blue Jays and Expos. Once SkyDome reaches the end of its life cycle, Canadians will learn whether they have an appetite for public stadium financing. They will also find the same forces that created and settled the centuries-old rivalry between Toronto and Montreal at the heart of it all.

The shame is that there is plenty of time to save the Expos but little hope of mobilizing the necessary will until Toronto is at death's door as well. By that time, it will be too late. Until Toronto feels the heat, Montreal will fend for itself. Even backed by a binding international agreement, this is the inevitable truth.

Trade is an area in which Canada constantly struggles with the competing pressures of deferring to American priorities and asserting an independent stance. Since the Cold War era, the notion of butting heads with the United States has made Canadian officials cringe because it strains the co-dependent relationship these neighbors share. With the rise of Toronto and decline of Montreal, support for such confrontations is generally lacking where the prospect of securing Toronto's success is missing.

> "This great waterway [is] a bond rather than a barrier between Canadians and Americans."
> —*Prime Minister Louis St. Laurent, 1959*

Mackenzie King permanently altered the balance of power in Canada by putting Clarence Howe in charge of the wartime economy. True to tradition, King's impact also expressed itself through the recruitment of new politicians.

In 1941, one of the prime minister's most trusted allies died unexpectedly. He tried to recruit a replacement from within but failed repeatedly. Those turning down the appointment consistently recommended an alternative: Louis St. Laurent.

St. Laurent was a successful lawyer who'd set his sights on early retirement and was reluctant to take the government appointment. The war, as it turned out, was Mackenzie King's trump card. The prime minister insisted that while Canadian soldiers were sacrificing their lives overseas, it was left to St. Laurent to make a contribution at home. St. Laurent agreed to become Minister of justice under the condition that he be relieved of this public office after the war. That's not how events unfolded.

When the war finally ended, St. Laurent was once again convinced that his calling to public service outweighed his calling to retirement. He decided to stay in politics and was immediately thrust into a scandal that ushered in the Cold War era.

For a brief period following World War II, Canada pursued a truly independent voice on the world stage as Louis St. Laurent strove to assert Canada's legitimacy as a neutral intermediary between hostile powers rising—the United States and Soviet Union. In 1946, that legitimacy was dashed when the Canadian government was forced to take action against its own officials spying on behalf of the Soviets.

The scandal was launched when it became clear that St. Laurent had been approached by a would-be defector from the Soviet embassy with evidence of a spy ring operating in Ottawa. Wary of damaging Canada's good relationship with the USSR, St. Laurent did not act on the allegations. Instead, he granted asylum to the whistle-blower and launched an extensive investigation.

This culminated in the arrest of 39 suspected spies and the revelation that Canada was leaking atomic secrets. Suddenly, the idea that Canada was an intermediary between the United States and Soviet Union seemed dangerous. It became impossible for Canada to maintain its neutrality.

Amidst these growing international tensions, Mackenzie King announced that he was stepping down as prime minister. As his last public service to the Canadian people, he once again twisted St. Laurent's rubber arm.

This time, instead of dangling wartime obligations, he dangled the prospect of real power. St. Laurent took the bait and, that same year, won the leadership of his party as well as the general election that followed. The soft-spoken man, dubbed Uncle Louis by supporters, became prime minister.

Canada, as it appears in the early 21st century, came together under Louis St. Laurent. Newfoundland joined the confederation. The trans-Canada highway was built. St. Laurent paid off the war debt and strengthened welfare programs. For all these domestic achievements, his most lasting contribution to Canadian history came in the form of his having accepted the necessity of allying with the Americans.

Canada and the United States are independent nations whose citizens place a high value on the symbolic freedoms they enjoy. Yes, there are contrasts between the neighbors. The Canadian government places a higher premium on public health care and education. The fact that slavery was never institutionalized in Canada is a huge historical distinction. However, the single most significant difference that exists between the allies, formally acknowledged while Louis St. Laurent was prime minister, is that Canada cannot afford for the United States to think of it as a threat.

Such has been the accepted political reality since the spy scandal of 1946 forced the Canadian government to choose sides by joining the United States in all-out war against the Soviets in 1950. The importance of maintaining a strong relationship with the United States turned the Soviets into an enemy for Canada. This same dynamic doesn't work in reverse.

It is irrelevant to the United States whether Canada approves of the countries it chooses for allies. Still, the United States is restricted in its own way by the border it shares with Canada, which represents an ideal staging ground from which the enemies of America could, in theory, wage war.

This is the core of America's firmest yet most seldom acknowledged military obligation. The United States is responsible for defending Canada's borders as well as its own.

During the early years of the Cold War era, this relationship was set in concrete. Canada and the United States were allies, protecting a common land mass against the perceived threat of Soviet aggression. These ties encouraged government officials to pursue stronger economic links as well, literally blasting away barriers that limited trade back and forth across the border.

The city of Montreal prospered throughout its history by offering the shortest shipping route from Europe and, thanks to a network of railway connections, easy access to most industrialized cities in North America. This came about because, though a network of locks and canals had been created to join the Great Lakes, most cargo was too heavy to transport through these shallow waterways. Between the early 19th and mid-20th centuries, commercial shipping to North America frequently involved boats headed to Montreal followed by trains to carry goods into the United States.

In the 1950s, the idea of creating an integrated seaway linking Canada and the United States was promoted by Canadian politicians. It was not a case of Canada deferring to the will of a stronger power. Rather, what makes the proposed St. Lawrence Seaway illustrative for this period is that the Canadian government was so keen to foster economic ties between Toronto and the United States that it pursued the seaway to the detriment of the port in Montreal.

By creating a waterway that passed straight through to America, it would become possible for shippers to circumvent Montreal altogether. Why were Canadian officials so eager to make this a reality? Because they felt the obvious disadvantage to Montreal was offset by the pronounced benefit such a channel would provide to Toronto in its place. The domestic impact was judged as balancing out while the international benefits were regarded as essential to Canadian interests.

The seaway project opened the port of Toronto to direct transport from Europe and promised greater integration with businesses in the United States. It provided Canada's golden city with stronger ties to the country's most important ally.

In 1959, the St. Lawrence Seaway was built. Commercial shipping through Toronto never entirely took hold and the port gradually fell into disrepair but the project had a direct impact on the balance of commercial power in Canada's

Though the St. Lawrence Seaway never turned Toronto (1926) into a North American shipping capital, nothing could stop the city's rise to prominence (Merrilees Collection / Library and Archives Canada / PA-161576).

economy. For decades, this initiative redirected business away from Montreal by allowing international ships to sail past the old port.

Canada's relationship with the U.S. not only influenced the shape of the national economy, it has also impacted the attitudes of its citizens. If such a thing as a national psyche exists in Canada, one of its primary components is a confused preoccupation, equal parts self-congratulation and self-loathing, with how Canada is different from America.

The more integrated the two become, the more people in Canada howl about losing their autonomy. The more exaggerated differences in public policy become, the more they wring their hands at the thought of being in America's doghouse. It is a mixed bag of conflicting emotions.

Stitched into this schizophrenia is a sense that Americans are risk-takers who, in virtue of their willfulness and resources, often succeed where others fail. They seem to get what they want.

This stereotype came into play in Montreal as soon as news started circulating about a rich New Yorker who, drawn rather than repelled by the struggles of the Expos, seemed to believe that committed investment was all that was needed to stabilize the franchise. It was a simple line of reasoning that had been heard before but, coming from a rich American with the resources to back it up, seemed like a revelation. This ushered in the final chapter in Montreal's depressing collapse, and it occurred during a period when the shine of the Blue Jays franchise first started to fade as well.

"No wonder everybody wants to leave Canada."
—*Jeffery Loria, arguing with a flight attendant, 2000*

Throughout 1999, the Montreal Expos were held hostage by Claude Brochu, who wanted to be paid for his share in the team based on the value of healthier franchises. This put the Expos, and newly appointed chairman Jacques Menard, in a delicate position.

No one was going to step forward as an owner in Montreal if they had to pay Brochu based on what the team would be worth in another market. In this bind, the Expos missed repeated deadlines imposed by Bud Selig for breaking ground on a new stadium. They were stuck.

The crisis in Montreal was so severe that few noticed when attendance at SkyDome fell to record lows and the Blue Jays endured financial headaches all their own. The severe hardship of the Expos made it almost impossible to find a new owner. The less severe hardship of the Blue Jays, on the other hand, was a precursor to hundreds of millions of dollars in public write-offs and the sale of the cash-strapped team.

The Expos were broke, would not be bailed out by the Quebec government, could not find a new owner and, by all accounts, were doomed. The Blue

Jays were broke, forced the Ontario government to accept a $300 million loss on SkyDome but successfully courted a new owner and, by all accounts, were on their way to making things work.

When all was said and done, the province of Ontario provided $300 million to the Blue Jays in indirect debt relief for SkyDome: $300 million free and clear.

When fans and journalists debate the divergent fates of the Expos and Blue Jays, wagging fingers at fans in Montreal as the root cause of their team's failure, no one talks about the $300 million the Blue Jays received.

The Blue Jays won two World Series titles. More power to them. Still, the financial restructuring by which the province wrote that debt off its books was critical to keeping the team afloat. Three hundred million dollars? Don't worry about it, Jays.

By 2000, the Blue Jays had a new owner. Media mogul Ted Rogers, trying to capitalize on a cable-sports programming model that Ted Turner pioneered in Atlanta, bought the team. Toronto's marquee media partnership was born.

For a time, it seemed that the Expos were back in business as well. Jacques Menard succeeded in courting an investor he believed was committed to keeping the Expos in Montreal. That investor was Jeffrey Loria who, just a few weeks prior to spring training 2000, formally purchased the team.

Brochu was bought out. Menard stepped down. Loria announced that he would turn the fortunes of the league's most troubled franchise around completely. What happened over the next 18 months was either a case of best intentions going horribly wrong or a case of deliberate fraud aimed at destroying what little credibility the team retained in Montreal.

The list of his decisions in those first months is downright dubious. He appointed his stepson, who had no experience or local contacts, as the team's president with a million dollar salary. He challenged the proposed stadium's only significant sponsor, Labbatt Breweries, to cough up more money. Labbatt walked away from the deal. He changed the design of the stadium, increasing its projected cost. The Quebec government withdrew its financial commitment, and the Expos lost their purchase-hold for an ideal downtown property where the stadium was to be located. Loria dropped all local broadcasters, leaving the team with no radio or TV coverage. Next, he told his partners that he needed cash from them to keep Montreal's team going. If the other investors failed to meet his demands, their shares would revert to him by default. The ownership group descended into chaos.

All this, just as Loria's first season got underway. It was a complete mess. The players, whose acquisitions Loria approved in moves touted as the beginning of a new era, were busts.

Hideki Irabu, for whom the Expos surrendered their best pitching prospects, collected only two wins. Graeme Lloyd suffered a family tragedy and missed the entire season. First baseman Lee Stevens pulled some of his weight with 22 home runs but, in a league where 22 home runs is what contending teams get from middle infielders, this was adequate at best. Loria had added payroll without making the team any better.

Two thousand was also a year of new beginnings in Toronto where the marriage between Blue Jays baseball and Rogers television was officially launched. The good news was that the Jays sent a daunting offense onto the field every day. Carlos Delgado was a triple-crown threat, batting .344 with 41 home runs and 137 RBIs. Five other Blue Jays hit over 20 home runs.

The bad news was that the Blue Jays could rarely keep opponents from putting runs on the board. They did well to finish with a winning record of 83–79.

Where they didn't do well was at the gate. Only four teams in the American League drew fewer fans than the Blue Jays and final attendance figures showed a robust 21 percent drop from the previous season, making 2000 the third consecutive year that attendance had fallen at SkyDome. This translated into huge losses for the new owner.

Things would get worse. Prior to the start of the 2001 season, Buck Martinez was appointed team manager. In fairness, it's not clear that any manager could have succeeded. David Wells had been traded to Chicago in exchange for Mike Sirotka, who would never pitch an inning in Toronto. The team's pitching was mediocre and there were fewer offensive fireworks to strike fear in the hearts of opponents.

The Blue Jays dropped to 80–82, once again near the bottom of the league in home attendance, and lost so much money it became a story in itself. Toronto lost more money than any other team during the biggest money-losing season ever in Major League Baseball. The only factor keeping this failure out of the glaring national spotlight was the even bigger problems facing the Expos.

So much false hope was raised and promptly dashed after Jeffrey Loria took over that, by 2001, the dark clouds over Olympic Stadium churned with more menace than ever. Under the auspices of making the team more competitive, Loria oversaw the acquisition of third baseman Fernando Tatis. The trade was regarded as a high-risk gamble offering the potential for a huge payoff if Tatis could find his way back to good health. Tatis played in only 41 games. Once again, Loria added payroll without making the team any better.

Montreal won 67 games, compounding what had already been the worst sequence of losing seasons in team history. If this didn't spell disaster, Loria made sure the coffin was nailed shut by firing Felipe Alou in mid-season. After that, Loria couldn't have stayed in Montreal. Expos fans hated him.

With both teams posting losing records, and empty seats plaguing Olympic Stadium and SkyDome, the Expos and Blue Jays had a rough go of it in 2001. Toronto's hopes had been pinned on an ambitious scheme devised by an aggressive entrepreneur, made viable by debt relief provided by the government.

Montreal's hopes were dashed by an owner who held no sway in local politics and could not generate any enthusiasm for a publicly funded stadium. This is all consistent with the history and character of the cities.

The only players who seemed to be missing were the feds but this perceived absence is just an illusion. By that time, Canada's political history had taken another critical turn.

For the first time since confederation, a prime minister had recaptured the control that was once wielded so effortlessly by John Macdonald himself. It is the single greatest failing of individuals running the Blue Jays and Expos during this period that they did not react to this shifting landscape.

The rivalry between these cities may have been settled but the same dynamics that brought it about two centuries earlier were still in place. In fact, they had stormed back to the fore.

While Major League Baseball twisted Toronto and Montreal into knots, the political balance of power in these cities underwent another significant change. The eventual rise of the most powerful leader in Canadian history would bind the history of their rivalry and the future of baseball together.

"Produce one line, one word that shows I was ever against Quebec."
—*John Diefenbaker, 1964*

Like all prime ministers, Louis St. Laurent discovered that the same issues he relied upon to secure power could be turned into ammunition for his political opponents. The St. Laurent government moved Canada out of its coveted position as mediator between the United States and the Soviet Union, choosing to ally as closely with the Americans in Cold War politics as in trade. This was perceived in some circles as a threat to Canada's traditional relationship with the Old World in England and France.

Enter John Diefenbaker, a lawyer from Saskatchewan who ran for a seat in public office in 1925, 1926, 1929, 1933 and 1938 but lost every time. He circulated in a political environment that included prominent anti-immigrant and anti-French lobbies. The persistent would-be politician brazenly carried this checkered baggage with him to Ottawa after finally winning a seat in the House of Commons in 1940.

By that time, Diefenbaker had become leader of the opposition. He would retain this role in federal politics until 1956 when the cracks in St. Laurent's armor finally began to show.

Though Canadians generally have little regard for true democracy, stubbornly sticking to party allegiances and considering a vote wasted unless it is cast for a winning candidate, they don't like their political leaders to stick this fact in their faces. When St. Laurent closed debate on a controversial proposal in Parliament, and when this became a hot-button issue in the national media, he came off as out of touch with average Canadians. This concern was amplified in 1956 when bickering between England and France, along with military action by Israel, generated a serious crisis in Egypt over control of the Suez Canal.

St. Laurent's secretary of external affairs, Lester Pearson, intervened and famously proposed using Canadian soldiers to establish a peacekeeping force in the region, thereby setting a precedent that the United Nations would pursue for the next 50 years. Louis St. Laurent, weary of the bickering Old World powers, did not improve his public stature in the affair.

Average Canadians, who'd been brought up on the idea that the roots of their country and culture traced back to the same places that St. Laurent was dismissing, didn't know what to think. John Diefenbaker was there to tell them.

In the election of 1957, Dief the Chief made the prime minister out to be an arrogant elitist whose presence in Ottawa was an insult to the founding peoples of the country. Diefenbaker turned St. Laurent's weariness with England and France into a question of national pride and voters went for it.

Louis St. Laurent was narrowly defeated in an election that most figured he would win in a landslide. John Diefenbaker had seized power.

Anyone paying attention to the lessons of Canadian history could not have been surprised by what happened next. Diefenbaker followed up his election platform with policies that flew in the face of his campaign.

The English and French roots of Canada's identity? Diefenbaker liked to make a big deal out of the fact that he was the first leader in Ottawa with neither English nor French roots and made it his personal mission to promote a vision of Canada that abandoned such distinctions.

Some genuinely good things came out of this position. First Nations, for example, were finally given the chance to vote. His policies also made it easier for immigrants to understand themselves as truly Canadian citizens with a real place in the national culture. His policies weren't necessarily negative, they just had nothing to do with the platform that got him elected.

Naturally, there were some negative consequences. The French in Quebec weren't excited to learn that their heritage had nothing to do with Canadian culture anymore. In fact, they were quite put out by the news.

Diefenbaker's timing couldn't have been worse. At the time of Diefenbaker's ascendance to power, French Quebecers were wallowing near the very bottom of the socio-economic spectrum.

No one in Canada has ever had it as bad as the First Nations but no one has ever come as close as the French in Quebec. Least educated. Most poorly paid. Least access to public services. Lowest proportion of industry ownership. Most under-represented in the public service. These things held true inside Quebec itself where the French constituted a majority of the population.

If the prime minister wanted to help Canada's most underprivileged he'd have done well to have paid some attention. This wasn't part of his vision for equality in Canada.

Diefenbaker's term in office was a crucial period in Quebec's history as masses of people discovered not only one another in urban centers such as Montreal but also that, between them, they shared great pride in their francophone heritage. It was a watershed period for Quebecois culture.

There were pressing new demands for better education and greater business opportunities for French Quebecers, along with the insistence that the language become more accepted in the corporate community. It was the Quiet Revolution and, with John Diefenbaker in Ottawa, it gathered a momentum that would forever change the face of Canadian politics by seriously calling the status of Quebec within the federation into question.

Busying himself with condemnations of communism at the United Nations, the promotion of nuclear disarmament and the introduction of a Bill of Rights that established his reputation as a champion of freedom around the world, Diefenbaker simply ignored the question of Quebec, setting it aside for successors like Lester Pearson and Pierre Trudeau. By the time leaders such as Pearson and Trudeau took over, the question had been transformed into a full-blown crisis.

John Diefenbaker was not the prime minister who succeeded in reclaiming the role in Canadian cities that was held by John Macdonald as a matter of course. However, by punting the question of Quebec to successors, he opened the door for it to happen. If Diefenbaker had not allowed the Quiet Revolution to evolve into crisis through inaction, if he'd taken the question of rising nationalism in Quebec more seriously, Canada might have never come to know Jean Chrétien.

> "The art of politics is ... a survival game played under the glare of lights."
> —*Jean Chrétien, 1985*

When Diefenbaker abandoned federal politics in 1967, he not only dumped the Quiet Revolution onto Lester Pearson's shoulders, he also opened the door for a populist politician who became the single most powerful leader in Canadian history. Though Pearson was a revered international statesman and his successor, Pierre Trudeau, a flamboyant icon, the future of the federal government and its role in cities like Toronto and Montreal would be shaped by a seemingly low-profile backbencher named Jean Chrétien.

Chrétien entered federal politics in 1963, overcoming long odds to defeat a popular incumbent and unexpectedly find himself as an anonymous MP in Ottawa. Chrétien quickly learned that his success hinged on being immune to the whims of Canada's fickle electorate.

He accomplished this by transforming himself into an effective manipulator of the machinery of government. As such, when Pierre Trudeau took power from Lester Pearson it didn't hurt Chrétien at all. Trudeau needed bureaucracy manipulators as much as anyone and Chrétien was game.

Over the next 12 years, Chrétien would propose a sweeping overhaul of federal policies related to First Nations, would oversee the day-to-day finances of the entire government and dabble in the national economy as minister of both industry and finance. In 1980, he and his boss came face to face with the separatist movement that could no longer be ignored in Quebec.

The very fact that Pierre Trudeau was faced with this question was, to the prime minister, irksome in itself. He was no great sympathizer of Quebec's demands. Though a Quebecer himself, Trudeau made his living trumpeting the greatness of Canadian diversity, within which French Quebecers were a minority. Inside Quebec, they wanted to be treated like the majority they were. Quebec's core demands flew in the face of Trudeau's whole vision for Canada.

In close collaboration with Chrétien, Pierre Trudeau won the 1980 referendum by proposing a compromise. Quebec wanted more power? Fine. Ottawa would be prepared to discuss constitutional reform so long as Quebec voted against separation. It was a winning strategy. The only problem was that, after the referendum victory, Trudeau had to deal with the expectation that he was actually going to retool the constitution.

Taking a typically aggressive approach, Trudeau announced that he was going to amend the constitution and that the provinces could play a part or not. This came to a head in 1981 when he faced a coalition of provinces, including Quebec, which opposed his framework for acknowledging the status of French-Quebec within Canada.

Quebec's collusion with this so-called Group of Eight eventually broke down as Premier René Lévesque waffled over whether to side with the other provinces against Trudeau or side with Trudeau against the other provinces. In one week that changed the course of Canadian history, Lévesque flipped to one side then flopped back to another and the political fallout led to Quebec's permanent isolation.

Without advising the other members of the Group of Eight, Lévesque publicly announced that Quebec had decided to back the prime minister. Eight days later he mysteriously announced that he'd been betrayed by the Group of Eight provinces and, in an expression of pure desperation, compared this supposed offense to Nazi Germany's infamous "Night of the Long Knives." It created a hailstorm of controversy that cast the province of Quebec outside the negotiations altogether.

Pierre Trudeau simply allowed his referendum foe to sink into political exile. The Canadian constitution was amended without Quebec's consent, an oddity that would resurface whenever the question of Quebec's status in

Canada was raised, and would also be the focus of another enormous constitutional review ten years later.

Emboldened by his insider role in these successes, Jean Chrétien made the ultimate power grab when Pierre Trudeau retired in 1984. Unfortunately, another strong candidate also had designs on replacing the outgoing prime minister.

John Turner was a typical fed, recruited into politics by Clarence Howe himself. When Trudeau stepped down, many pegged Turner as his natural successor. Chrétien, who'd won his first seat in Parliament by defeating a heavily favored foe, took the challenge.

What Chrétien didn't realize was that Pierre Trudeau was behind the scenes bolstering Turner's campaign. This intervention sank Chrétien's bid and represented, in his eyes, a truly bitter betrayal. He withdrew from politics altogether.

John Turner took control of Trudeau's party and accepted the worst job in representative democracy. He replaced a controversial 16-year incumbent. By 1984, Canadian voters were eager for a change.

Turner felt he represented that change and, though there was still time left on the mandate he assumed as prime minister, opted to call a snap election. He suffered a devastating loss. Watching from the sidelines, Chrétien must have been shaking his head.

John Turner went from prime minister to opposition leader in the blink of an eye. Shell shocked by the abruptness of this massive blunder, he might have backpedaled out of the spotlight. That wouldn't have suited his personality. Instead, Turner went on the offensive and tried to rebuild his party by tearing strips off the person who beat him in the snap election of 1984: Brian Mulroney.

Mulroney's policies represented the ultimate realization of the realignment that Louis St. Laurent had initiated during the Cold War. With Mulroney in power, Canada's inextricable bond to its superpower neighbor came of age through the total integration of their economies. Free trade with the United States was not the only act that Brian Mulroney undertook as prime minister. He also introduced a wildly unpopular national sales tax. However, free trade might as well have been the only measure he introduced because it destroyed his party.

Brian Mulroney understood that free trade was a looming reality and that he couldn't have prevented it without alienating Canada from its most important trading partner. Canadians, ever sensitive to the notion that they are just Americans with a weak dollar, hated the idea and John Turner jumped all over it. Turner's criticism of free trade played well in the media. To his discredit, it also came to characterize his public persona.

Turner was a critic with no credibility as a leader. In 1998, he got his second crack at winning an election but the results were no better than they had been four years earlier. As much as Canadians despised free trade and distrusted Brian Mulroney, John Turner could not make them believe that he had anything better to offer. In 1990, Turner retired.

Jean Chrétien's 30-year war of attrition was finally over. He was the obvious choice to replace Turner just as Prime Minister Mulroney stepped into the arena of constitutional reform. Mulroney wanted to bring Quebec in from the cold and cement his reputation as the prime minister who secured Canada's unity. He tried twice to create conditions that would allow Quebec to sign the constitution.

His first effort was called the Meech Lake accord. Meech Lake gave all provinces greater control over immigration and the power to withdraw from inter-governmental cost sharing deals but also formally recognized Quebec as a "distinct society," awarding it a special veto power over future constitutional amendments. This proposal failed.

Mulroney tried again two years later. The Charlottetown Accord was basically Meech with a few minor amendments to appease those who'd opposed the reform in 1990. In Quebec, the accord was shot down because it was not regarded as providing sufficient recognition by sovereigntists and because it seemed to offer way too much power to Quebec in the eyes of federalists. Outside Quebec, it failed because of the concessions it made to Quebec and because of the common perception that it didn't offer a lot of benefits to anyone other than the separatists.

Chrétien let Mulroney dig his own grave. Mulroney had become anathema among most Canadians who believed he'd sold the country out to America and failed to bring Quebec into the constitution despite having spent his entire second term trying. In 1993, Mulroney retired and turned the country over to his successor, Kim Campbell.

For a few brief months Campbell acted as the only female prime minister in Canadian history. She called an election later that year and only then did it become clear just how much damage Mulroney had done. Campbell was blown out of the water.

At long last, Jean Chrétien was prime minister. Thanks to Brian Mulroney, Chrétien's chief political opponents had been transformed into a marginal lobby with no power whatsoever. In Quebec, Mulroney's failed constitutional efforts gave rise to a renewed separatist movement so brazen that a federal party, campaigning on the promise of independence, carried Quebec in the '93 election. Every party, other than Chrétien's, was in shambles.

Chrétien ruled with near absolute control for over a decade, never suffering defeat at the polls. In his time as prime minister, he survived another referendum in Quebec and established a new model for federal involvement in the affairs of Canadian cities such as Toronto and Montreal.

Chrétien is the figure upon which the future of Major League Baseball in Canada hinges, not because he is keen on stadium financing, but because he created a framework in which the very possibility of ballpark development rests on the same factors that launched Toronto's rivalry with Montreal. Hopes for another Canadian World Series hang in the balance.

> "We weren't supposed to be here!"
> —*Minnesota outfielder Torii Hunter, on advancing to face Anaheim, 2002*

Baseball fans in Canada, if any have the endurance to stay up and watch the late-night playoffs, may be encouraged by watching the Anaheim Angels and Minnesota Twins play in the American League championship series. Neither of these teams are big spenders. Neither was given much of a chance at being in this position when the 2002 season started.

It seems to fly in the face of conventional wisdom for two relatively small clubs to have gotten this far. This is the mythic exception that proves the rule and, for most, is taken as evidence that the first round of the playoffs is too short to produce results that truly reflect the talent of competing teams.

Maybe so, but the fact that the Twins and Angels are playing in mid-October is enough to make even the most jaded fan dream of scenarios in which their hopeless team might do the impossible. It's a huge damper to think that the commissioner of baseball worked so hard to make this match-up impossible by pushing for Minnesota's contraction.

It's even more depressing to think that the only reason the franchise was taken off the commissioner's hit list is that politicians warmed to the idea of building a new stadium in Minneapolis. This is all disheartening because it underscores the fact that the status quo is still alive and well in baseball, which is exactly the opposite of what optimists want to take away from an Anaheim-Minnesota showdown.

During the series' first game, Bud Selig sits in the Metrodome, frowning like an exiled Napoleon, forced to watch the team he tried to trash play for a chance at the biggest prize in the business. Bud Selig, slouched in his seat, cringing under the deafening noise of the league's loudest stadium, looks every bit like the Grinch hearing the sound of Christmas cheer floating up from Whoville.

The commissioner's sour mug takes much of the joy out of an unlikely match-up. It also underscores the fact that nothing has changed insofar as the prerequisites for success in Major League Baseball are concerned.

> "[If] we do not act ... we will not be talking about a new system of transfers to the provinces, we'll be talking about no transfers at all."
> —*Jean Chrétien's finance minister, Paul Martin, 1995*

Jean Chrétien inherited a government so far in debt that, on an annual basis, it accrued billions of dollars in compounded interest charges. Pure mathematics required that the enormous budgetary deficit be curtailed or else Canada ran the risk of simply going bankrupt.

The axe fell in 1995 when Chrétien tabled a budget that cut spending by $29 billion. For every new dollar that the federal government brought in, it proposed to eliminate seven dollars in expenses. This radical action had sweeping impacts, the most severe of which was the decrease in provincial transfer payments.

Under the Canadian constitution, provinces are mandated to deliver key public services as well as to legislate and manage urban development. In carrying out these responsibilities, all provinces depend on the financial support of the federal government. With the implementation of the 1995 budget, the total federal contribution to provinces was scaled back by 17 percent.

Naturally, this didn't please anyone in Canada and seemed to please the people of Quebec the least. Quebec continued to receive much more money in transfers than any other province, except Ontario, but the optics of this budgetary cut-back were horrible. The federal government had proposed to do less in Quebec while keeping more revenues for itself. It was a perfect breeding ground for the renewed separatist movement.

Shortly after the federal budget was introduced, while Canadians were still gasping at the projected spending cuts, the premier of Quebec again proposed separation. Another referendum was called and the provincial government slickly worded the question in a vague manner, asking whether voters supported changing the relationship between Quebec and Canada. As prime minister, Jean Chrétien again faced the question of Quebec.

Chrétien shifted tactics for this second bout. Whereas in 1980, he supported Trudeau in offering Quebec a new constitutional deal, in 1995 he knew that after three failed efforts to bring Quebec into the constitution no such promise would do.

Instead, Chrétien chose to put the onus on the sovereigntists themselves. Rather than try to conjure up some new carrot to dangle in front of Quebecers, he challenged the separatists to prove that they were truly offering a more attractive alternative.

On the day of the referendum, the vote was too close to call. No one knew what would happen. There is evidence to suggest that both sides engaged in ballot tampering and electoral fraud. At the end of the day, Canada was held together by 0.4 percent.

For all the drama of the referendum, it was not the most significant byproduct of Jean Chrétien's radical fiscal reform. Rather, the most enduring impact of the 1995 budget, other than making it tougher on the poor and sick to be poor and sick, was on the capacity of provincial and municipal governments to keep Canada's cities from falling apart.

Cities such as Toronto and Montreal were hit from two ends simultaneously. On one hand, Chrétien's government revised its role in critical areas such as social housing, effectively shifting such functions to the lower levels. On the other, the accompanying reduction in financial transfers limited the capacity of provinces to undertake new functions. Provinces had less money and more responsibility. This was especially significant because, at the time, Canadian municipalities were coming to grips with the staggering cost of maintaining old cities that refused to stop growing.

The difference between the pipes, roads and housing that existed in Canadian cities during that period and those that needed to exist in order to support a healthy quality of life was $40 billion. Provinces and cities were scrambling just to manage existing responsibilities. They were feeling the squeeze even before Jean Chrétien withdrew funding from the provinces and, by extension, the cities.

In this way, two forces collided. The massive infrastructure pressure of a $40 billion gap slammed into the suffocating constraints of a 17 percent revenue decrease.

There was little money for necessary capital upgrades in cities like Toronto, where a private toll highway was built to serve daily commuters, and Montreal, where half the city's drinking water leaked into the ground through rusted pipes before ever reaching the homes of citizens. The country's books were balanced by changing the way governments in Canada addressed these types of pressing issues. Ironically, this adjustment actually transformed Ottawa into a more important player than ever because competition for the money that remained became a matter of survival.

What eventually replaced the old system of provincial transfer payments was a series of grant programs that provided direct funding for individual projects. In effect, Chrétien had circumvented the provinces.

His framework took money out of transfer payments and redirected it into grants through which cities competed against one another for access to project-specific funding. All municipalities would compete for access to funds. Toronto and Montreal would compete against their own suburbs. This is the dynamic that made a wave of amalgamation necessary.

Jean Chrétien put his adminstration back on the urban scene by making it difficult for major initiatives to be contemplated by provinces alone. Thereafter, the governments of Ontario and Quebec signed deals that both symbolized and solidified this reality.

Under the new paradigm, cost-sharing partnerships worth billions of dollars were launched, turning local urban problems into national political issues. The fiscal re-balancing of 1995 brought two centuries of history full circle by transforming large-scale developments into joint projects. On the long list of potential deals impacted by these agreements, sports facilities such as baseball stadiums stand out for obvious reasons.

Unless they cover costs out of their own budgets, cities and provinces would have to tie stadium deals to partnerships under which pooled funds are managed. This is Jean Chrétien's historic legacy. It directly impacts the future prospects of the Blue Jays and Expos.

"What do you want from me?"
—*Giants slugger Barry Bonds, defending his World Series performance, 2002*

Contested on the West Coast, between the Anaheim Angels and San Francisco Giants, the 2002 World Series is one of the least watched ever. The games end too late and too few people know enough about either team to bother staying up. Just the same, it is an exciting and engaging series between two determined teams.

The Angels overcame heavy odds by beating the Yankees prior to outlasting the Minnesota Twins. The Giants, powered by perhaps the most dangerous hitter ever in Barry Bonds, knocked the Atlanta Braves out of the opening round, saving all baseball fans from the embarrassment of the Tomahawk Chop, before defeating the St. Louis Cardinals to earn a spot in the final.

The World Series turning point comes in Game 6. With the Angels still recovering from the 16-run pounding two days earlier, they fall behind 5–0 at home. With a comfortable lead in what could be the deciding game, Barry Bonds is poised to accept his first championship and first World Series MVP on the same night.

In the 7th inning, however, the Angels come to life and Bonds plays an unwilling part in his own undoing. It all starts with a three-run home run that sends the Anaheim crowd into a frenzy by drawing the Angels back within striking distance. The following inning, after a leadoff home run and a string of hits, Bonds misplays a ball in the outfield and allows the potential go-ahead run to move into scoring position.

This forces manager Dusty Baker to go to his bullpen ahead of schedule, and becomes the most famous lowlight of the series when the very next batter brings that runner home, forcing Game 7. If there is such a thing as momentum in baseball, it swings in favor of the Angels.

Anaheim follows this unlikely comeback by sending a rookie pitcher to the mound in the deciding game, tempting fate by daring to become the first team ever to win with such a youngster on the hill. Though something of a let-down after the fireworks a night earlier, there is dancing in Disneyland as the Angels complete their playoff run with a 4–1 win over the Giants.

The Angels are not America's adopted team. They are unloved and their victory is uncelebrated. The against-all-odds championship is not an inspiration to optimists who hope to see baseball succeed in Canada, primarily because the Angels are still up for sale and struggling to find a buyer despite having won the World Series.

The Angels put a fine team together on a small budget then crossed their fingers and got lucky. That's not a recipe for long-term success. Not in baseball.

> "Now it's Toronto's turn to get its waterfront right."
> —*Robert Fung, Toronto Waterfront Revitalization Task Force, 2000*

The future of baseball in Canada and the history of Toronto's rivalry with Montreal are bound by more than Chrétien's aggressive maneuver. The old waterfronts where both cities came of age are implicated as well. The most likely properties on which ballparks could be built are located down by the ports and rail yards where this whole story began.

The most prestigious development site in Canada is Toronto's downtown waterfront. It is isolated from the city core by an elevated expressway that discourages pedestrian and local traffic but features 2000 acres of land left behind from the earliest days of Toronto's history.

In the 1950s, the promise of increased activity promoted by the St. Lawrence Seaway never fully materialized. In 1972, the federal government stepped in to purchase large parcels of the site and directly sponsor the development of a mixed-use community.

Poor stakeholder management and rampant land speculation turned this vision into a spotty, high-rise reality. By 1989, the project was scrapped and the site was setaside for another day.

That day came in 2000 when the fledgling Toronto Waterfront Revitalization Task Force issued a report calling for the removal of the elevated expressway, the creation of new residential neighborhoods and the incorporation of venues supporting Toronto's bid to host the 2008 Olympics. Without public support none of it could be realized because project funding was expected to come, in part, from government coffers and Ottawa was among the largest landowners in the patchwork of competing interests on the site.

When Beijing beat Toronto for the honor of hosting the 2008 Games, much of the momentum for this redevelopment, along with hundreds of millions in funding that had been pledged by government, was lost. The impact of this failure stretched to the baseball diamond as well.

The waterfront stadium would have become available just as the Blue Jays got serious about stadium renewal. It might have been perfect.

With no Olympics coming to Toronto, this scenario will never play out. The new 2002 waterfront plan does not include a stadium component despite the fact that SkyDome will be obsolete long before the 30 year vision for the

The Gardiner Expressway was a critical step in Toronto's surrender to both suburban sprawl and the demands of the automobile (1959), and isolated the waterfront district whose redevelopment would preoccupy politicians for decades (G. Lynney / Library and Archives Canada / PA-111447).

site expires, and the waterfront is the best space upon which a new downtown stadium could be located.

Whether a new stadium is ever constructed on this controversial site, in which politicians and business leaders have a long-standing interest, or SkyDome itself undergoes a major overhaul funded by taxpayers to keep it from becoming a liability like the Big O, the future of baseball in Toronto hinges on some form of public stadium fianancing for the Blue Jays and the government of Canada. The fact that the team is not yet lobbying for this public support is the biggest reason that the Expos have so little hope of being bailed out.

In Montreal, the dilapidation of Olympic Stadium is not a future worry but an alarming reality. Major League Baseball is openly looking for the quickest, easiest way to dump the franchise into the hands of investors and legislators in a city eager to build a new stadium. The crises that Toronto will spend the next ten years trying to avoid are already running wild in Montreal.

Former minority owners of the Expos are still in the process of suing Bud Selig and Jeffrey Loria for fraud. Commissioner Selig has tried to slip out of this lawsuit by petitioning to have the case thrown out of court based on a geographic technicality.

His lawyers have argued that, since most of the activity cited in the lawsuit actually took place in New York, the lawsuit filed in Florida ought to be tossed. This effort has been recognized for the evasive maneuver that it is, and the judge has stated the case can justifiably be pursued.

Still, there's not much reason for fans of the Montreal Expos to celebrate. The former Expos owners likely have no intention of channeling court winnings back into baseball. Plus, Jeffrey Loria relinquished the team's purchase hold on a piece of downtown property that had been under government control and might have served as the ideal location for a new stadium. The Expos are running out places to turn for help.

Even after ceding its status as Canada's premier city to Toronto, Montreal's familiar old fallbacks remain. There are sites on the waterfront that need to be redeveloped and all the important stakeholders have their eyes on public support. Local investors recognized the area as a potential goldmine.

The showpiece property in the middle of this site is Bickerdike Pier. Though it continues to be used for the storage and processing of goods, Bickerdike Pier is usually one of the first parcels mentioned whenever downtown redevelopment is discussed. It's clear that something is going to be built on this site, the only question is what.

As in Toronto, many different political agendas will have to be aligned before any project sees the light of day. The forces that have shaped Montreal since Canada's earliest days are still at play. Granted, there's nothing to say that they won't come together in a perfectly transparent manner.

Except, public stadium financing is a reckless gamble. The story of Montreal's rivalry with Toronto suggests that reckless gambles have rarely been taken without some less-than-transparent dealing. If the league can put enough pressure on political insiders willing to mock valid procedures set up to prevent scandal and ensure fairness, baseball could thrive.

The Toronto Blue Jays announced $69 million in losses over the 2002 season. It is impossible to envision a future for baseball in Toronto that does not include an enormous amount of pressure being applied by the commissioner's office towards the development of a new stadium.

The Montreal Expos don't lose very much money because there's no money for the franchise to lose. The Expos are as dead as any team has ever been in baseball yet, despite the funeral preparations already underway, there is still a sliver of hope. That hope turns on the possibility that a new stadium could still be constructed close to downtown.

In both scenarios, the dubious key is to manufacture the appearance of agreement between taxpayers' money and baseball-friendly development along the waterfronts where these cities waged their rivalry. Nothing could be more consistent with the country's history, and baseball's current strategy. If Major League officials were to succeed in over-riding processes that protect against bad decisions in Canada, ballparks could be on the horizon.

> "Red Sox get ... extra revenue, the Expos get a great place to play."
> —*Anonymous source, cited in reports that the Expos may move to Boston, 2002*

Bud Selig is not behaving like a person trying to find backroom dealmakers sympathetic to his league's appetite for free money. As a fitting postscript to the 2002 season, a new proposal for relocating the Expos has come to light. This proposal brings the whole debacle of the past year full circle.

Not long ago, John Henry needed help dumping the Marlins so he could buy the Red Sox. Bud Selig helped ease the way for a franchise flip that eventually saw Jeffrey Loria abandon Montreal. Henry is now looking for ways to increase revenues in Boston and Major League Baseball is full of ideas.

The commissioner has already confirmed that his office is actively looking into having the Expos play a portion of their home schedule in locations other than Montreal next season. One of those locations could be Boston.

Though Henry has already approved a 7 percent increase in the price of tickets at Fenway Park, the most expensive venue at which to watch a baseball game, he is still looking for ways to further maximize cash flow at Boston's aging classic. As the story goes, senior officials at the Major League front office are discussing the idea of moving the Expos to Fenway as a temporary home prior to relocating the team to a new city permanently. Revenues from Expos games would become free money for Henry.

Everyone vehemently denies that this scenario is being considered. Yes, the league plans to hear petitions from various cities on the topic of Expos relocation. Yes, Puerto Rico may be a destination for the Expos for parts of its home schedule in 2003. No, Fenway Park is not currently on the table.

For once, there's reason to believe these denials. On the face of it, the idea that the commissioner would once again manipulate franchise movement to the benefit of John Henry seems preposterous.

However, it's not because this manipulation is wrong or unfair that Bud Selig won't do it. Rather, the simple fact of the matter is that the other major league owners, who all hold equal shares in the Expos franchise, will never allow this asset to be turned over for Henry's sole benefit.

If there were some practical way that they could all share in revenues generated by such a scheme, it might fly. If revenues were split among all the owners, Henry would have no reason to go through the headache of setting up the Fenway deal. It will never happen.

If the Expos play anywhere other than Montreal next season it will apparently be in San Juan. This location won't be selected because Major League Baseball is eyeing Puerto Rico as a potential long-term market. It will be the only neutral site to which the owners can agree.

Puerto Rico is just about as far from Canada as it gets. The chasm between league officials and the power brokers in Canada who could help them achieve their ends seems very wide. For fans in Montreal, short of crossing their fingers and praying that the Blue Jays fall so far so fast that an iron will to save baseball is generated before the Expos disappear, only the repeating cycles of history offer any real hope.

Montreal has seen teams come and go. Influence peddlers of all stripes have always found a way around legitimate channels and into the sometimes dimly lit halls of Canadian political power. Baseball took shape and grew up in Canada, in the midst of a rivalry that was settled while a series of baseball teams streamed in and out of existence.

Montreal came out on the short end of its rivalry with Toronto and has never kept a baseball team yet. But if it all points to one fact, if any certainty can be drawn from the mess, it's this: baseball will be back.

"Montreal isn't sustainable ... [baseball] is going to address relocation **very soon.**"
—*Former U.S. presidential advisor Frederick Malek, 2002*

Bibliography

In developing my argument, I made use of facts drawn from the following sources. I highly recommend these books, reports and websites for any reader seeking a deeper understanding of the histories of Canada, Toronto, Montreal, urban development in the United States or any other issue addressed in this book.

Books

Auf der Maur, Nick. *The Billion Dollar Game: Jean Drapeau and the 1976 Olympics.* Toronto: Lorimer Press, 1976.
_____. *Le Dossier Olympique.* Montreal: Editions Quebec-Amerique, 1976.
Berchman, F.R. *Opportunity Road: Yonge Street 1860–1939.* Toronto: Natural Heritage/Natural History, 1996.
Brown, William. *Baseball's Fabulous Montreal Royals.* Montreal: Robert Davies, 1996.
Careless, J.M.S. *Toronto to 1918: An Illustrated History.* Toronto: James Lorimer, 1984.
Chisholm, J.A. *The Speeches and Public Letters of Joseph Howe.* Vol. 2. Halifax: McChronicle, 1909.
Cooper, J.I. *Montreal: A Brief History.* Montreal: McGill-Queen's Press, 1969.
Firth, Edith. *The Town of York (1815–1834).* Toronto: University of Toronto Press, 1966.
Forbes, E.R. *The Maritime Rights Movement 1919–1927: A Study in Canadian Regionalism.* Montreal: McGill-Queen's University Press, 1980.
Gibbon, John. *Our Old Montreal.* Toronto: McLelland & Stewart, 1947.
Glazebrook, G.P. *The Story of Toronto.* Toronto: University of Toronto Press, 1971.
Gubbay, A. *The Mountain and the River.* Montreal: Trillium Books, 1981.
Guillet, Edwin. *Toronto: From Trading Post to Great City.* Toronto: Ontario, 1934.
Hodge, Gerald. *Planning Canadian Communities.* Toronto: ITP Nelson, 1998.
Hounsom, Eric. *Toronto in 1810.* Toronto: Ryerson Press, 1970.
Jacobs, J. *The Question of Seperatism.* New York: Random House, 1980.
Jedwab, Jack. *Jackie Robinson's Unforgettable Season of Baseball in Montreal.* Montreal: Editions Image, 1996.
Jenkins, Kathleen. *Montreal: Island City of the St. Lawrence.* New York: Doubleday, 1966.
Leacock, Stephen. *Leacock's Montreal.* Toronto: McLelland & Stewart, 1948.
Linteau, P.A. *Histoire de Montréal depuis la Confédération.* Montreal: Editions du Boreal, 1992.
Mann-Trofimenkoff, Susan. *The Dream of Nation.* Toronto: Macmillan, 1982.
Masters, D.C. *The Rise of Toronto.* Toronto: University of Toronto Press, 1947.
Mays, John B. *Emerald City: Toronto Visited.* Toronto: Viking Press, 1994.

Mulvany, C.P. *Toronto: Past and Present*. Toronto: Caiger, 1884.
Perry, David. *Financing the Canadian Federation*. Toronto: Canadian Tax Foundation, 1997.
Roberts, Leslie. *Montreal: From Mission Colony to World City*. Toronto: Macmillan Press, 1969.
Sewell, John. *The Shape of the City*. Toronto: University of Toronto Press, 1993.
Simpson, J. *The Spoils of Power*. Toronto: Collins, 1988.
Stevenson, Garth. *Unfulfilled Union*. Toronto: Macmillan, 1979.
West, Bruce. *Toronto*. Toronto: Doubleday, 1979.

Reports

Berman, D. "Put a Lid on It—Toronto's Skydome Has Become a World-Class Disaster." *Canadian Business* 71, 1998.
Bradford, N. "Why Cities Matter." Canadian Policy Research Networks, Discussion Paper, 2002.
Brunt, Stephen. "Endgame." *Report on Business*, August 2002.
Crombie, David. *Interim Report*. Royal Commission on the Future of the Toronto Waterfront, 1989.
_____. *Regeneration: Toronto's Waterfront and the Sustainable City*. Royal Commission on the Future of the Toronto Waterfront, 1992.
DeMause, N. "Skydome: Then and Now." *This Magazine* 32, 1999.
Feldstein, R. *The Repatriation of the Constitution*. University of Ottawa, Faculty of Law.
Foster, P. "Money Pit: Where Did $461 Million Go?" *Toronto Life* 33, 1999.
Hill, S.R. "Baseball in Canada." *Indiana Journal of Global Legal Studies*. 2000.
Latzko, David. *Who Won the Major League Baseball Strikes?* Wilkes University, Department of Business and Economics, 1997.
Long, Eric. "The 1994 Baseball Strike Revisited: A Better Impasse Analysis." *Southern Illinois University Law Journal* 22, 1997.
Lorinc, J. "Stealing Home: Is Skydome Really Bust." *Report on Business*, February 1999.
Sancton, A. "Differing Approaches to Municipal Restructuring in Montreal and Toronto." *Canadian Journal of Regional Science*, Spring/Summer 1999.
Shivers, J. "Goodbye Expos." *Talking Sports* 20, 1999.
Staudohar, Paul. "The Baseball Strike of 1994-95." *Monthly Labour Review* 120, 1997.
Towards a Canadian Urban Strategy—Framework for Government of Canada Involvement in Urban Affairs. Canadian Institute of Planners, 2002.

Websites

Amateur Athletics Foundation of Los Angeles, Sports Library: www.aafla.org. General factual information about the roots of baseball in Ontario, the relocation of Brooklyn Dodgers, and Lord Killanan.
American Association of Port Authorities: www.aapa-ports.org. General historic and factual information about the shipping industry in Montreal.
Association for Canadian Studies: www.acs-aec.ca. Profile of Canada's role in World War II.
Atlantic Institute for Market Studies: www.aims.ca. General historic and factual information about economic factors impacting the maritime provinces.

Ballparks.com. Stadium dimensions and data.
BallparksofBaseball.com. Stadium dimensions and data.
BaseballAlmanac.com. General stadium information.
BaseballLibrary.com. Facts and statistics.
BaseballReference.com. Facts and statistics.
Baseball-Statistics.com. Facts and statistics.
Boston Globe: www.boston.com. General historic information about urban development and the Backbay District.
Bread not Circuses: www.breadnotcircuses.org. General factual information about the financial and tax framework for SkyDome.
Bronx Center Project: www.vnc.bc.ca. General historic information about the development of the Bronx neighborhood and urban renewal projects.
Buffalo Bisons: www.bisons.com. General historic information about Montreal baseball in 1890.
Business Week Magazine: www.businessweek.com. Outline of factors impacting Detroit's downtown revival plan.
Canada-Quebec Infrastructure Program: www.infrastructurecanada.gc.ca. General factual information about the role of federal funding in infrastructure projects.
CanadaInfo.com. Prime ministerial profiles
Canadian Broadcast Corporation: www.history.cbc.ca. Prime ministerial profiles, 1967 De Gaulle event in Montreal and general historic information.
Canadian Coalition for Nuclear Responsibility: www.ccnr.org. Overview of the nuclear industry during World War II.
Canadian Museum of Civilization and Canadian War Museum: www.civilization.ca. Overview of the Naval Bill controversy.
Canadian Parks and Recreation Association: www.cpra.ca. General historic and factual information about the roots of baseball in Montreal.
Canada's Cities—Unleash Our Potential: www.canadascities.ca. General factual information about infrastructure deficit and intergovernmental relations affecting urban affairs.
Canada's Digital Collections: www.collections.ic.gc.ca. Prime ministerial profiles, speeches and general historic information about Toronto and Montreal.
CBSSportsline.com. Boxscore information.
Citizen's Budget Committee of NY: www.cbcny.org. Letter to New York mayor Rudolph Giuliani about stadium financing.
City of Montreal: www.ville.montreal.qc.ca. General historic information from the Montréal à 350 ans project.
CNNMoney.com. Factual information about Enron's role in the Houston, Texas, economy.
Department of Finance: www.fin.gc.ca. General factual information about the 1995 budget and the provincial transfer system.
Department of National Defence and Canadian Forces: www.dnd.ca. Outline of factors at play in Canada during World War I.
Detroit Free Press: www.freep.com. General factual information about land assembly strategy for stadium development.
Doug Pappas' Business of Baseball: www.roadsidephotos.sabr.org. General factual information about Major League Baseball strike history and franchise sales.
Emerald Necklace Conservancy: www.emeraldnecklace.org. General historic information about Olmstead's Backbay park network.
Empire Club of Canada: www.empireclubfoundation.com. Prime ministerial speeches and keynote addresses.
ESPN.com. Boxscore information.

Federal Deposit Insurance Corporation: www.fdic.gov. Outline of economic factors impacting Houston.
Federal Reserve Bank of Dallas: www.dallasfed.org. Historic overview of the Texas oil industry.
Fenway Community Development Corporation: www.fenwaycdc.org. General historic information about urban development and the Backbay District.
Field of Schemes: www.fieldofschemes.com. Factual information about public contributions to stadium development and also franchise sales.
Firstworldwar.com. General historic information about Canada's role in World War I.
Forbes Magazine: www.forbes.com. General factual data and information about reported Major League Baseball franchise values and revenues.
Fraser Institute: www.oldfraser.lexi.net. Description of dispute settlement under North American Free Trade Agreement.
Globe and Mail: www.globeandmail.ca. General factual information about lawsuits and the Major League Baseball labor negotiations in 2002.
Great Lakes St. Lawrence Seaway System: www.greatlakes-seaway.com. General historic information about the St. Lawrence Seaway project.
Historical Society of Washington, DC: www.citymuseumdc.org. General historic information about urban development in the United States.
Hofstra University: www.hofstra.edu. General historic information and outline of factors impacting port expansion and the shipping industry in Montreal.
Houston Chronicle: www.chron.com. General factual information about the stadium development plan in 1996.
Independent Budget Office of New York: www.ibo.nyc.ny.us. Evaluation of the economic impact and public benefit of stadium financing.
International League: www.ilbaseball.com. General historic information about international league and expansion of professional baseball in Canada.
Jimcrowhistory.org. General historic information about Branch Rickey and Jackie Robinson.
Journal of San Diego History: www.sandiegohistory.org. General historic information about the development of San Diego and its Gaslamp District.
Library and Archives Canada: www.canadiana.org. General factual information about factors impacting the rebellions of 1837–1838.
Library of Congress: www.memory.loc.gov. General historic information about American cities and urban development.
Log Cabin Chronicles: www.tomifobia.com. Profile of Prime Minister Laurier.
Major League Baseball: www.mlb.com. General historic facts and information about the Major League Baseball strike of 1981.
Marquette University, School of Law: www.law.marquette.edu. Overview of sporting facility financing in North America.
Massachusetts Institute of Technology: www.mitalliance.org. General historic information about urban development in Detroit.
McGill University: www.arts.mcgill.ca. General factual information about the impact of the St. Lawrence Seaway on Montreal's economy.
Metropolitan Sports Facilities Commission: www.msfc.com. General factual information about the development of Comerica Park and the planned urban village.
Minneapolis-St. Paul City Pages: www.citypages.com. General factual information about the stadium financing framework in Minnesota and Milwaukee.
Montreal Port Authority: www.port-montreal.com. Overview of federal involvement in the shipping industry in Montreal and factual information about redevelopment strategies.

National Center for Policy Analysis: www.ncpa.org. Overview of issues linking the North American Free Trade Agreement and stadium subsidies.
National Library of Canada: www.nlc-bnc.ca. Prime ministerial profiles, the Riel uprising and general historic information about Toronto and Montreal.
New York Public Library: www.nypl.org. General factual information and reference material about the history of the Bronx.
New York Times: www.nytimes.com. General factual information about lawsuits and Major League Baseball labor negotiations in 2002.
Northeastern University Magazine: www.numag.neu.edu. General historic information about urban development and the Backbay District.
Ontario Handgun Association: www.teapot.usask.ca. Historic overview of Canadian weapons control measures and government interventions.
Oregon Historical Society—Oregon Urban History Project: www.ohs.org. General historic information about urban development in Portland and the surrounding area.
Oregon House Committee on Smart Growth and Commerce: www.arcweb.sos.state.or.us. Public discussion about economic impact and justification for stadium financing.
Organization of American States: sice.oas.org. General factual information about the North American Free Trade Agreement.
Paralympics.org. Overview of 1976 Paralympic Games in Toronto.
People's History Coalition: www.buffalonian.com. Overview of factors impacting the rebellions of 1837–1838.
Portland Development Commission: www.pdc.us. General factual information about urban renewal in Portland, Oregon.
Red Sox Connection: www.redsoxconnection.com. General historic and factual information about the history of franchise, Huntington Grounds and Fenway Park.
Régie des installations olympiques: www.rio.gouv.qc.ca. Overview of the 1976 Montreal Olympics.
Save Fenway Park: www.savefenwaypark.com. "Homefield Advantage" report.
Save the Expos: www.savetheexpos.com. General factual information about the financial framework for Olympic Stadium.
Selkirk College: www.selkirk.bc.ca. Full text of the Front de Liberation du Québec (FLQ) Manifesto.
Simon Fraser University Magazine: www.peak.sfu.ca. Profile of Prime Minister King, and an overview of Canadian immigration policies.
SuperBuild Program: www.superbuild.gov.on.ca. General factual information about the role of federal funding in infrastructure projects.
Toronto Blue Jays: www.toronto.bluejays.mlb.com. General factual information about Toronto franchise history.
Toronto Port Authority: www.torontoport.com. General historic information about the administration of the port in the 19th century.
Toronto Public Library—Virtual Exhibit "All Aboard Toronto": www.tpl.toronto.on.ca. The role of railway development in the growth of Toronto.
Toronto Star: www.thestar.com. General historic information about the history of baseball in Toronto and Montreal.
Turtle Trader: www.turtletrader.com. Profile of John Henry.
United States Senate Committee on the Judiciary: www.judiciary.senate.gov. Finneran comments on proressional sports and economic activity.
Uniting Canada: www.uni.ca/history. General historic information about Quebec seperatism and referendum history.
University of Kansas: www.ku.edu. General historic information about Canada's wartime shipbuilding industry.

University of Michigan Magazine: www.pub.umich.edu. Overview of factors impacting Detroit's downtown revitalization program.
University of Texas at Austin, School of Architecture: www.ar.utexas.edu. Urban planning history case studies.
University of Toronto: www.chass.utoronto.ca. Pierre Trudeau debates.
Urban League of Portland: www.ulpdx.org. General factual information about development in Portland, Oregon.
Vanderbilt University, School of Law: www.law.vanderbilt.edu. Overview of the North American Free Trade Agreement and the sporting industry.
York University: www.chem.yorku.ca. General factual information about factors impacting the rebellions of 1837–1838.

Index

Alexander, Doyle 72
Allan, Hugh 42–43, 62
Alomar, Roberto 109, 111–112, 162
Alou, Felipe 6–7, 22, 110, 124, 153–154, 168
Alou, Moises 124, 153
Armas, Tony, Jr. 74, 89, 101, 161
Ashby, Andy 48, 69, 116
Atwater Park 141–142

Bailey, Bob 24–25
Baker, Dusty 59, 178
Ballpark at Arlington 27
Bank Act 41–42, 44
Barfield, Jesse 49, 58, 71, 94
Barrett, Michael 22–23, 33, 75, 81, 97, 101, 161
Baseball origins 37
Beeston, Paul 35, 48, 99–100
Bell, George 58, 94, 108–109
Blue Monday 59–60
Bonds, Barry 70, 83–84, 115, 156, 178
Borden, Robert 88, 117–121, 134
Borders, Pat 111
Boston, urban history 3–4
Bowa, Larry 157
Brenly, Bob 83, 105
Brochu, Claude 91, 152–156, 166
Bronfman, Charles 13
Bronx, urban history 129–130
Brown, Kevin 69
Buckner, Bill 113
Burke, Tim 95
Burley, Craig 92
Burnitz, Jeromy 21
Bush, George W. 27
Bush, Homer 38

Cabrera, Orlando 7, 9, 67–68, 74, 81, 101, 161
Cameron, Mike 38
Caminiti, Ken 50
Campbell, Kim 174
Canadian National Railway 142, 144
Canadian Pacific Railway 42–43, 62, 64, 144

Canseco, Jose 50, 109, 155–156
Carter, Gary 25, 59, 110
Carter, Joe 96, 107–109, 111–114, 162
Cartier, George Etienne 41
Chavez, Eric 114
Chen, Bruce 21, 27, 33, 75
Chrétien, Jean 171–177
Clancy, Jim 49, 71, 94
Clark, Champ 89
Clemens, Roger 153, 155
Clemente, Roberto 6
Cleveland, Reggie 99
Clinton, Bill 125
Cold War 162, 164, 169
Colon, Bartolo 51, 76, 80–81, 83, 89–90, 101, 122, 133, 151–152, 161
Comerica Park 55–56
Comiskey Park 150
Cone, David 111–112
Conscription 118–120, 136
Contraction 6–9, 28, 30, 33, 39–40, 57, 83, 100, 106, 126, 132–133, 142
Cordero, Wil 81, 90
Cosby, Bill 9–10
Cromartie, Warren 25
Cross, James 12
Cruz, Jose, Jr. 8, 33, 73, 106, 161
Cyr, Louis 97

Daulton, Darren 112
Dawson, Andre 59, 95
Day, Zach 67
De Gaulle, Charles 11
Delgado, Carlos 6, 9, 22, 27–28, 33, 47, 51, 65, 67–69, 73, 75, 95–96, 114, 131, 151, 153, 155, 161, 168
Dempster, Ryan 81, 83
Deshields, Delino 109
Detroit, urban history 54–55
Diefenbaker, John 169–171
Drapeau, Jean 34, 103–104
Dravecky, Dave 104
Durham, Ray 114
Dykstra, Lenny 112

Eaton, Timothy 44
Eckersley, Dennis 109, 111
Eckstein, David 28
Eischen, Joey 75
Enron Field 31
Escobar, Kelvim 26, 28, 68, 75, 107, 115, 122
Exhibition Stadium 35–36, 58, 77, 94
Expo '67 10–11, 103–104
Eyton, Trevor 78

Fairly, Ron 24
Fanning, Jim 59
Fehr, Donald 123, 127
Fenway Park 3–5, 182–183
Fletcher, Darrin 38, 65–66, 99–100, 124
Flood, Curt 70
Floyd, Cliff 81, 83, 89–91, 97, 101–102, 105–106, 161
Franco, Julio 80
Francoeur, Joseph-Napoléon 117
Fregosi, Jim 113
Front de Libération du Québec (FLQ) 12–13
Fryman, Woodie 59
Fung, Robert 179

Gagne, Eric 116
Galarraga, Andres 7, 95
Gamboa, Tom 150
Garciaparra, Nomar 6, 14
Garvey, Steve 59
Gaston, Cito 107–108
Giambi, Jason 47
Giuliani, Rudolph 128, 130
Glavine, Tom 51–52, 80, 89–90, 111, 133
Godfrey, Paul 77–78
Graney, Jack 99
Great Depression 121, 135, 137, 146–147
Greene, Shawn 80, 153, 155
Griffin Alfredo 49, 58
Grissom, Marquis 109–110
Gruber, Kelly 109
Guerrero, Pedro 59
Guerrero, Vladimir 7, 9, 21, 23, 28, 31–33, 39, 51, 56, 66, 68, 73–75, 80–81, 83, 89–90, 96–97, 105, 116, 122, 133, 151, 153, 155–157, 161
Gullickson, Bill 59
Guzman, Juan 110–111
Gwynn, Tony 124

Halladay, Roy 8, 25–26, 38, 47, 51, 66, 69, 74, 83, 96, 101, 107, 122, 131, 151, 182
Hamilton, Joey 155
Harrison, Tommy 97
Henderson, Rickey 108–109, 111–113
Hendrickson, Mark 107
Henke, Tom 94, 108, 110–112
Henry, John 3–5, 102, 182–183
Hentgen, Pat 112, 153

Herges, Matt 125–126
Hermanson, Dustin 155
Herzog, Whitey 58
Hill, Ken 110
Hinske, Eric 8–9, 26, 32, 38, 47, 74–75, 96, 106–107, 114, 162
Hitchcock, Sterling 50
Hitler, Adolf 136
Hochelaga, annexation to Montreal 63–64
Hooton, Burt 59
Houston, urban history 30–31
Howe, Clarence 133, 137–139, 147, 163, 173
Howe, Joseph 40–41
Hudson, Orlando 107, 131, 162
Hudson, Tim 114
Hunt, Ron 24
Hunter, Torii 175
Huntington Grounds 4

Ilitch, Mike 55
Interleague play 57
Irabu, Hideki 32, 167

Jacobs Field 69
Jarry Park 10, 12–13, 23–25
Jeter, Derek 14, 131
Johnson, Randy 33, 102
Jones, Andruw 51, 89
Jones, Chipper 51, 90
Justice, David 114

Keri, Jonah 23
Kerrigan, Joe 93
Key, Jimmy 72, 94, 108–109, 111
King, Mackenzie 134–136, 163
Koch, Billy 114–115
Koufax, Sandy 106
Kruk, John 112

Langevin, Hector 65
Langston, Mark 102
Lanier, Bob 30,
Laporte, Pierre 12–13
Lastman, Mel 82–83
Laurier, Wilfred 64–65, 85, 87–88, 117, 134
Lawrence, Joe 38
Lee, Bill "Spaceman" 34, 59
Lévesque, René 172
Lichtenhein, Sam 141
Lloyd, Graeme 89, 167
Loaiza, Esteban 22, 47, 51, 66–67, 73, 100
Lopez, Felipe 74–75
Loria, Jeffrey 5, 7, 39, 91, 102, 115, 151, 156–157, 166–168, 181–182
Lorimier Grounds/Stadium 147, 149

Macdonald, John 42, 44, 60, 62, 64–65, 117, 135, 169
Macias, Jose 73, 75, 80–81
Mackenzie, William Lyon 15, 17

Index

Mackenzie Rebellion 17, 19, 37
Maddux, Greg 51
Maldonado, Candy 107
Malek, Frederick 183
Malton, Sam 149
Maple Leaf Stadium 98–99
Maris, Roger 84
Martinez, Buck 22, 25, 50, 56, 131, 168
Martinez, Dennis 95, 110
Martinez, Pedro 5–6, 39, 100, 153–154
Mayberry, John 49
McCain, John 49
McGriff, Fred 94, 108–109
McGwire, Mark 84, 109
McHale, John 54
Menard, Jacques 91, 166–167
Miller, Justin 47, 66
Millwood, Kevin 132
Minaya, Omar 9, 21, 27, 39, 66–67, 75–76, 81, 89, 102
Minzberg, Sam 160
Molitor, Paul 111–113
Monday, Rick 59–60
Mondesi, Raul 8–9, 27–28, 33, 51, 56, 68, 73–75, 80, 106, 161
Montreal, city/urban planning 145–146, 148
Montreal Royals 6, 141–142, 147
Montreal waterfront/harbor/port 17, 42–43, 62–64, 85–86, 144, 165, 179, 181–182
Mordecai, Mike 68
Morris, Jack 107, 110–111
Morton, Carl 12, 24
Moseby, Lloyd 49, 58, 71, 94
Moss, Damian 90
Mulroney, Brian 173–174
Musial, Stan 106
Mussina, Mike 50

NAFTA 156, 159, 162
Naval Service Act 87–88
Nicholson, Jack 112
Nixon, Otis 111

Ohka, Tohmo 66, 96, 105, 161
O'Leary, Troy 39–40, 52, 68, 116
Olerud, John 109, 112, 124
Olmsted, Frederick Law 3
Olympic Stadium 6–7, 10, 14, 22–23, 25, 28–29, 34–35, 52, 56, 65, 68, 74, 78–79, 84, 89–90, 94, 103–104, 110, 115, 121, 131, 149–150, 152, 154, 156–157, 159, 168, 181
Olympics/Olympic Games 25, 34–35, 81–83, 92, 103, 179
Owens, Eric 101

Parris, Steve 22, 122
Parrish, Larry 25, 59
Patriotes Rebellion 19–20, 37
Pavano, Carl 39, 66–67
Pearson, Lester 10–12, 104, 170–172

Pearson Cup 92–93
Perez, Pascual 95
Person, Robert 56
Phelps, Josh 107, 131, 162
Pohland, Carl 5, 53

Quiet Revolution 171

Raines, Tim 6, 59, 95, 109
Reames, Britt 132
Reardon, Jeff 59, 95
Rebellion Losses Bill 20
Reciprocity Treaty 41
Relocation 13, 30, 98, 130, 158–159, 181
Ricciardi, J.P. 8, 39, 74, 80, 95–96, 100, 106, 114, 131, 151, 162
Rickey, Branch 148–149
Riel, Louis 46
Robinson, Frank 6–7, 33, 68–69, 75, 89–90
Robinson, Jackie 6, 148–149
Rodriguez, Alex 70, 122–123, 156
Rodriguez, Henry 7, 28–29, 39, 153
Rogers, Buck 93
Rogers, Steve 24, 59–60
Rogers, Ted 53, 167
Runnells, Tom 110
Ruth, Babe 37, 99, 128–129, 142

St. Laurent, Louis 163–163, 169–170
St. Lawrence Seaway 144, 165, 179
Santana, Johan 100
Schilling, Curt 33, 100, 105, 112
Schneider, Brian 67, 89, 101
Selig, Bud 3, 5, 7–8, 13, 28, 39, 50, 53, 57, 70, 83–84, 91–92, 97, 99, 102, 106, 115, 123, 126, 133, 140, 149, 156, 158, 160, 166, 175, 181–182
Separatist(ism) 12–13, 15, 37, 40–41, 116, 120, 125, 174, 176
Shea Stadium 128
Sheffield, Gary 89
Simpson, Robert 44
Singleton, Ken 24–25
Sirotka, Mike 168
SkyDome 7, 14, 25, 32, 38, 51, 53, 68, 74–75, 78–79, 92, 95, 107–108, 112, 131, 150, 153, 156, 159–160, 162, 166–168, 179–180
Smith, Bryn 95
Smith, Dan 132
Smoltz, John 51, 53
Sosa, Sammy 23, 84
Staub, Rusty 12
Steinbrenner, George 97, 105–106, 126, 128
Stephen, George 42, 60, 62
Stevens, Lee 28, 66–67, 76, 168
Stewart, Dave 109, 111–112
Stewart, Scott 116
Stewart, Shannon 8, 27, 67–68, 106–107
Stieb, Dave 49, 58, 71, 94, 108–109, 111
Stoneman, Bill 12, 24

Stottlemyre, Todd 108–109
Strickland, Scott 21, 27
Strike 40, 58, 70, 72, 106–108, 114–115, 121, 123–126, 133, 152
Sunlight Park 98
Suzuki, Ichiro 38
Sweezey, Bob 135

Taillibert, Roger 34, 103
Tarte, Joseph 64–65, 85, 87–88
Tatis, Fernando 32, 67, 73–75, 80–81, 101, 161, 168
Taylor, Charles 4
Tejada, Miguel 114
Terrorist(ism) 13, 68, 128, 140, 150–151
Toronto Baseball Grounds 98–99
Toronto, city/urban planning 145–146, 148
Toronto waterfront/harbor/port 15, 17, 23–24, 44–46, 61, 64, 77, 81–82, 85–86, 93, 144, 165, 179–180, 182
Torre, Joe 83, 160
Torrez, Mike 24
Tosca, Carlos 56, 67–69, 73–74, 95, 107, 131
Trudeau, Jean-Charles 147
Trudeau, Pierre 12, 23, 93, 104, 171–173
Tupper, Charles 41, 64, 117
Turner, John 173–174
Turner, Ted 167
Turner Field 133

Ueberoth, Peter 71
Upshaw, Willie 49, 58, 71
Urbina, Ugueth 6

Valenzuela, Fernando 59
Vaugh, Mo 21, 96–97
Vazquez, Javier 9, 21, 28, 31, 51, 67, 80, 90, 101, 161

Ventura, Jesse 53, 57
Ventura, Robin 50
Vidro, Jose 7, 9, 22–23, 27–28, 51–53, 56, 67, 83, 90, 101, 133, 154, 161

Walker, Larry 109–110, 123, 152
Walker, Pete 74–75
Wallach, Tim 59, 95, 109
War Measures Act 12, 118
War Supply Board 137
Ward, Duane 108, 110–112
Wells, David 14, 93, 108–109, 111–112, 131, 140, 155, 168
Wells, Vernon 8, 66, 68, 73, 75, 96, 162
Wetteland, John 110, 152
White, Devon 107, 109, 113
White, Rondell 50, 153
Whitman, Walt 44
Whitt, Ernie 49
Wilkerson, Brad 52, 67, 90, 97, 161
Williams, Jimy 108
Williams, Mitch "Wild Thing" 112–113
Wilson, Tom 38, 67
Winfield, Dave 111
World War I 117–118, 120, 134
World War II 136–137, 147–148, 163
Wrigley Field 132

Yankee Stadium 13, 128–130
Yonge Street 15, 44–45, 61
Yorkville, annexation to Toronto 61–62
Yoshii, Masato 73, 75
Youmans, Floyd 95

Zito, Barry 114

www.ingramcontent.com/pod-product-compliance
Lightning Source LLC
Chambersburg PA
CBHW030110170426
43198CB00009B/563